Lecture Notes in Computer Science 9687

Commenced Publication in 1973
Founding and Former Series Editors:
Gerhard Goos, Juris Hartmanis, and Jan van Leeuwen

Editorial Board

David Hutchison
Lancaster University, Lancaster, UK
Takeo Kanade
Carnegie Mellon University, Pittsburgh, PA, USA
Josef Kittler
University of Surrey, Guildford, UK
Jon M. Kleinberg
Cornell University, Ithaca, NY, USA
Friedemann Mattern
ETH Zurich, Zürich, Switzerland
John C. Mitchell
Stanford University, Stanford, CA, USA
Moni Naor
Weizmann Institute of Science, Rehovot, Israel
C. Pandu Rangan
Indian Institute of Technology, Madras, India
Bernhard Steffen
TU Dortmund University, Dortmund, Germany
Demetri Terzopoulos
University of California, Los Angeles, CA, USA
Doug Tygar
University of California, Berkeley, CA, USA
Gerhard Weikum
Max Planck Institute for Informatics, Saarbrücken, Germany

Márk Jelasity · Evangelia Kalyvianaki (Eds.)

Distributed Applications and Interoperable Systems

16th IFIP WG 6.1 International Conference, DAIS 2016
Held as Part of the 11th International Federated Conference
on Distributed Computing Techniques, DisCoTec 2016
Heraklion, Crete, Greece, June 6–9, 2016
Proceedings

 Springer

Editors
Márk Jelasity
University of Szeged
Szeged
Hungary

Evangelia Kalyvianaki
City University London
London
UK

ISSN 0302-9743   ISSN 1611-3349   (electronic)
Lecture Notes in Computer Science
ISBN 978-3-319-39576-0   ISBN 978-3-319-39577-7   (eBook)
DOI 10.1007/978-3-319-39577-7

Library of Congress Control Number: 2016939991

LNCS Sublibrary: SL5 – Computer Communication Networks and Telecommunications

Printed on acid-free paper

This Springer imprint is published by Springer Nature
The registered company is Springer International Publishing AG Switzerland

Foreword

The 11th International Federated Conference on Distributed Computing Techniques (DisCoTec) took place at Aquila Atlantis Hotel in Heraklion, Greece, during June 6–9, 2016. It was organized by the Institute of Computer Science of the Foundation for Research and Technology Hellas and the University of Ioannina, Greece. The Dis-CoTec series is one of the major events sponsored by the International Federation for Information Processing (IFIP). It comprises three conferences:

- COORDINATION, the IFIP WG6.1 International Conference on Coordination Models and Languages
- DAIS, the IFIP WG6.1 International Conference on Distributed Applications and Interoperable Systems
- FORTE, the IFIP WG6.1 International Conference on Formal Techniques for Distributed Objects, Components and Systems

Together, these conferences cover a broad spectrum of distributed computing subjects, ranging from theoretical foundations and formal description techniques to systems research issues.

Each day of the federated event began with a plenary speaker nominated by one of the conferences. The three invited speakers were Tim Harris (Oracle Labs, UK), Catuscia Palamidessi (Inria, France), and Vijay Saraswat (IBM T.J. Watson Research Center, USA).

Associated with the federated event were also two satellite workshops, that took place on June 8–9, 2016:

- The 9th Workshop on Interaction and Concurrency Experience (ICE) with keynote lectures by Uwe Nestmann (Technische Universität Berlin, Germany) and Alexandra Silva (University College London, UK)
- The Final Public Workshop from the LeanBigData and CoherentPaaS projects

Sincere thanks go to the chairs and members of the Program and Steering Committees of the involved conferences and workshops for their highly appreciated efforts. Organizing DisCoTec 2016 was only possible thanks to the dedicated work of the Organizing Committee, including George Baryannis (Publicity Chair) and Vincenzo Gulisano (Workshops Chair), with excellent support from Nikos Antonopoulos and Alkis Polyrakis of PCO-Convin. Finally, many thanks go to IFIP WG6.1 for sponsoring this event, Springer *Lecture Notes in Computer Science* for their support and sponsorship, and to EasyChair for providing the refereeing infrastructure.

April 2016   Kostas Magoutis

Preface

This volume contains the proceedings of DAIS 2016, the 16th IFIP International Conference on Distributed Applications and Interoperable Systems, sponsored by the IFIP (International Federation for Information Processing) and organized by the IFIP Working Group 6.1.

DAIS was held during June 4–7, 2016, in Heraklion, Crete, Greece, as part of DisCoTec, the 11th International Federated Conference on Distributed Computing Techniques, together with FORTE (the 36th IFIP International Conference on Formal Techniques for Distributed Objects, Components and Systems) and COORDINATION (the 18th IFIP International Conference on Coordination Models and Languages).

There were 34 submissions for DAIS. Each submission was reviewed by at least three, and on average 3.8, Program Committee members. The committee decided to accept 13 full papers and three short papers, resulting in an acceptance rate of 38 % for full papers. Out of the 13 accepted full papers, five were chosen after a shepherding process, during which a committee member helped the authors implement the improvements required by the reviewers.

The accepted papers represent a compelling sample of the state of the art in the area of distributed applications and interoperable systems. Cloud computing and services received a large emphasis this year. The proceedings include contributions on resource management (optimizing energy consumption, adaptive optimization of Hadoop parameters, predicting resource usage, and an investigation of erasure coding libraries for redundancy) as well as techniques for cloud-based data processing and computing (shuffling methods, GPU access from virtual machines, and edge-cloud computing). In the area of decentralized systems, we have contributions on self-organizing DHTs, decentralized social networks, and content distribution systems. The area of Byzantine fault tolerance is also represented as well as the emerging area of complex event processing, where performance, load balancing, and language support are investigated.

The conference was made possible by the work and cooperation of many people working in several committees and organizations that are listed in these proceedings. In particular, we thank the Program Committee members for their commitment and thorough reviews and for their active participation in the discussion and shepherding phases, and all the external reviewers for their help in evaluating submissions. We would like to thank the publicity chair, Valerio Schiavoni, for his excellent work in publicizing DAIS 2016. We would also like to thank Tim Harris, our invited keynote speaker. Finally, we also thank the DisCoTec general chair, Kostas Magoutis, and the DAIS Steering Committee chair, Rui Oliveira, for their constant availability, support, and guidance.

April 2016

Márk Jelasity
Evangelia Kalyvianaki

Organization

DisCoTec Steering Committee

Elie Najm (Chair)	Telecom-ParisTech, France
Rocco De Nicola	IMT Lucca, Italy
Kurt Geihs	University of Kassel, Germany
Farhad Arbab (Coordination)	CWI, The Netherlands
Rui Oliveira (DAIS)	University of Minho, Portugal
Jean-Bernard Stefani (FORTE)	Inria, France
Alain Girault	Inria, France
Uwe Nestmann	TU Berlin, Germany
Michele Loreti	University of Florence, Italy
Jim Dowling	KTH, Sweden
Marjan Sirjani	Reykjavik University, Iceland
Frank de Boer	CWI, The Netherlands
Lea Kutvonen	University of Helsinki, Finland
John Derrick	University of Sheffield, UK
Gianluigi Zavattaro	University of Bologna, Italy

DAIS Steering Committee

Alysson Bessani	Universidade de Lisboa, Portugal
Sara Bouchenak	INSA Lyon, France
Jim Dowling	KTH Royal Institute of Technology, Sweden
Frank Eliassen	University of Oslo, Norway
Pascal Felber	Université de Neuchâtel, Switzerland
Karl Goeschka	Vienna University of Technology, Austria
Rüdiger Kapitza	Technical University of Braunschweig, Germany
Kostas Magoutis	FORTH-ICS and University of Ioannina, Greece
Rui Oliveira	Universidade do Minho, Portugal
Peter Pietzuch	Imperial College London, UK
Romain Rouvoy	University of Lille 1, France
Franois Taiani	Université de Rennes 1, France

DAIS 2016 Program Committee

Program Committee Chairs

Márk Jelasity	University of Szeged, Hungary
Evangelia Kalyvianaki	City University London, UK

Publicity Chair

Valerio Shiavonni   Université de Neuchâtel, Switzerland

Program Committee Members

Luciana Arantes   Université Pierre et Marie Curie-Paris6, France
Carlos Baquero   HASLab, INESC TEC and University of Minho,
                                   Portugal
Sonia Ben Mokhtar   LIRIS CNRS, France
Alysson Bessani   Universidade de Lisboa, FCUL/LaSIGE, Portugal
Andrea Bondavalli   University of Florence, Italy
Sara Bouchenak   INSA Lyon, France
Jian-Nong Cao   Hong Kong Polytechnic University, Hong Kong, SAR
                                   China
Miguel Correia   IST/INESC-ID, Portugal
Paolo Costa   Microsoft Research Cambridge, UK
Wolfgang De Meuter   Vrije Universiteit Brussel, Belgium
Jim Dowling   KTH, Sweden
Frank Eliassen   University of Oslo, Norway
Ittay Eyal   Cornell University, USA
David Eyers   University of Otago, New Zeland
Pascal Felber   Université de Neuchâtel, Switzerland
Kurt Geihs   Universität Kassel, Germany
Karl M. Goeschka   FH Technikum Wien, Austria
Franz J. Hauck   University of Ulm, Germany
K.R. Jayaram   IBM Research, USA
Vana Kalogeraki   Athens University of Economics and Business, Greece
Rüdiger Kapitza   TU Braunschweig, Germany
Attila Kertesz   University of Szeged, Hungary
Benjamin Mandler   IBM, Israel
Evangelos Markatos   University of Crete, FORTH-ICS, Greece
Miguel Matos   HASLab, INESC TEC and University of Minho,
                                   Portugal
Rene Meier   Lucerne University of Applied Sciences and Arts,
                                   Switzerland
Alberto Montresor   University of Trento, Italy
Kiran-Kumar   Harvard School of Engineering and Applied Sciences,
    Muniswamy-Reddy   USA
Marta Patino   Universidad Politecnica de Madrid, Spain
Peter Pietzuch   Imperial College London, UK
Hans P. Reiser   University of Passau, Germany
Altair Santin   Pontifical Catholic University of Paraná, Brazil
Spyros Voulgaris   VU University Amsterdam, The Netherlands

Additional Reviewers

Abreu, Vilmar
Baraki, Harun
Behl, Johannes
Ceccarelli, Andrea
Dar, Kashif Sana
Gonçalves, Ricardo
Huu Tran, Tam
Kambona, Kennedy
Köstler, Johannes
Lollini, Paolo
Maia, Francisco
Marynowski, João Eugenio
Mendes, Ricardo
Obelheiro, Rafael
Rakotondravony, Noelle

Renaux, Thierry
Robu, Bogdan
Rodriguez Avila, Humberto
Saey, Mathijs
Salaün, Gwen
Sartakov, Vasily
Shoker, Ali
Swalens, Janwillem
Taubmann, Benjamin
Timo, Hönig
Tomaras, Dimitris
Vianello, Valerio
Zacheilas, Nikos
Zoppi, Tommaso

Systems Challenges in Graph Analytics
(DAIS 2016 Keynote)

Dr. Tim Harris

Oracle Labs, Cambridge, UK
timothy.1.harris@oracle.com

Abstract. Graphs are at the core of many data processing problems, whether that is searching through billions of records for suspicious interactions, ranking the importance of web pages based on their connectivity, or identifying possible "missing" friends on a social network. This talk will discuss the challenges in building large, scalable, in-memory graph analytics systems. Many of these challenges come from the way that graph algorithms behave differently based on the structure of the input graph: a planar road network graph can produce a significantly different load on the machine's memory system from a low-diameter social network graph. It can be necessary to select particular algorithms for these different cases, and to make contrasting decisions over how the machine's resources are allocated. Finally, we face challenges simply from the scale at which we operate: making efficient use of the hardware in new SPARC machines with over 4000 threads.

Speaker: Tim Harris leads the Oracle Labs group in Cambridge, UK. His research interests span multiple layers of the stack, including parallel programming, VMM/OS/runtime-system interaction, and opportunities for specialized architecture support for particular workloads. He has also worked on the implementation of software transactional memory for multi-core computers, and the design of programming language features based on it. Tim has a BA and PhD in computer science from Cambridge University Computer Laboratory. He was on the faculty at the Computer Laboratory from 2000–2004 where he led the department's research on concurrent data structures and contributed to the Xen virtual machine monitor project. He was at Microsoft Research from 2004, and then joined Oracle Labs to found the Cambridge office in 2012.

Contents

Enhanced Energy Efficiency with the Actor Model on Heterogeneous Architectures

Yaroslav Hayduk$^{(\boxtimes)}$, Anita Sobe, and Pascal Felber

University of Neuchâtel, Neuchâtel, Switzerland
{yaroslav.hayduk,anita.sobe,pascal.felber}@unine.ch

Abstract. Due to rising energy costs, energy-efficient data centers have gained increasingly more attention in research and practice. Optimizations targeting energy efficiency are usually performed on an isolated level, either by producing more efficient hardware, by reducing the number of nodes simultaneously active in a data center, or by applying dynamic voltage and frequency scaling (DVFS). Energy consumption is, however, highly application dependent. We therefore argue that, for best energy efficiency, it is necessary to combine different measures both at the programming and at the runtime level. As there is a tradeoff between execution time and power consumption, we vary both independently to get insights on how they affect the total energy consumption. We choose frequency scaling for lowering the power consumption and heterogeneous processing units for reducing the execution time. While these options showed to be effective already in the literature, the lack of energy-efficient software in practice suggests missing incentives for energy-efficient programming. In fact, programming heterogeneous applications is a challenging task, due to different memory models of the underlying processors and the requirement of using different programming languages for the same tasks. We propose to use the actor model as a basis for efficient and simple programming, and extend it to run seamlessly on either a CPU or a GPU. In a second step, we automatically balance the load between the existing processing units. With heterogeneous actors we are able to save 40–80 % of energy in comparison to CPU-only applications, additionally increasing programmability.

1 Introduction

Energy efficiency of data centers and clouds has become a major concern. As claimed in 2012 by a Greenpeace report [6], current cloud computing systems consume the same amount of energy as a whole country such as Germany and India. While going *green* is from the users' and operators' perspective often done voluntarily or for economic benefits, today's systems reach physical limitations—the so-called "power wall"—that enforce focusing on energy-efficiency [5].

Usually, work on improving energy efficiency is limited to isolated strategies. For instance, on a data center level, power consumption is reduced by adaptively shutting down nodes; on a single system level, power consumption is

Published by Springer International Publishing Switzerland 2016. All Rights Reserved
M. Jelasity and E. Kalyvianaki (Eds.): DAIS 2016, LNCS 9687, pp. 1–15, 2016.
DOI: 10.1007/978-3-319-39577-7_1

reduced by providing more efficient hardware or runtime support and by dynamically adapting the CPU frequency using dynamic voltage and frequency scaling (DVFS) [4]. While these approaches are effective per se, we believe that software and hardware have to be considered together to best enable energy-efficient resource usage. In general, the energy consumption E of an application relates to its power consumption P and its execution time T ($E = P \cdot T$). Hence, to reduce energy consumption, one can either radically (1) reduce the power consumption (usually at the cost of execution time) or (2) reduce the execution time (usually at the cost of power consumption).

As shown by Trefethen et al. [24] the CPU frequency has a major impact on power consumption. We therefore exploit the CPU frequency scaling features of Linux where possible and use predefined "governors".

To reduce the execution time, a possible way is to exploit all available hardware resources, e.g., graphical processing units (GPUs). Programming applications that run both on CPUs and GPUs is a challenging task as parts of a program might be better targeted at a CPU, while other parts are data parallelizable and run more efficiently on GPUs. As it might be necessary to provide two versions of the same application (e.g., CUDA/C++), we focus our contributions especially on programmable solutions for heterogeneous applications.

As a basis we rely on the *actor model* [10]. The model offers a high degree of isolation between its main entities, called actors. Actors enable seamless interoperability between heterogeneous components [1], allowing us to differentiate between actors running on a CPU or GPU and consequently support *heterogeneous actors*. Actors are useful for data parallelizable applications; they, however, might cause overhead if applications are iterative and maintain state.

In this paper we investigate several strategies for implementing heterogeneous actors focusing on iterative applications. We start from a manually crafted and optimized implementation, in which an actor running in Scala calls the CUDA/GPU code written in C/C++ using the Java native interface (JNI). Later, we propose to decouple this design by using a middleware component, RabbitMQ.[1]

Another solution is to use a domain-specific language (DSL) for generating both CPU and GPU code. Frameworks such as Delite [21], which provide automatic code generation, expect the entire application to be written with the DSL and executed by the provided runtime. With actors it is desirable to be able to decide on a fine-grained level whether a task, encapsulated in an actor, should execute on a CPU or on the GPU. Therefore, we adapt the actor model by introducing heterogeneous actors, which can be programmed using Delite DSLs.

From a programmer's point of view we show that the heterogeneous actors based on DSLs represent the simplest solution and lead to a reduced energy consumption of up to 40 % in comparison to CPU-only actor implementations, with JNI actors allowing for savings of up to 80 %. We present our final contribution, which is a scheduler that balances workload among GPU and CPU resources.

The rest of the paper is organized as follows. We introduce the generic ideas on power consumption and execution time reduction in Sect. 2, providing

---

[1] http://www.rabbitmq.org.

implementation details on heterogeneous actors in Sect. 3. The load balancing of actor tasks is introduced in Sect. 4. In Sect. 5 we describe the hardware and software setup used for evaluation. We present and analyze results in Sect. 6 and discuss related work in Sect. 7. We conclude in Sect. 8.

2   Improving Energy Efficiency

One way to reduce the energy consumption is to decrease the power consumption ($E = P \cdot T$). This can be achieved either by influencing the hardware (e.g., by changing the frequency of a CPU), or by lowering the resource usage of the application itself (e.g., only use a single CPU with a sequential program). Another way is to focus on the improvement of the application's performance. In the following sections we discuss mechanisms for both approaches in detail.

2.1   Reducing Power Consumption

The overall power consumption of a machine is highly influenced by the power consumption of the CPU. Although CPUs become more and more energy-efficient, the overall energy consumption increases as we usually trade power for performance [3]. We focus on two strategies that are easy to configure: (1) the level of parallelism and (2) the voltage/frequency of a CPU.

If the level of parallelism (i.e., thread count) of an application is not properly chosen, the performance and the power consumption are negatively affected. For example, the system scheduler might interfere with the program execution, impeding the application's performance.

The power consumption of a CPU can be influenced by changing the CPU frequency. The Linux kernel provides a tool, `cpufreq`,[2] allowing us to configure *governors* that automatically set the desired CPU frequency. Specifically, we are interested in three governors. (1) **Performance**: the CPU will be automatically set to the highest available frequency; (2) **Powersave**: the CPU will be automatically set to the lowest available frequency; (3) **Ondemand (DVFS)**: the governor monitors the CPU utilization and, if it is on average more than 95 %, the frequency will be increased. The dynamic approach with the *ondemand* governor is the most promising, as it provides DVFS to fit the needs of an application.

2.2   Reducing Execution Time

If the performance gain is significant, it can be translated into a reduction of the total energy consumption. Concurrent programming is one measure to reduce execution time. Programming with threads and locks, however, is challenging.

The actor model has been introduced by Hewitt et al. [10] as a popular mechanism for implementing parallel, distributed and scalable systems. An actor is an independent, asynchronous object with an encapsulated state that can only be

---

[2] https://www.kernel.org/doc/Documentation/cpu-freq/governors.txt.

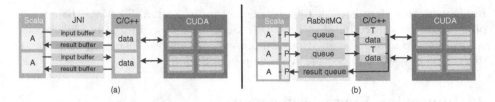

Fig. 1. Heterogeneous actors using (a) JNI and (b) RabbitMQ.

modified locally based on the exchange of messages. Considering a typical data-parallel algorithm as an example, we can easily design an application with a set of dedicated worker actors performing the required computations and a separate coordination entity actor that distributes the data and collects the results. In contrast to a classical multithreading approach we do not need to account for synchronizing shared memory accesses. For our actor implementations we use Akka[3], an official platform to manage actors in Scala.

Actors allow for interoperability not only on a single CPU but also across its boundaries. Communication, however, is not yet supported between different kinds of processors such as GPUs.

3   Enabling Heterogeneous Actors

To reduce the energy consumption while ensuring programmability, we exploit heterogeneous computing (CPU/GPU programming) with the help of actors. For GPU programming CUDA is a de facto standard.[4] CUDA provides a C/C++ binding for communicating with the GPU. As a GPU is a co-processor, the CPU is always necessary for communication, management, and data exchange. While with C/C++ and CUDA the program would be tightly interwoven, the actor model provides inherent decoupling by separating tasks into actors. As stated before, the communication between actors on different processors is not straightforward. As such, we provide support for actors that are able to run on either a GPU or a CPU, calling them *heterogeneous actors*. In what follows, we present three different possibilities for implementing heterogeneous actors.

JNI. The Java native interface (JNI) can be used for communicating with native libraries written in C/C++, supporting the communication with the GPU. In data-parallel programs, actors responsible for interacting with the GPU are initialized with a portion of input data (see Fig. 1(a)). A copy of the actor-local data is propagated to the actor-local GPU memory as well. In each GPU actor the final result is then stored in a result buffer, which can be accessed from either C or Scala using JNI.

RabbitMQ. An alternative for decoupling CPU and GPU code is to use a middleware component like RabbitMQ.[5] RabbitMQ enables the communication

---

[3] http://akka.io.

[4] http://docs.nvidia.com/cuda/cuda-c-programming-guide/index.html.

[5] http://www.rabbitmq.org.

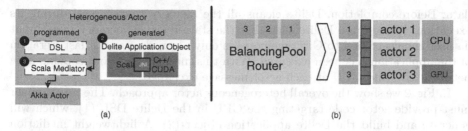

Fig. 2. (a) Heterogeneous actors using DSLs from the programmer's view. (b) BalancingPool Router in Akka.

(via queues) between programs written in different languages and amongst distributed machines. By using RabbitMQ we can connect CPU actors with GPU actors. Communication is supported via a proxy (P in Fig. 1(b)) that passes data from Akka to RabbitMQ. On the C/C++ side, each actor is associated with one thread (T) that waits for work in its RabbitMQ queue and, once available, fetches and forwards the data to the GPU for processing. The data is still isolated and accesses do not have to be synchronized. Upon completion, threads dispatch their result to the shared RabbitMQ result queue. The results are then collected and merged by a coordination actor in Akka. With RabbitMQ it is still necessary to provide both the CPU and the GPU implementations. It also requires the development of custom code to interact with the communication middleware (the proxy is not part of Akka).

DSL. For the DSL implementation we base our efforts on Delite [20], a framework that provides high level DSLs and runtime for heterogeneous programming. Delite expects that the programmer writes the entire application in the provided DSLs and executes the generated code in a dedicated runtime environment. As it is not always feasible to write the entire application in a DSL, our goal is to provide finer control to the programmer such that only some parts of his application have to be written in a DSL. In particular, only heterogeneous actors will be written in one of the Scala-like intuitive DSLs provided by Delite.

To support the execution of generated code from the actor environment, we need to provide custom communication facilities. Delite currently supports communication to generated Scala code with an intermediate packaging step into a *Delite application object*. To interact with this object (stored in a JAR file), so-called *Scopes* are needed as entry points [21]. They are limited, however, to mapping simple Scala data types to generated Scala code and they cannot forward data from Scala to the generated C++/CUDA code. As a first measure, we enhanced Scopes with a JNI method for forwarding data to the generated C++/CUDA code. We further extended Scopes to automatically load the generated C++/CUDA code and enable the interaction between Scala and C++/CUDA, which was not supported by Delite.

Another limitation of Delite is the lack of support for applications that maintain state between iterations. Typically, upon start-up the generated C++ code allocates main memory and GPU memory for storing input and intermediate data. Before completion, Delite cleans all the memory that it used during its execution. We adapted Delite such that the state-relevant memory (e.g., input dataset chunks copied to GPU memory) is only cleaned after the last iteration of the application has been executed. With this measure we avoid copying data between CPU and GPU at each actor message exchange.

In Fig. 2 we show the overall heterogeneous actor approach. The programmer must provide actor code targeting the GPU in the Delite DSL (1), which will generate and build the Delite application object (2). A lightweight mediation part in Scala (3) is required to convert Akka messages into data structures for the Delite application object and vice versa. We also provided support for Delite-generated CUDA code to return the result to the calling Scala code.

4   Resource Load Balancing with Heterogeneous Actors

Since the CPU and the GPU have different performance characteristics, load imbalances can happen. Hence, this section focuses on efficient workload balancing strategies for runtime and energy reduction.

To distribute work among actors on a CPU, Akka provides so called *Routers* that schedule messages targeted to a set of actors accomplishing a similar task. Specifically, the *BalancingPool router* embraces "work-stealing"[6] by balancing workload dynamically among worker actors. When an actor accesses its mailbox to fetch the next available message to be processed, Akka transparently forwards that request to a shared message queue started by the BalancingPool Router (see Fig. 2). Since the mailbox queue is shared, any worker actor should be capable of processing any message in the queue. Hence, Akka imposes a requirement for worker actors to be stateless, thus limiting its usage for iterative applications.

To overcome this limitation, we propose to use the following strategies. First, to enable iterative applications to be used with routers, we encapsulate all state required for the execution into messages. Each message contains the required context for having it processed on either the GPU or the CPU. For example, to avoid copying input data on each iteration, we store a pointer to it in a message. Also, to avoid synchronization issues between the CPU and the GPU memory, the message also contains a result object, stored in CPU memory, to which all implementations write intermediate results for the next iteration.

For actors running on both processing units, both implementations are required and any of the strategies discussed in Sect. 3 can be used. Also, since for iterative applications, the behavior will be repetitive, it is likely that the number of actors running on a CPU/GPU will not change at runtime. Hence, it is sufficient to find the optimal actor CPU/GPU configuration at startup. As such, at application start we introduce a brief profiling phase. For each configuration (e.g., 0 GPU actors/8 CPU actors; 1 GPU actor/7 CPU actors; etc.), we measure the execution time using 1 % of messages to be processed. Once finished, we select the configuration with the lowest execution time and use it for the processing of remaining messages.

---

[6] The actual implementation more precisely follows a *work-sharing* approach.

To summarize, our approach enables actors, independent of whether they run on the CPU or GPU, to request work when required, thus leading to reduced idle time and more balanced workloads.

5 Experimental Setup

Hardware. Our experiments are executed on a server equipped with an AMD FX-8120 (8 cores, no hyperthreading) CPU and an NVIDIA GeForce GTX 780 Ti (2880 CUDA cores) with 3 GB of RAM. We use a hardware power meter (Alciom PowerSpy v2.0) that periodically reports the system power in Watts.

Software. We base our evaluations on the well-known k-means [2] algorithm used for splitting an input dataset into different clusters. K-means is a good case study as it exhibits iterative and processing-intensive characteristics representative for data-parallelism. We further focus on k-means as it is a well-understood algorithm that can be represented in a straightforward manner in Delite's OptiML DSL. As such, we chose depth over breadth regarding our analysis, presenting the results of k-means only. Despite exclusively focusing on k-means, the core premise of heterogeneous actors is applicable for implementing other iterative algorithms (e.g., coordinate descent, logistic regression, deep belief learning with a restricted Boltzmann machine).

We used the thread-based STAMP [17] implementation of k-means as a basis for creating the actor version. For the actor-based implementation the following data structures are required: (1) input matrix; (2) current cluster center matrix; (3) points to cluster center *map* (holds the current cluster center index for each input point); (4) per-cluster member count structure (holds the number of points assigned to each cluster).

Parallel Implementation with Actors. Our actor-based algorithm uses two types of actors: *iteration actors* (Algorithm 1) and *worker actors* (Algorithm 2). While a typical thread-based version maintains a shared copy of the current cluster center matrix and the per-cluster member counts, the actor-based version maintains a private copy of these data structures in each of the worker actors.

Algorithm 1. K-means iteration actor.

Data: input set, number of clusters, number of workers
Result: clusters
Initialize K cluster centers
foreach *Worker* **do**
 | Create workers and pass partial input set
while *Termination condition is not met* **do**
 | Send current cluster centers to worker actors
 | **foreach** *Worker* **do**
 | | Receive partial results
 | Compute final cluster centers by merging partial results

Algorithm 2. K-means worker actor.

Data: partial input set, current cluster center
Result: local cluster centers, local member count
foreach *Assigned input point* **do**
| Assign point to the closest cluster center
| Update the local cluster centers matrix and member count
Send local cluster centers and cluster counts to iteration actor

---

The iteration actor then merges the data sent by each of the worker actors to calculate the final cluster centers.

Heterogeneous Implementation with JNI. For the heterogeneous implementation we extend the baseline actor implementation. Specifically, we execute the worker actor code on the GPU, while leaving the iteration actor unchanged for execution on the CPU. We further preserve the communication patterns between worker actors and the iteration actor. We reimplemented the worker actor to access the GPU resources by calling the C/CUDA code using JNI with the help of shared byte buffers as shown in Fig. 1(a). Each worker actor connects to a C implementation that starts two CUDA kernels, one for finding the closest cluster center for each input point (on block memory), and one for finding the total number of points that changed clusters as compared to the previous iteration (on GPU global memory). Once the GPU execution has finished, the results are transferred to the result buffer and to the iteration actor.

Heterogeneous Implementation with RabbitMQ. In this implementation we reused the CUDA code of the worker actor from the JNI implementation, but adapted the communication pattern between Scala and C/CUDA. Each worker actor now includes a proxy (as shown in Fig. 1(b)) that is responsible for marshaling the messages and sending them to the RabbitMQ queue. Once work is available, the aforementioned CUDA implementation is launched, omitting the shared byte buffers. In the end, a proxy actor connecting to the iteration actor transfers the results.

Heterogeneous Implementation using a DSL. We define the worker actor's logic using OptiML [19]—a Delite DSL. Next, we write the mediation code to connect to the generated code (Fig. 2). The mediation code extracts the current cluster centers from an Akka message, converts them to a Delite array (to map the `Rep` data structures in the DSL), and then calls that generated code with the array as input. Once the result is available, the mediation code converts it to an Akka message and forwards it to the iteration actor.

Heterogeneous Work Balancing Implementation. For the implementation of the work balancing use case any of the before mentioned implementations can be used. We decided to use JNI as it showed the best performance (see Sect. 6). We define the worker actor code just like in the heterogeneous implementation with JNI, but the worker actors are able to execute on both the CPU and the GPU. To enable load balancing, we require stateless actors, hence moved their state to messages (see Sect. 4). The profiling uses 1 % of the overall workload for testing each possible configuration, hence we allow the programmer to set the number of desired iterations manually.

System Configuration. K-means is a representative candidate for this evaluation as it is able to work on different input sizes. For the first three implementations of k-means (CPU/GPU), we chose a default data set from the STAMP benchmark with 65,536 input rows and 16 clusters. To test the profiling and selection process of the best share of CPU/GPU actors we use three different datasets: *small* (4,096 rows), *medium* (10,240), *large* (131,072). We set the worker actor count to match the CPU core count (i.e., 8). To enable efficient load balancing, the iteration actor divides the work into more tasks than the number of worker actors (32 tasks per iteration). As the run times can be considerably reduced with a GPU, we increased the load to gather reasonable results. The profiling takes 450 iterations per configuration, with an overall benchmark length of 5,000 iterations. We run each implementation 5 times and take the median execution time and power readings; the energy is then calculated out of these two values.

6   Results and Discussion

In this section we discuss the results of the different k-means implementations from Sect. 5 with respect to power consumption and execution time, and relate them to energy consumption.

6.1   Reducing Power Consumption

We investigate the reduction of power consumption by varying the number of workers, as well as the governors impacting the frequency of the CPU. The default governor is *ondemand*; its goal is to provide good performance when work is available and downscaling of the frequency otherwise (DVFS).

On the left side of Fig. 3 we present the power consumption of the three CPU-only Scala implementations (seq: sequential, par: parallel thread-based, act: actor). We scale the number of threads/actors (4, 8, 16, 32) in separate runs and average the results for each chosen frequency. The sequential implementation consumes the least power since only one core is used while the others are idling. The *ondemand* governor depends on CPU utilization and, since k-means is CPU-intense, power consumption of the *ondemand* and *performance* governors is comparable. The *powersave* governor sets the CPU to the lowest frequency, hence power consumption is reduced. The difference between the *powersave* and other two governors is 70 W for the parallel implementations and around 40 W for the sequential implementation.

The middle part of Fig. 3 shows the impact of the governors on the execution time. The sequential algorithm using the *powersave* governor is about 3 times slower than with any other governor. The parallel implementations exhibit a slowdown of about 2 times if the *powersave* governor is used.

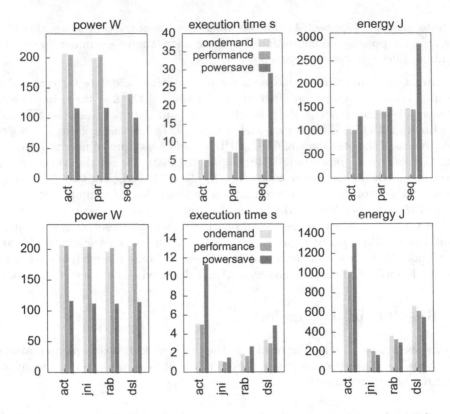

Fig. 3. Comparison of the power consumption (left), execution time (middle), and energy (right) using different governors. The top graphs refer to CPU execution. The bottom graphs include one bar for CPU-only execution and three bars for mixed execution (CPU/GPU).

Based on power and execution time measurements, we can compute the energy consumption as shown in Fig. 3 (right). The actor implementation outperforms the parallel and the sequential implementations. We can further see that, while the *powersave* governor decreases the power consumption, the execution time is significantly higher. This leads to higher energy consumption than when using the *ondemand* and *performance* governors. In general, the *ondemand* governor seems to be the best choice independent of the type of implementation.

6.2   Reducing Execution Time

This section focuses on execution time reduction and its impact on energy consumption. In the heterogeneous implementation, CPU actors cooperate with the GPU in different ways. We compare the JNI implementation (jni) with RabbitMQ (rab) and DSL actors (dsl) as described in Sect. 5. We also vary the frequencies for the CPU running the remaining code.

Figure 3 shows the power consumption (left), execution time (middle) and energy consumption (right). We see that the power consumption is not impacted by the usage of the GPU. The reason is that in this hardware setup the GPU is more energy-efficient than the CPU, hence running code on the CPU is more expensive in terms of power consumption. All GPU implementations execute faster than CPU implementations, yielding lower total energy consumption (Fig. 3 (right)). The DSL implementation in *powersave* mode consumes 540 J, which is lower than the 1,001 J of the actor implementation in *ondemand* mode. In contrast to the CPU-only execution, we see that reducing the CPU frequency with the *powersave* governor does not have a drastic impact on performance. Therefore, the best choice would be the *powersave* governor in the heterogeneous scenarios.

With respect to the different implementations, JNI provides the most direct way of communication with the GPU. This implementation does not provide the decoupling nor the flexibility for seamlessly exchanging the code to be executed on the GPU or the CPU. While the RabbitMQ implementation provides the possibility of exchanging worker (GPU) code, it still requires the programmer to implement the actual GPU code in C/CUDA. In comparison, by using heterogeneous actors with the DSL, programmers only need to provide the worker code for message processing in one of the Delite DSLs.

In terms of the lines of code required to implement k-means, JNI implementation is the most energy-efficient one, it requires 336 lines for the k-means logic written in CUDA and C, as well as 67 lines for providing JNI functionality (communication logic). RabbitMQ uses the same k-means logic as JNI, but requires another 337 lines for the communication logic. In comparison, our DSL implementation does not require communication logic because it is automatically generated by Delite. Hence, the overall effort for the DSL implementation is as low as 39 lines of code.

From a programmer's point of view heterogeneous actors with DSL represents the best solution, with better energy efficiency than CPU-only implementations. However, from an energy-efficiency point of view heterogeneous actors with JNI are preferable, as with it is possible to reduce the energy consumption of up to 80 % in comparison to a solution running on the CPU.

6.3 Resource Load Balancing with Heterogeneous Actors

This section presents our proposed load balancing approach. We execute the profiling phase as well as the full run on all datasets and combine the prediction capability of the profiling phase. Clearly, the execution time of the full running phase will be a multitude higher than the execution time of the profiling phase. Therefore, we normalize all values to the execution time of the first configuration. Figure 4 presents the results for different dataset sizes showing that the profiling phase can mimic the execution time of the remaining workload reasonably well. In more detail, for the *small* dataset we see that the problem is not scaled significantly to amortize overheads associated with executions on a GPU. When using the *medium* dataset we see that the most efficient configuration is composed of

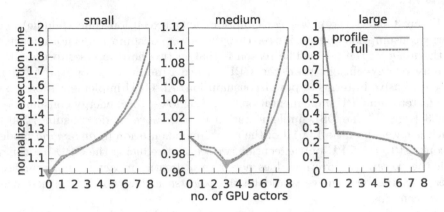

Fig. 4. Normalized execution time of the profiling phase as well as of the remaining workload using different configurations of CPU/GPU actors.

3 GPU actors and 5 CPU actors. When we use a *large* dataset (e.g., also the STAMP sample dataset from our former experiments), it is always beneficial to process all the workload using GPU actors.

The energy consumption reveals the same trends, however, we further noticed that with increased load, the CPU tends to use its turbo frequencies and hence draws about 20 W more than in the experiments before. In the case of the *large* dataset the CPU has a significantly higher power value if it shares work with the GPU while the execution time is not reduced significantly. Therefore, from an energy consumption point of view any sharing of work with the CPU in our hardware setup would be disadvantageous. With the *medium* and *small* dataset the load is not as high, hence sharing the work between the CPU and the GPU leads to slightly increased power consumption but lower execution time, and in total to lower energy consumption.

7   Related Work

In general, research on hybrid computing rarely considers energy efficiency. Researchers focus more on performance improvements (e.g., [25]) or develop power estimation models [11,14]. The trend of using graphical processing units (GPUs) for scientific programming became popular as there is a potential for significant performance improvement over executing only on a CPU. With the radical reduction of execution time, GPUs can in turn reduce the total energy consumption, providing means for energy-efficient programming [13,18]. Nevertheless, if the gains in execution time of GPU implementations are not high enough, the energy consumption might increase as compared to a CPU-only implementation [18].

The PEACH framework [9], for example, combines performance and power metrics to guide the scheduling on both CPU and GPU, but it focuses on defining a theoretical model rather than a practical implementation capable of working with real-world applications. Researchers working on SEEP [12] aim at helping programmers to produce energy-aware software. Their approach considers continuous energy monitoring of specific code paths helping to identify energy-hungry code. They mainly target, however, embedded systems capable of executing a single task. On the programming language level the authors of [8] divide a program into phases for which specific CPU frequencies are assigned. This approach does not only necessitate fine-grained monitoring of energy and execution time, but also requires that a program exclusively occupies a single core of a CPU. In [15] the authors propose a hybrid OpenMP/MPI programming model for power-aware programming. They use this model to steer the level of parallelism as well as the current frequency of a CPU.

The SPRAT [22] environment can automatically select the proper execution processor (either CPU or GPU) at runtime for energy efficiency. Migration is, however, quite expensive as the current state of the application must be saved when moving from one processor to another. There are a number of approaches for scheduling work between the CPU and the GPU. They can be broadly divided into performance/cost models (e.g., HEFT [23]), offline training [16], as well as work stealing [7]. A performance/cost model requires determining the approximate runtimes and data transfer times beforehand for each processing unit. For developers this requirement is hard to meet.

8 Conclusion

In this paper we tackle the problem of reducing energy consumption of parallel programs in heterogeneous environments. As energy depends on both power consumption and execution time, we investigate the impact of each independently. We first reduce the power consumption with the help of frequency scaling. We then reduce the execution time by running parts of an application on a GPU, while the sequential parts remain on the CPU. We evaluate a number of strategies for heterogeneous actors regarding their energy efficiency and programmability. JNI and RabbitMQ provide a more direct way of accessing a GPU, while the DSL implementations provide a concise and simple way for building heterogeneous actors. In a first step all heterogeneous implementations require manual assignment to the best processing unit. Hence, our final contribution enables automatic sharing of resources among actors yielding the highest energy efficiency. Our contributions lead to significant reductions of energy consumption in the range of 40–80 % as compared to CPU-only implementations.

References

1. Agha, G.: Actors programming for the mobile cloud. In: Symposium on Parallel and Distributed Computing (ISPDCP), pp. 3–9. IEEE (2014)
2. Alpaydin, E.: Introduction to Machine Learning. MIT press, Massachusetts (2004)
3. Barroso, L.A., Hölzle, U.: The case for energy-proportional computing. IEEE Comput. 40(12), 33–37 (2007)

4. Beloglazov, A., Buyya, R., Lee, Y.C., Zomaya, A., et al.: A taxonomy and survey of energy-efficient data centers and cloud computing systems. Elsevier Adv. Comput. **82**(2), 47–111 (2011)
5. Cai, C., Wang, L., Khan, S.U., Tao, J.: Energy-aware high performance computing: a taxonomy study. In: International Conference on Parallel and Distributed Systems (ICPADS), pp. 953–958. IEEE (2011)
6. Cook, G.: How clean is your cloud? Report, Greenpeace International, April 2012
7. Faxén, K.F.: Wool-A work stealing library. ACM Comput. Architect. News **36**(5), 93–100 (2009)
8. Freeh, V.W., Lowenthal, D.K.: Using multiple energy gears in MPI programs on a power-scalable cluster. In: Symposium on Principles and Practice of Parallel Programming (PPoPP), pp. 164–173. ACM (2005)
9. Ge, R., Feng, X., Burtscher, M., Zong, Z.: PEACH: a model for performance and energy aware cooperative hybrid computing. In: Conference on Computing Frontiers, pp. 1–24. ACM (2014)
10. Hewitt, C., Bishop, P., Steiger, R.: A universal modular ACTOR formalism for artificial intelligence. In: International Joint Conference on Artificial Intelligence (IJCAI), pp. 235–245. Morgan Kaufmann Publishers (1973)
11. Hong, S., Kim, H.: An integrated GPU power and performance model. In: International Symposium on Computer Architecture (ISCA), pp. 280–289. ACM (2010)
12. Hönig, T., Eibel, C., Kapitza, R., Schröder-Preikschat, W.: SEEP: exploiting symbolic execution for energy-aware programming. In: Workshop on Power-Aware Computing and Systems (HotPower), pp. 1–4. ACM (2011)
13. Huang, S., Xiao, S., Feng, W.: On the energy efficiency of graphics processing units for scientific computing. In: International Parallel & Distributed Processing Symposium (IPDPS), pp. 1–8. IEEE (2009)
14. Kasichayanula, K., Terpstra, D., Luszczek, P., Tomov, S., Moore, S., Peterson, G.D.: Power aware computing on GPUs. In: Symposium on Application Accelerators in High-Performance Computing (SAAHPC), pp. 64–73. IEEE (2012)
15. Li, D., de Supinski, B.R., Schulz, M., Cameron, K., Nikolopoulos, D.S.: Hybrid MPI/OpenMP power-aware computing. In: International Parallel & Distributed Processing Symposium (IPDPS), pp. 1–12. IEEE (2010)
16. Luk, C.K., Hong, S., Kim, H.: Qilin: exploiting parallelism on heterogeneous multiprocessors with adaptive mapping. In: IEEE/ACM International Symposium on Microarchitecture (Micro), pp. 45–55. ACM (2009)
17. Minh, C.C., Chung, J., Kozyrakis, C., Olukotun, K.: STAMP: stanford transactional applications for multi-processing. In: International Symposium on Workload Characterization (IISWC), pp. 35–46. IEEE (2008)
18. Rofouei, M., Stathopoulos, T., Ryffel, S., Kaiser, W., Sarrafzadeh, M.: Energy-aware high performance computing with graphic processing units. In: Workshop on Power Aware Computing and Systems (HotPower), p. 11. ACM (2008)
19. Sujeeth, A., Lee, H., Brown, K., Rompf, T., Wu, M., Atreya, A., Odersky, M., Olukotun, K.: OptiML: an implicitly parallel domain-specific language for machine learning. In: International Conference on Machine Learning (ICML), pp. 609–616. ACM (2011)
20. Sujeeth, A.K., Brown, K.J., Lee, H., Rompf, T., Odersky, M., Olukotun, K.: Delite: a compiler architecture for performance-oriented embedded domain-specific languages. ACM Trans. Embed. Comput. Syst. **13**(4s), 1–25 (2014)

21. Sujeeth, A.K., Rompf, T., Brown, K.J., Lee, H.J., Chafi, H., Popic, V., Wu, M., Prokopec, A., Jovanovic, V., Odersky, M., Olukotun, K.: Composition and reuse with compiled domain-specific languages. In: Castagna, G. (ed.) ECOOP 2013. LNCS, vol. 7920, pp. 52–78. Springer, Heidelberg (2013)
22. Takizawa, H., Sato, K.: SPRAT: runtime processor selection for energy-aware computing. In: International Conference on Cluster Computing (Cluster), pp. 386–393. IEEE (2008)
23. Topcuouglu, H., Hariri, S., Wu, M.Y.: Performance-effective and low-complexity task scheduling for heterogeneous computing. IEEE Trans. Parallel Distrib. Syst. **13**(3), 260–274 (2002)
24. Trefethen, A.E., Thiyagalingam, J.: Energy-aware software: challenges, opportunities and strategies. Elsevier J. Comput. Sci. **4**(6), 444–449 (2013)
25. Yang, C., Wang, F., Du, Y., Chen, J., Liu, J., Yi, H., Lu, K.: Adaptive optimization for petascale heterogeneous CPU/GPU computing. In: International Conference on Cluster Computing (Cluster), pp. 19–28. IEEE (2010)

Evaluating the Cost and Robustness
of Self-organizing Distributed Hash Tables

Sveta Krasikova, Raziel C. Gómez, Heverson B. Ribeiro, Etienne Rivière[✉],
and Valerio Schiavoni

Université de Neuchâtel, Neuchâtel, Switzerland
{sveta.krasikova,raziel.gomez,heverson.ribeiro,etienne.riviere,
valerio.schiavoni}@unine.ch

Abstract. Self-organizing construction principles are a natural fit for large-scale distributed system in unpredictable deployment environments. These principles allow a system to systematically converge to a global state by means of simple, uncoordinated actions by individual peers. Indexing services based on the distributed hash table (DHT) abstraction have been established as a solid foundation for large-scale distributed applications. For most DHTs, the creation and maintenance of the overlay structure relies on the exploration and update of an already stabilized structure. We evaluate in this paper the practical interest of self-organizing principles, and in particular gossip-based overlay construction protocols, to bootstrap and maintain various DHT implementations. Based on the seminal work on T-Chord, a self-organizing version of Chord using the T-Man overlay construction service, we contribute three additional self-organizing DHTs: T-Pastry, T-Kademlia and T-Kelips. We conduct an experimental evaluation of the cost and performance of each of these designs using a prototype implementation. Our conclusion is that, while providing equivalent performance in a stabilized system, self-organizing DHTs are able to sustain and recover from higher level of churn than their explicitly-created counterparts, and should therefore be considered as a method of choice for deploying robust indexing layers in adverse environments.

1   Introduction

The scale and complexity of distributed systems have dramatically increased in the last decade. Among the abstractions that allow building large-scale distributed services, DHTs (distributed hash tables) play a fundamental role. Applications of DHTs are numerous, ranging from communication backbone [2,9] to file systems [3] and media streaming [1]. DHTs are at the heart of many industrial large-scale storage systems such as Amazon S3/Dynamo [4].

A DHT is a decentralized index, where each node is responsible for a small disjoint subset of the index. Nodes are organized in some overlay network. The base structure of this overlay allows establishing routing paths towards the node

© IFIP International Federation for Information Processing 2016
Published by Springer International Publishing Switzerland 2016. All Rights Reserved
M. Jelasity and E. Kalyvianaki (Eds.): DAIS 2016, LNCS 9687, pp. 16–31, 2016.
DOI: 10.1007/978-3-319-39577-7_2

responsible for a given object (based on the *key* of this object, typically a hash of its name or its content). Additional links are added to this base structure in order to provide faster routing, and to exploit redundancy for tolerating crash faults. A plethora of DHTs structures have been proposed. For instance, based on rings [24, 25, 29], based on a prefix-trees [20], based on the Butterfly graphs [18], based on De Bruijn graphs [8]; or using clusters of complete graphs [10].

One of the defining characteristics of large-scale distributed systems is their instability: due to their size, nodes are expected to join and leave regularly, a phenomenon called *churn*. Being able to tolerate high levels of churn is a key requirement for large-scale decentralized systems.

In the classical method to build DHTs, a new node will gradually *navigate* an existing structure to find its neighbors, and inform nodes that should connect to it. Under churn, or when there are concurrent nodes arrivals, this process may lead to an inconsistent state due to conflicts in the concurrent join or repair processes. To avoid this, joins and repairs should ideally be performed as form of transactions, first contacting all nodes involved in the operation, locking them, applying the change, and finally unlocking them to ensure the atomicity of the overlay changes. A more widespread method is to have all nodes join in sequence, but this means that constructing a network requires a time that is linear in the number of nodes. It is also unclear how this process of sequential joins can be coordinated without a centralized authority. Both methods are costly, error-prone and non-scalable. The reason why these issues have received little attention in the literature (with the exception of [11]) is the overuse of simulations for DHT evaluations, where simplified models removed the need for atomic structure updates.

Gossip-based overlay construction has been proposed as an alternative to the explicit construction and maintenance of overlay networks. When designed properly, gossip-based algorithms can indeed provide self-stabilization guarantees [5]. This means that they are able to recover from any chaotic or incorrect state, as a self-stabilizing system is constantly converging to one of its correct states. Gossip-based protocols are based on simple pairwise interactions between nodes. Nodes typically only have a limited view of the whole system; this view is nevertheless sufficient to take local decisions and implement global behaviour without requiring complex multi-node operations. Two similar frameworks were proposed for gossip-based overlay construction: Vicinity [26] and T-Man [12]. They offer generic construction services allowing users to specify how nodes select their neighbors in the target structure. By converging gradually to the perfect set of neighbors on each node, Vicinity and T-Man create global structures autonomously. The use of a Peer Sampling Service [14] is required to provide convergence guarantees. Gossip-based overlay construction protocols allow bootstrapping a new structure from any state, such as a previously existing structure or even random connections [11].

In their seminal work, the authors of T-Man [12] present the gossip-based construction of Chord [25] as an application of their framework. The resulting system, named T-Chord, is evaluated through cycle-based simulations without considering the impact of churn. We are interested in this work in evaluating the cost, performance and robustness of gossip-constructed DHTs deployed in adverse environments. In addition to T-Chord, we contribute three novel gossip-constructed DHTs using the T-Man framework, namely T-Pastry (following [24]), T-Kademlia (following [20]) and T-Kelips (following [10]). We deployed all four DHTs in a cluster of up to 600 independent nodes and evaluated the cost, performance and robustness of the resulting DHTs structures including when subject to various level of churn. Our findings are the following: the overlays constructed by gossip provide similar performance to the explicitly-constructed ones, or better performance, when there is no churn. They impose a permanent but steady bandwidth consumption at each node (typically within 2 to 10 KB/s), but are able to (1) perform better under churn and (2) recover to a stable structure faster than DHTs using regular, explicit construction. We also make general observations on the convergence of DHT links using gossip, which can vary widely in performance depending on the nature of the created graph and the mean by which each node selects its neighbors.

The rest of the paper is organised as follows. We review related work in Sect. 2. We present the principles of T-Man in Sect. 3, and its use for constructing the four DHT structures in Sect. 4. We detail our experimental results in Sect. 5, before concluding in Sect. 6.

2   Related Work

We discuss related work on the evaluation of DHTs and gossip-based protocols as deployed systems. We are not aware of any work evaluating the performance of gossip-constructed DHTs deployed in the field.[1]

The study of regular DHTs deployed over the internet has sparkled significant interest in the last decade. The authors of [27] analyze the lookup performances of Kad, a Kademlia-inspired DHT [20], to identify optimal configuration sweetspots for routing efficiency. Several studies reveal that Kademlia presented slowness issues affecting its routing performance [22]. The Vuze/Azureus network has been subject of a profiling analysis [6] to characterize the dynamics of its underlying DHT, in particular in the presence of churn. Similar simulation studies for Tapestry and OneHop exist [17]. The authors of [23] study the performance of the Bamboo DHT under churn using a real implementation and network emulation. Analytical studies can help in modeling the expected performance of DHTs, in stable environments [27] or under churn [28].

Studies of gossip protocols deployed *in the wild* offer concrete evidence of their effectiveness but are not numerous. The *BuddyCast* gossip protocol was implemented and deployed to support social recommendation, peer and content discovery, in the context of the Tribler P2P social network [21]. LayStream [19] stacks multiple gossip-based protocols to provide an efficient and churn-resilient dissemination overlay for online video-streaming. LayStream uses T-Man [12] to construct a spanning tree that considers network costs, but does not require a DHT.

---

[1] The one-hop DHT at the core of S3/Dynamo [4] uses gossip and is deployed, but it targets a stable data center environment with less faults and a complete graph structure.

3 Gossip-Based Overlay Construction

This background section describes the gossip-based overlay construction protocol T-Man [12], that we use to bootstrap DHTs in the rest of this paper. The goal of a T-Man instance is to construct for each peer a *view*, which contains contact information for a number *neighbor* peers. Unless otherwise noted, we use instances for which the view size is *bounded* to a maximum of c peers. Neighbors are selected according to a *distance function*. The basic principle of T-Man is to periodically look for the "best" neighbors, among the ones in the current view and candidates obtained by exchanges with other peers. Peers are ranked according to the distance function, and the c closest are kept as neighbors. In case of a tie, other criteria can be used for ranking, or simply a random pick.

In order to guarantee convergence, a T-Man instance must rely on an underlying instance of the Peer Sampling Service (PSS) [14]. The PSS also creates a view of bounded size at each peer, but with the goal that the resulting overlay resembles a random graph as much as possible, guaranteeing a strong resilience to partitions and good recovery properties. This graph is constantly evolving, providing a stream of fresh random peers to each node. The PSS is in charge of inserting new peers in the system and bootstrapping the views for the T-Man instances. The PSS is typically implemented by means of gossip-based interactions itself. The use of the random peers from the PSS allows nodes to avoid ending in a state where the current selection of neighbors is a local minima that is not the global minima, with no possibility to learn about neighbors that belong to the latter [26].

T-Man interactions follow the classical gossip framework. Each peer features two threads. The *active* thread is in charge of initiating exchanges, and the *passive* thread is in charge of answering these requests. The active thread triggers an exchange every Δ time units. It selects the partner either from its T-Man view or from the PSS; more typically, alternating between the two options. The partner selection is normally based on the *age* of the entry, i.e. the time since its inception by the active thread of the corresponding node during an exchange. *Older* links are tested first in order to get rid of links to failed peers within a bounded time. The initiator selects from its view the set of entries it wishes to share with the partner (typically, all of them if entries are not associated with

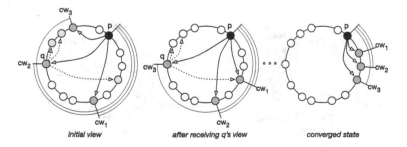

Fig. 1. Convergence of a peer p's view towards clockwise ring neighbors with T-Man.

heavy payloads as will be the case in the remainder of this paper). After the exchange, on both sides peers p and q consider the union of their current view and the received entries to form a new view in the SELECTTOSEND function. Entries are sorted according to the specific distance function d associated with this T-Man instance, and on both sides the c first entries are kept as the new view.

We illustrate the process of overlay construction using T-Man with a simple example of a ring in Fig. 1. This example will be the basis for the two of the DHT constructions described in the next pages, T-Chord and T-Pastry. Each peer has a identifier id, drawn from a large circular space (e.g., $[0..2^m - 1]$). We define distance cw as the *clockwise* distance on the ring, i.e., $cw(p.id, q.id) = (2^m + q.id - p.id) \bmod 2^m$. In this example, the size of the view is $c = 3$, therefore the goal of peer p is to converge towards its three *successors* on the ring. We see that, by interacting with peer q, p learns about peers that minimize distance cw and eventually converges to the three closest peers.

4   Four Gossip-Based Self-Organizing DHTs

We present in this section the four DHTs used in our evaluation. In the interest of space, we focus our description on the overlay structure aspect, that is built using gossip. Other aspects, such as the routing process, data storage and replication, use the mechanisms presented in the original papers [10,20,24,25]. For each DHT, we provide a list of T-Man instances (Table 1) used to construct the different sets of links each node must possess to form the global structure. We will first present all of the instances as operating independently (as illustrated on the right hand side of Fig. 3) and revisit this by presenting runtime optimisations in Subsect. 4.5. There exists two types of links in each structure. *Mandatory* links are required to ensure correct routing towards the peer responsible for a given key. *Optional* links are not required for correctness but allow to speed up routing, or provide redundant links for robustness.

4.1   T-Chord

We start by describing the self-organizing version of Chord [25], T-Chord, originally proposed in [12]. The structure is shown in Fig. 2 (left). A node p is assigned

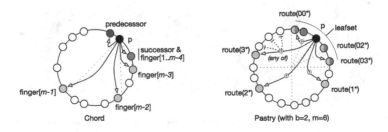

Fig. 2. Ring-based DHTs: Chord [25] and Pastry [24].

Table 1. T-MAN instances (inst.) in T-Chord, T-Pastry, T-Kademlia and T-Kelips.

View	Distance function	Size	Criticality
T-Chord ($m + 1$ instances)			
successors	cw (from $p.id$)	3	critical
predecessor	ccw (from $p.id$)	1	optional
$m - 1$ inst.: f_i, $i \in [0..m - 1]$	cw (from $p.id + 2^i$)	1 each	optional
T-Pastry ($2 + (m.2^b)/b$ instances)			
leafset (inc)	cw (from $p.id$)	8	critical
leafset (dec)	ccw (from $p.id$)	8	critical
$(m.2^b)/b$ instances: RT$_\pi$, $\pi \in q.id.\text{pre}(\{0..m/b\}) \times \{0..2^b - 2\})$	pd (from each prefix π_i of $p.id$, plus one non-common digit)	1 each	optional
T-Kademlia (m instances)			
bucket B_i with $i \in [0..m - 1]$	xor (from each prefix π_i of $p.id$, plus one non-common bit)	3 each: crit. (1st), opt. (others)	
T-Kelips ($G = \sqrt{\bar{N}}$ instances)			
p's group $G_{p.id\%G}$	sg (from $p.id\%G$)	∞	critical
$G - 1$ instances: other groups G_i with $i \in [0..G - 1]\backslash(p.id\%G)$	sg_i (from i)	3 each: crit. (1st), opt. (others)	

a bit identifier $p.id$ in $m = 128$ bits, determining its position on a ring. The first view links to the set of mandatory *successors*. It uses the cw distance function defined in the previous section. While the original Chord algorithm uses a single successor neighbor, using a set of $c = 3$ successors allows routing around failures and implementing replication. A single-neighbor view links to the *predecessor* of the node. The distance function is the counterclockwise distance ccw, where $ccw(p.id, q.id) = (2^m + p.id - q.id) \bmod 2^m$. Node p is responsible for the range of keys following its predecessor and including its own key. The predecessor is used in the original Chord to implement reparation procedures. In T-Chord, the constant convergence towards the optimal peers does not require the presence of the predecessor. Maintaining it allows to compare against the original structure and speed up the convergence of the predecessor's successor list by initiating exchanges that would otherwise only happen through random selection via the PSS. Finally, a set of long-range neighbors, or *fingers*, allows efficient routing on the ring, which otherwise would take O(N) steps, N being the number of nodes. Each finger must point to the node that is the immediate successor to the finger *destination*, covering increasing portions of the ring. Each finger f_i's destination is at a double distance on the ring from the destination of the previous finger f_{i-1}: the first finger points to $p.id + 2^1$ and is effectively the first successor, while the last finger points halfway across the ring to $p.id + 2^{m-1}$. The distance function is therefore cw, with the distance computed from this destination rather than from $p.id$. Fingers allow O($\log N$) routing costs, but are not mandatory for routing correctness. We note that there is conceptually one instance of T-Man *per finger*, leading to $1+1+m-1 = m+1$ T-Man instances in addition to the mandatory PSS, as shown in Fig. 3. We explain in Sect. 4.5 how the exchanges for these multiple instances can be grouped. Furthermore, in practice only instances for longer fingers need to be enabled, i.e., instances that target a destination that is before the farthest successor can be disabled as they would be duplicates of the successors.

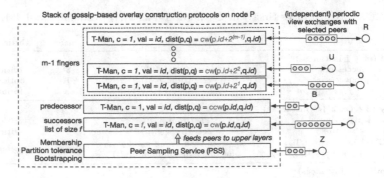

Fig. 3. T-Chord: stack of $m+1$ T-Man instances and the PSS on peer P.

4.2   T-Pastry

T-Pastry creates the structure of Pastry [24] by gossip using a set of T-Man instances. The structure of Pastry as seen from a node p is shown in Fig. 2 (right). Similarly to Chord, node p has an identifier $p.id$ in $m = 128$ bits. This identifier is represented as digits in base 2^b. Figure 2 uses $b = 2$ but our implementations of T-Pastry and Pastry in Sect. 5 uses $b = 4$. Each node maintains two sets of immediate neighbors on the ring, in both directions. These mandatory links form the *leafset*. Two instances of T-Man are required, using previously-defined distance functions cw and ccw and a view size of $c = 8$ for each. In addition, each node maintains a *routing table* (RT). The goal of the RT is to link to nodes that allow matching a prefix with a target key k that is longer than the common prefix between $p.id$ and k. The RT allows $O(\log N)$ routing hops. For instance, in Fig. 2, p with $p.id$ starting with 01* links to nodes that allows matching 02*, 2*, 3*, etc. The RT is organized as a set of $\frac{m}{b}$ rows, one per increasing prefix length, and 2^b columns, one per digit value. A key difference with T-Chord is that multiple nodes can be selected for a given RT entry, e.g., any node in the upper left quartile of the ring is adequate for the entry 3*. This property allows selecting any of the eligible nodes for this RT entry, in particular based on network proximity. We do not make use of this possibility in our implementation, as our cluster testbed does not have heterogeneous links. Each of the RT entry can be (conceptually) filled by one T-Man instance for which the distance is set as pd (binary prefix distance) to a target prefix π_i of $p.id$, of $i \in [0..\frac{m}{b}]$ digits: $pd(\pi_i, q.id) = 0$ if $\pi_i = q.id.\mathtt{pre}(i))$, where $q.id.\mathtt{pre}(i)$ is the prefix of $q.id$ of i digits, and ∞ otherwise. The total number of T-Man instances for the RT is $(m.2^b)/b$. While this number seems to indicate a large amount of independent T-Man instances running concurrently, this is merely a conceptual description. We explain in Subsect. 4.5 how instances are actually grouped and merged by the runtime.

4.3   T-Kademlia

Kademlia [20] is a DHT design allowing prefix routing based on the XOR metric. Nodes have identifiers in $m = 160$ bits and the structure as seen by a node p is depicted in Fig. 4 (left). It can be modeled as a binary tree, where for each prefix π of $p.id$, a *bucket* represents the set of nodes with a prefix that differs in the $|\pi| + 1^{\text{th}}$ bit. For instance, peer p with $p.id =$1011 and $m = 4$ considers 4 buckets, containing nodes with prefixes 0, 11, 100, 1010, respectively. The binary tree is not materialized–instead, the goal of each node is to find at least one representative neighbor in each bucket, if such a node exists. T-Kademlia uses m T-Man instances, one per bucket. Each instance B_i with $i \in [0..m - 1]$ is parametrized with a prefix π_i of $p.id$, with $|\pi_i| = i - 1$, to which one bit is added, which is the complement of the ith bit of $p.id$. The distance function used for each instance B_i is xor, where $xor(\pi_i, q.id) = \pi_i \oplus q.id$. The *first* link to a bucket is considered mandatory, as routing requires being able to resolve any prefix towards a destination key. Extra optional links are kept (2 in our implementation, hence a view size of $c = 3$ links) in order to tolerate faults.

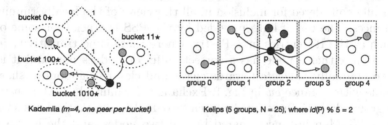

Fig. 4. Kademlia [20] and Kelips [10] DHTs.

4.4   T-Kelips

Our last DHT is T-Kelips, which emerges the structure of Kelips [10] by using a total of $G = \sqrt{\tilde{N}}$ instances of T-Man, $\tilde{N}$ being an estimation of the number of nodes provided when bootstrapping the DHT. Such an estimate can be obtained using a gossip aggregation protocol [13] or using the interval density approach described in [15] on the PSS's view. The structure of Kelips is simple and allows O(1) routing at the cost of O(G) connections, more than for previous designs. The set of nodes is split into G groups. Each node must know all members of its group, as well as at least one representative in each of the other groups. Routing requires two steps: locating the appropriate group for target key k, as $k \bmod G$, and locating the node responsible for k in the group, this time using advertised responsibility ranges, as done in the O(1) DHT at the heart of S3/Dynamo [4]. The original Kelips construction mechanisms uses gossip principles for node detection but without the clear guarantees for convergence allowed by the use of a PSS and T-Man instances stack. We formalize

T-Kelips as the combination of two views. The first view contains all members of p's group. The distance function is *same group*, or sg, where $sg(p.id, q.id) = 0$ if $p.id \bmod G = q.id \bmod G$, and ∞ otherwise. Unlike previously mentioned T-Man instances, the size of this view is unbounded, and all links therein are mandatory. The remaining $G-1$ other instances contain each links to one group, excepting the one $p's$ belong to. Each instance $i \in [0..G-1] \backslash (p.id \bmod G)$ is equipped with distance sg_i, defined as $sg(i, q.id) = 0$ if $i = q.id \bmod G$, and ∞ otherwise. The view at each instance is bounded to $c = 3$. We consider the first link to be mandatory and the remaining two to be optional.

4.5 Optimisations and Interactions with the PSS

So far we considered multiple, independent instances of T-Man interacting with the other corresponding instances on other nodes, as illustrated for T-Chord in Fig. 3. As previously detailed, all instances rely on the existence of the PSS in order to guarantee convergence. This interaction happens in two forms. First, gossip partners can be selected from the PSS. We alternate between a selection in the T-Man view and the PSS view. Second, the nodes in the PSS view are automatically considered for inclusion in all the views of the locally running T-Man instances. The use of links provided by the PSS is crucial for some of the views, such as the RT entries in T-Pastry, where there is no transitivity in the node selection: either a node has a correct suffix or it does not, and it is not possible to gradually *navigate* towards closer and closer neighbors as shown in the example with distance cw in Fig. 1. Exchanges for multiple T-Man instances are also grouped: an interaction between two nodes automatically exchanges views for *all* T-Man instances shared by the two nodes, and the gossip cycle Δ is the same for all instances. The implementation allows however defining each instance separately–the grouping is handled automatically by the T-Man runtime. This allows a simple and principled definition of the gossip stack while maximizing convergence speed, and is made possible thanks to the small payload (a single m bits identifier) associated with each of the entries.

5 Evaluation

We present in this section the evaluation of T-Chord, T-Kademlia, T-Pastry and T-Kelips using a prototype implementation. For Pastry, we include comparison figures against an implementation following the explicit construction and main-tenance mechanisms of the original paper [24]. For space reasons, we leave the comparison of the other explicitly-constructed DHTs to future work.

We leverage the Splay framework [16] for our experiments. All protocols and the T-Man runtime are coded in Lua. We use a cluster of 12 dual-core Intel Core2 machines (24 cores in total), each with 2 GB of RAM and interconnected using a switched 1 Gbps network. We deploy up to 600 nodes over this cluster. The PSS we use is an implementation of the framework in [14]. The view size is $c = 10$. Two parameters S and H allow setting the compromise between the randomness quality of the PSS overlay (S) and the ability to quickly discard failed peers (H). We use $S = c/2 - 1 = 4$ and $H = 1$. The gossiping period Δ for both the PSS and T-Man instances is set to 5 s. We consider crash failures only, and leave the evaluation of the impact of other failures models such as omissions and fail-recovery failures, to future work.

We study the convergence of the four structures in Sect. 5.1 and their routing efficiency in Sect. 5.2. The network costs for constructing the four DHTs using gossip are evaluated in Sect. 5.3. Finally, we conclude in Sect. 5.4 by observing the behaviour of the protocols under churn and comparing against the explicitly-constructed Pastry implementation.

5.1 Overlay Convergence in a Stable Network

We start by analyzing the speed of convergence towards the target structure of the four DHTs. For each node, after each T-Man exchange, the set of neighbors in each of the views is compared to what would be selected by an omniscient observer. Mandatory and optional links, as defined in Table 1, are considered separately. This omniscient selection would pick the c peers with the smaller distance (e.g., for T-Chord's *successors* and *fingers*, or for T-Pastry's *leafsets*) or, when multiple peers are equally *close* to the node, consider valid any random set of c peers among the ones at this distance (e.g., for T-Pastry's *RT entries* of T-Kademlia's *buckets*).

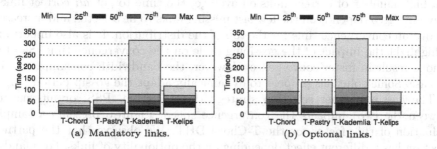

Fig. 5. Convergence of links in gossip-based DHTs.

Figure 5 presents convergence results for mandatory (Fig. 5a) and optional (Fig. 5b) links. We use a representation based on stacked *percentiles* throughout this section. The white bar at the bottom represents the minimum value, the pale grey bar on top the maximal one. Intermediate shades of grey represent the 25th, 50th–the median–, and 75th percentiles. The median time for a T-Pastry node to learn all of its mandatory links is 5 cycles (25 s). For both T-Chord and T-Pastry, all nodes reach mandatory links convergence within 12 cycles (60 s). For T-Kelips, it takes twice as much time, which is explained by the higher number of mandatory links ($O(\sqrt{N})$ entries, ≈ 50 average in practice). T-Kademlia has the slowest convergence of mandatory links (up to 65 cycles, or 5.4 min in the worst case). Other experiments (not shown) show that this worst-case time increases linearly with the network size, leading to poor scalability.

It is interesting to understand the reason for this slow convergence. The distance function used, *xor*, is discrete and transitive: if a node n_1 is close to node n_2, who is in turn close to node n_3, then there is a higher probability that n_1 be close to n_3, than it would be with a random node. This property typically allows speeding up the overlay convergence, as nodes *gradually* learn about closer and closer peers. However, the nature of the overlay built by T-Kademlia prevent this gradual selection from happening. Indeed, a peer in a bucket B_i of peer p contains neighbors starting with a prefix π_i whose last (i^{th}) bit differs from the ith bit of *p.id*. These neighbors may themselves have neighbors that would minimize p's *xor* distance, but they are selected among all eligible neighbors and in a single bucket (a B_j for which π_j has the same $i-1$ bits as π_i and the same i^{th} bit as *p.id*). A result is that the probability for these peers to be of interest to p is the same as the one for peers drawn randomly from the PSS, explaining that the convergence performance is similar to what would happen by considering random peers only, and its duration evolves linearly in the number of nodes. Optional links in T-Kademlia are selected similarly to the mandatory ones, and their convergence shows similar performance. The same similar behaviour for the two types of links is displayed by T-Kelips, and for the same reason. Optional links differ in their definition from mandatory ones for both T-Chord and T-Pastry. In both cases, the latter are more numerous but can accommodate a lazy construction. Their convergence is indeed slower–while our evaluation of the percentage of correct links (not shown) shows that nodes converge quickly to a high number of correct links on average, the time to get *all* correct links, shown in Fig. 5 depends on the few last missing links to be selected and increases the overall convergence time for the top of the distribution. It is also important to highlight the impact of the gossiping cycle on the convergence time. Shorter periods result in faster convergence. However, the bandwidth consumption will increase. Some solutions propose to dynamically adapt the gossip period [7].

The gossip partner selection strategy (from T-Man, PSS, or alternating between the two) impacts the convergence speed. Figure 6 presents a sample evaluation of this factor for the T-Chord DHT. We observe that the partner selection has a different effect depending on the optionality of links. For mandatory links, formed of the *successors* view, selecting partners from the PSS only is the fastest, leading to convergence in less than 8 cycles (40 s). Selecting partners

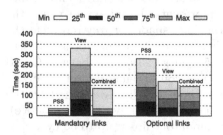

Fig. 6. Partner selection in T-Chord.

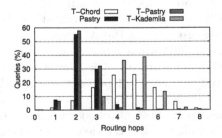

Fig. 7. Overlays routing efficiency.

from the view leads to up to 65 cycles (5.4 min) for convergence, with a linear distribution. The *combined* (alternating between the two) strategy has good general case convergence but also incurs outliers converging in up to 26 cycles (2.2 min). This behavior can be explained based on the nature of the successors lists. A node p who has node q selected as its current successor can ask for q's successors, but it is unlikely that those will be closer to p than they are to q, and will replace the current successors of p. It is only when p is connected to its very close neighbors that these will help to converge by sharing their views and in particular their predecessor. Random interactions are more efficient in this case for fast convergence. Interestingly, the opposite is true for optional links (fingers): random interactions through the PSS yield the slowest convergence, while using the combined approach is slightly faster than using the views only. For T-Kad we observe that selecting partners from the PSS only is the slowest option among the strategies, leading to a median convergence time of 24 cycles (2 min), while selecting from the view yields 9 cycles (45 s) and using the combined strategies requires 11 cycles (55 s). We observe the same lack of pattern for T-Pastry and T-Kelips but in the interest of space we do not present those results. This shows that there does not seem to be a one-size fits all for this parameter; we leave the automatic adaptation of gossip-based overlay construction protocol for future work and use the combined selection in the remaining of our evaluation.

5.2 Routing Efficiency

Our next benchmark evaluates the efficiency of routing in the converged DHTs structures. We evaluate the routing costs by sending 50 queries per node to randomly generated keys for a total of 30,000 queries. Figure 7 shows the distribution of the number of hops in each of the structures, with the exception of T-Kelips where this number is always 1 (in the same group) or 2 (general case) by construction. We see that the routing performance is on par with the expectations, in particular, T-Pastry can deliver queries as efficiently as Pastry: 50 % of the queries reach the destination in at most 2 hops, while outperforming T-Kademlia and T-Chord, where 50 % of the queries require 4 hops.

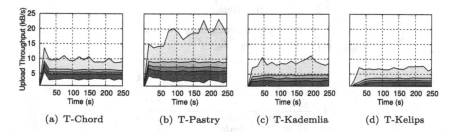

(a) T-Chord   (b) T-Pastry   (c) T-Kademlia   (d) T-Kelips

Fig. 8. Upload throughput in a static scenario for the four DHTs.

5.3   Bandwidth Consumption

We evaluate the network bandwidth cost of the gossip-based construction of
DHTs. This aspect has been one of the criticized aspects of gossip-based protocols, in particular for dissemination. With the constant and regular exchanges
of information, even in a stabilized network, gossip-based protocols indeed incur
a constant network cost for these exchanges. We do not consider techniques for
auto-adapting the gossip cycle Δ such as [7] but present in Fig. 8 the bandwidth
consumed by the four DHT, as the distribution of upload costs per node, as a

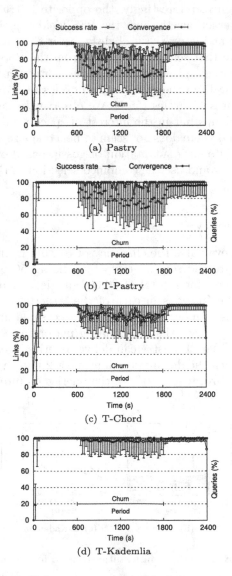

(a) Pastry

(b) T-Pastry

(c) T-Chord

(d) T-Kademlia

Fig. 9. Mandatory links convergence and lookup success under churn.

function of time. As expected, this distribution remains stable over time; with a small spread that is for the most part due to our fixed-time range aggregation. For all four DHTs, the bandwidth requirement is around 3 to 10 KB/s, up to 20 KB/s for T-Pastry. We believe these numbers remain reasonable in a wired environment; we leave the implementation of bandwidth capping mechanisms, in particular at the level of the aggregation of T-Man instances by the library, as future work (one solution being to send to a partner only the peers that have a potential interest for its own views rather than the whole set).

5.4 Behaviour Under Churn

Figure 9 presents the evolution of the overlay structures (convergence of the mandatory links, compared to an offline trace of online nodes in the system) and the success rates for lookups, when the system is subject to churn. We compare the behavior of Pastry to three of the gossip-based DHTs. We leverage Splay's ability to replay churn traces and orchestrating the creation and failure of peers. We use same churn trace for all four systems: the system starts in a stable state with 150 nodes. During the churn period of 20 min, indicated by the arrow on the figures and starting at time 10 min, every minute 15 % of the nodes are *replaced*: one node goes down and another one goes up. New nodes are fresh nodes and we leave the consideration of recovering nodes to future work. This results in the arrival of 450 new nodes and the departure of the same amount of nodes in the duration of the churn period. The churn period is followed by a stable period of 10 min. We observe that T-Kademlia is the least affected by churn: the lookup success rate is close to 100 % and the deviation from the correct state is insignificant. Once the system stabilizes, it immediately converges to the correct state again. The high success rate during churn is a result of the presence of redundant links in the routing table. T-Chord, likewise, converges to the ideal state right after the end of the churn period. Its lookup correctness is however more impaired compared to T-Kademlia during the churn. The performance of regular Pastry is more impaired by churn than that of T-Pastry, as the structure diverges more from the ideal and the lookup success rate is more impacted.

6 Conclusion

We have presented in this paper the design and evaluation of DHTs using gossip-based overlay construction principles. Following T-Chord based on T-Man [12], we presented the design of T-Pastry, T-Kademlia and T-Kelips. We evaluated the four DHTs using the Splay framework on up to 600 nodes, and under churn. The results indicate that gossip-based overlay construction is a sound approach for large and dynamic system: while it requires a constant bandwidth consumption, it is able to bootstrap overlays in very short times without concerns about the structure correctness or degradation. For one representative system compared against its explicitly-constructed counterpart (Pastry), the overlay resulting from the gossip-based construction shows better ability to handle and recover from churn.

Acknowledgments. The research leading to these results has received funding from CHIST-ERA under project DIONASYS, and from the Swiss National Science Foundation (SNSF) under grant 155249.

References

1. Castro, M., Druschel, P., Kermarrec, A.-M., Nandi, A., Rowstron, A., Singh, A.: SplitStream: high-bandwidth multicast in cooperative environments. In: SOSP (2003)
2. Castro, M., Druschel, P., Kermarrec, A.-M., Rowstron, A.: Scribe: A large-scale and decentralized application-level multicast infrastructure. IEEE JSAC **20**, 100–110 (2002)
3. Dabek, F., Kaashoek, M. F., Karger, D., Morris, R., Stoica, I.: Wide-area cooperative storage with CFS. In: SOSP (2001)
4. DeCandia, G., Hastorun, D., Jampani, M., Kakulapati, G., Lakshman, A., Pilchin, A., Sivasubramanian, S., Vosshall, P., Vogels, W.: Dynamo: Amazon's highly available key-value store. In: SOSP (2007)
5. Dolev, S.: Self-Stabilization. MIT Press, Cambridge (2000)
6. Falkner, J., Piatek, M., John, J.P., Krishnamurthy, A., Anderson, T.: Profiling a million user dht. In: ACM IMC (2007)
7. Felber, P., Kermarrec, A.-M., Leonini, L., Rivière, E., Voulgaris, S.: Pulp: an adaptive gossip-based dissemination protocol for multi-source message streams. Springer PPNA **5**(1), 74–91 (2012)
8. Fraigniaud, P., Gauron, P.: D2B: A De Bruijn based content-addressable network. Theorical Computer Science (2006)
9. Gupta, A., Sahin, O.D., Agrawal, D.P., El Abbadi, A.: Meghdoot: content-based publish/subscribe over P2P networks. In: Jacobsen, H.-A. (ed.) Middleware 2004. LNCS, vol. 3231, pp. 254–273. Springer, Heidelberg (2004)
10. Gupta, I., Birman, K., Linga, P., Demers, A., Van Renesse, R.: Kelips: Building an efficient and stable P2P DHT through increased memory and background overhead. In: IEEE P2P (2003)
11. Jelasity, M., Montresor, A., Babaoglu, O.: The bootstrapping service.In: ICDCSW 2006
12. Jelasity, M., Montresor, A., Babaoglu, O.: T-Man: Gossip-based fast overlay topology construction. Computer Networks (2009)
13. Jelasity, M., Montresor, A., Babaoglu, O.: Gossip-based aggregation in large dynamic networks. ACM TOCS **23**(3), 219–252 (2005)
14. Jelasity, M., Voulgaris, S., Guerraoui, R., Kermarrec, A.-M., Van Steen, M.: Gossip-based peer sampling. ACM TOCS **25**, 8 (2007)
15. Kostoulas, D., Psaltoulis, D., Gupta, I., Birman, K.P., Demers, A.J.: Active and passive techniques for group size estimation in large-scale and dynamic distributed systems. J. Syst. Softw. **80**(10), 1639–1658 (2007)
16. Leonini, L., Rivière, E., Felber, P.: Distributed systems evaluation made simple (or how to turn ideas into live systems in a breeze). In: NSDI (2009)
17. Li, J., Stribling, J., Morris, R., Kaashoek, F., Gil, T.M.: A performance vs. cost framework for evaluating DHT design tradeoffs under churn. In: INFOCOM (2005)
18. Malkhi, D., Naor, M., Ratajczak, D.: Viceroy : A scalable and dynamic emulation of the butterfly. In: ACM PODC (2002)
19. Matos, M., Schiavoni, V., Rivière, E., Felber, P., Oliveira, R.: LayStream: composing standard gossip protocols for live video streaming. In: IEEE P2P (2014)

20. Maymounkov, P., Mazières, D.: Kademlia: a peer-to-peer information system based on the XOR metric. In: Druschel, P., Kaashoek, M.F., Rowstron, A. (eds.) IPTPS 2002. LNCS, vol. 2429, p. 53. Springer, Heidelberg (2002)
21. Pouwelse, J.A., Garbacki, P., Wang, J., Bakker, A., Yang, J., Iosup, A., Epema, D.H., Reinders, M., Van Steen, M.R., Sips, H.J. et al.: Tribler: A social-based peer-to-peer system. Conc. and Comp.: Pract. and Exp. (2008)
22. Rhea, S., Chun, B.-G., Kubiatowicz, J., Shenker, S.: Fixing the embarrassing slowness of OpenDHT on planetlab. In: WORLDS (2005)
23. Rhea, S., Geels, D., Roscoe, T., Kubiatowicz, J.: Handling churn in a DHT. In: USENIX ATC (2004)
24. Rowstron, A., Druschel, P.: Pastry: scalable, decentralized object location, and routing for large-scale peer-to-peer systems. In: Guerraoui, R. (ed.) Middleware 2001. LNCS, vol. 2218, p. 329. Springer, Heidelberg (2001)
25. Stoica, I., Morris, R., Liben-Nowell, D., Karger, D.R., Kaashoek, M.F., Dabek, F., Balakrishnan, H.: Chord: A scalable peer-to-peer lookup protocol for internet applications. IEEE/ACM ToN 11, 17–32 (2003)
26. Voulgaris, S., van Steen, M.: VICINITY: a pinch of randomness brings out the structure. In: Eyers, D., Schwan, K. (eds.) Middleware 2013. LNCS, vol. 8275, pp. 21–40. Springer, Heidelberg (2013)
27. Wang, C.-C., Harfoush, K.: On the stability-scalability tradeoff of DHT deployment. In: IEEE INFOCOM (2007)
28. Wu, D., Tian, Y., Ng, K.-W.: Analytical study on improving DHT lookup performance under churn. In: IEEE P2P (2006)
29. Zhao, B.Y., Huang, L., Stribling, J., Rhea, S.C., Joseph, A.D., Kubiatowicz, J.D.: Tapestry: A resilient global-scale overlay for service deployment. IEEE JSAC 22, 41–53 (2004)

Mignon: A Fast Decentralized Content Consumption Estimation in Large-Scale Distributed Systems

Stéphane Delbruel[1]([⊠]), Davide Frey[2], and François Taïani[1]

[1] Université de Rennes 1, IRISA – ESIR, Rennes, France
{stephane.delbruel,francois.taiani}@irisa.fr
[2] Inria, Rennes, France
davide.frey@inria.fr

Abstract. Although many fully decentralized content distribution systems have been proposed, they often lack key capabilities that make them difficult to deploy and use in practice. In this paper, we look at the particular problem of content consumption prediction, a crucial mechanism in many such systems. We propose a novel, fully decentralized protocol that uses the tags attached by users to on-line content, and exploits the properties of self-organizing kNN overlays to rapidly estimate the potential of a particular content without explicit aggregation.

Keywords: Decentralized systems · Content consumption · Estimation

1   Introduction

User-generated content (UGC) services have grown extremely fast over the last few years [1,37]. In order to support this growth, current services typically exploit private data centers owned by large companies such as Google, Sony and Amazon. These data centers are further augmented with Content Distribution Networks (CDNs) and caching servers positioned at points-of-presence (PoP) within the infrastructure of Internet Service Providers (ISPs) [16].

This approach tends to favor big players, and to concentrate the industry in the hands of a few powerful actors. For several years now, both academia and practitioners have therefore sought to explore alternative designs to implement social online services in general, and UGC video services in particular. One strategy espouses a fully decentralized organization [2,5,18,24,28], in which each individual user (through her computer or set-top box) provides resources to implement the system's overall services, including storage [24,29,30], indexing [9], queries [3,19], recommendation [4–6], caching [13], and streaming [8,14].

To ensure their scalability, most of these services primarily rely on *limited interactions* (e.g. with a small set of neighboring nodes) and *local information* (e.g. users profiles, bandwidth, latency, tags). The use of local information is

M. Jelasity and E. Kalyvianaki (Eds.): DAIS 2016, LNCS 9687, pp. 32–46, 2016.
DOI: 10.1007/978-3-319-39577-7_3

one of the key reasons why these services scale. Too strong a focus on locality, however, constrains the range of decisions that can be taken by individual nodes, and their ability to adapt to phenomena occurring at a global scale.

In an attempt to address this limitation, we focus, in this paper, on the particular problem of *global predictions* in large-scale decentralized systems, with an application to the placement of videos in a decentralized UGC video service. Being able to predict where a new video is likely to be consumed is a crucial ability for decentralized services that often lack the tightly integrated global infrastructure of large players. It can help inform storage and caching decisions in order to best exploit the resources these services can rely on [32,33].

More precisely, we consider the problem of a newly uploaded videos that must be stored and replicated within a peer-to-peer system in the countries where it is more likely to be viewed. We have shown in a previous work that the tags attached to videos are a good predictor of a video's view distribution [11]. Unfortunately, individual peers do not by default have access to the past videos and tags consumed within individual countries, and this information can be costly to aggregate explicitly. In this paper, we therefore propose *Mignon*, a novel *decentralized content consumption estimation mechanism* that is fast and scalable and eschews the need for any global aggregation. Mignon exploits the properties of self-organizing similarity overlays [5,21,36] and delivers estimations that are on average within 0.6 % (respectively 13 %) of an exhaustive view aggregation on a MovieLens (respectively YouTube) dataset.

2   Problem Statement and Related Work

We consider a global decentralized P2P UGC service, in which each user contributes her resources to the system. As we focus on video placement and view prediction, we assume our service can store and retrieve videos from users' machines [29,31,34]. As is now common in many on-line services, we also assume that the past activity of users can be used to predict their affinity with new content (Fig. 1). More precisely, the individual devices of users (Alice and Bob, label **1**) store the list of videos they have consumed (their *video profile*, label **2**). Each video is associated with a set of descriptive tags provided by its uploading user [15,17] (label **3**). Here for instance, Alice has viewed a BBC video with the tag '*news*' (⊗), and a video on environmental protection with the tags '*news*', and '*animals*' (⊗ ☻). The tags of the videos viewed by a user form her *tag profiles* (label **4**): [⊗:2,☻:1] for Alice and [☻:1] for Bob.

We rely on a tag-based *affinity function* f that measures a user's affinity with new videos (**5**) [5,11]. The only assumptions we make about f is that its result is correlated with the probability that this user will watch the video (**6**).

2.1   Placing New Videos: The Prediction Problem

When uploading a new video, copies of this video should ideally be placed in storage locations close to where it might be most consumed. This is because

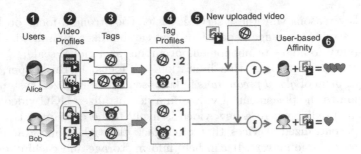

Fig. 1. Using tags to predict users' affinity with a new video

Table 1. Top 3 countries for *bollywood* (left) and *favela* (right)

country	#views	%age	country	#views	%
India	200,956,055	39.8%	Brazil	19,834,633	47.9%
United-States	124,461,447	24.7%	United-States	14,468,608	34.9%
United-Kingdom	29,506,586	5.8%	United-Kingdom	1,701,496	4.1%

the viewing patterns of many videos in UGC services present clear geographic trends [7], which are strongly correlated with a video's tags [11]. Table 1 shows for instance how the tags *"bollywood"* and *"favela"* follow clearly distinctive geographic distributions in a Youtube dataset analyzed in an earlier work [11]. Correctly predicting the geographic distribution of a video's views is particularly important in decentralized systems that often lack the caching infrastructure of large integrated services. In Fig. 2 for instance, Dave must decide whether to store his new video in the USA or in France. This decision should be driven by the video's likely future popularity in both countries, which can be estimated as the sum of all user affinities in each country.

Obtaining this aggregated sum efficiently is unfortunately challenging in a large P2P system. Dave could trigger a P2P aggregation in the USA and France [27], but such an approach would require computing the similarity between the new video and every user in each country, a slow and costly operation.

In this paper, we therefore investigate how such a sum can be efficiently, rapidly, and accurately estimated in a fully decentralized system while involving only a small subset of the users in a given country.

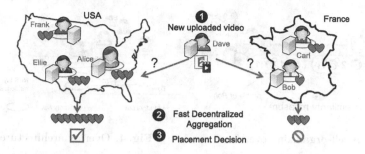

Fig. 2. Placing new videos based on aggregated affinity

2.2 Related Work

A number of works have been proposed to perform aggregation operations in decentralized peer-to-peer systems [20,27]. These works typically use an epidemic procedure in which nodes repeatedly interact with other random peers in a pair-wise fashion. They often further rely on a peer-sampling protocol [22,35] to maximize the diversity of interactions between peers. Following this strategy, averaging can for instance be implemented in the following manner: all peers p_i start with an initial value v_i^0. A given peer p_i then periodically selects another random peer p_j returned from the peer sampling service, and both peer update they respective value to $\frac{(v_i+v_j)}{2}$. This procedure guarantees that all nodes progressively converge to a value that is increasingly close to the average of all initial values $\frac{1}{N}\sum_{i=1}^{N} v_i$. The number of rounds required to attain a given aggregate accuracy primarily depends on the distribution of the original data [20].

This aggregation procedure can be used to estimate the size of a network, with all nodes but one starting with a value of 0, and one node (the initiator) a value of 1: all nodes will converge to a value of $\frac{1}{N}$ [27]. Combined with the above averaging protocol, such a size estimation can provide an estimate of the sum of the original peer values $\sum_{i=1}^{N} v_i$. Unfortunately, this approach is ill-suited to our case, as it would require the tags of every new video to be propagated to the entire network before any estimation may take place, incurring both additional latency and high network costs for every new upload.

3 Fast Decentralized Sum Estimation

Instead of launching an expensive aggregation every time a new video is uploaded, we propose a cheaper mechanism to estimate the aggregated affinity of a video. Our approach exploits a similarity-driven overlay [5] that interconnects all the users in a country. In the following we first briefly describe similarity-driven overlays, and then present the details of our approach.

3.1 Self-Organizing Overlays

Similarity-driven overlay networks organize peers according to their similarity [21], with a wide range of applications [3,5,6,12,13]. In this work, we consider

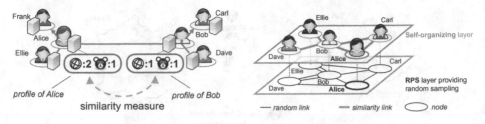

Fig. 3. A self-organizing overlay   **Fig. 4.** Overlay architecture

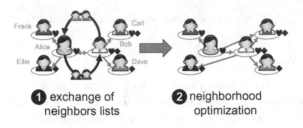

Fig. 5. Peer-to-peer neighborhood optimization

gossip-based similarity driven overlays, whose working is depicted in Figs. 3, 4 and 5. The machine of each user holds the user's profile: in our case the list of viewed videos and their attached tags (Fig. 3). Starting from random neighborhoods the overlay eventually connects each peer to its k most similar other peers in the network, according to some similarity metric (e.g. Jaccard's coefficient, or Cosine Similarity).

This construction uses two greedy mechanisms (Figs. 4 and 5). With the first mechanism, a peer (e.g. Alice) regularly polls an underlying and constantly evolving Random Peer Sampling (RPS) overlay [22] to obtain a set of random peers from the rest of the system. In Fig. 4 for instance, Alice might discover Dave through the RPS layer. If Dave turns out to be a better neighbor for Alice than Bob (upper self-organizing layer), Alice will replace Bob by Dave in her neighborhood. This stochastic process ensures that the system eventually converges to an optimal state. The convergence might however be very slow.

To speed up convergence, peers use a second '*neighbor-of-neighbor*' mechanism (Fig. 5). The intuition is that if Alice is similar to Bob, and Bob to Carl, then Carl might be similar to Alice. Peers therefore periodically exchange their current neighbors lists (Step **1** in Fig. 5), and use the new peers they discover to optimize their neighborhoods (Step **2**). This mechanism greatly accelerates convergence (usually in $log(N)$ rounds [21]), but might get stuck in a local minimum, and is therefore complementary to the stochastic mechanism of Fig. 4.

3.2   Mignon: Fast Decentralized Estimation

In this paper we propose *Mignon*, a protocol that employs the similarity-driven overlay we have just described to estimate the aggregated affinity of a new video with all the users in a country. To this end, all the users in a country participate in a similarity-driven overlay whose similarity function is the affinity function f of Fig. 1. When one of these users uploads a new video, v, she additionally creates a new virtual peer P_v, whose profile contains the tags associated with v.

Our estimation problem simply consists in computing the sum of the similarities between P_v and every other user in the country. To compute this sum exhaustively, either at peer P_v or using a standard aggregation protocol, we would either have to collect the profiles of all other nodes at P_v, or disseminate the profile of P_v to every other node. In both cases, the delay and the resulting network cost would be prohibitive for very large networks.

Instead, in Mignon, the uploading user simply impersonates the virtual peer by having it join the similarity-based overlay. In a very short time (generally logarithmic in the size of the network [21]), P_v obtains its k-nearest neighbors. Once this happens, the uploading user exploits the content of the KNN and RPS neighborhoods of P_v to estimate the video's aggregated affinity without any further network exchanges.

The key to the approach consists in considering the affinity values of users found in the KNN and RPS views of P_v as samples taken from a monotonically decreasing function. Figure 6 shows this pictorially in two examples. The black vertical lines represent the affinity values of the users found in the KNN and RPS views of P_v. Mignon uses these values to interpolate the function's shape, from which we derive an aggregated affinity by integration. The values obtained from the KNN neighbors constitute the first k consecutive samples, while those in the RPS represent randomly chosen samples distributed along the rest of the x-axis. To associate each of them with an x-coordinate (which the RPS does not indicate), we rely on a network-size estimation protocol [25] that provides us with the length of the x-axis, and assume that the RPS samples are equally spaced along this axis.

It should be noted that the inherent cost of size-estimation does not offset the benefits provided by our approach in terms of delay and network cost. First, the size estimation protocol does not need to be run for every video upload. Rather, in a setup consisting of set-top boxes that are almost always on, the protocol can run every few days. Second, protocols like Sample & Collide [25] can estimate the size of the network within a reasonable error margin at a minimal cost. We evaluate the impact of protocols like Sample & Collide in Sect. 4.3. In the following we describe the two interpolation techniques we use in Mignon.

Trapezoidal Rule. The first technique we consider is the trapezoidal rule, a well-known method for approximating the integral of a function. The rule replaces the function to be integrated with a sequence of linear segments and computes the integral as the sum of the areas of the corresponding trapezoids.

Polynomial Interpolation. As a second estimation mechanism, we consider a polynomial interpolation. Specifically, we compute the polynomial of degree $n-1$ that goes through all of the n samples in the KNN and RPS. We then use this polynomial to compute the values associated with the users that are not among the samples.

4 Evaluation

We evaluate Mignon on two distinct datasets. The first consists of an adaptation of the YouTube dataset we introduced in our previous work [10,18]. It contains $590,897$ videos, each associated with a set of tags —11.18 per video on average, with a total of $705,415$ distinct tags— and with a popularity vector that provides an estimated number of views per country. We extracted videos and tags directly from YouTube, while we computed the number of views for videos and tags by crossing YouTube data with information from Alexa Internet Inc.[1] as described in [10], with the following equation.

$$\mathbf{views}(v)[c] \simeq \frac{\widehat{\mathbf{p}}_{yt}[c] \times \mathbf{pop}(v)[c]}{\sum\limits_{\gamma \in World} \left(\widehat{\mathbf{p}}_{yt}[\gamma] \times \mathbf{pop}(v)[\gamma]\right)} \times tot\_views(v) \tag{1}$$

where $\mathbf{views}(v)[c]$ is the number of views of video v in country c, $\mathbf{p}_{yt}[c]$ is the proportion of Youtube views in country c at the time our data set was collected, and $\mathbf{pop}(v)[c]$ is a popularity vector issued from our ground hypothesis in [10], i.e. a number proportional to the share of video v's views in country c. To evaluate Mignon, we "reinterpreted" this dataset by considering each country as if it was a single user. Our modified dataset therefore consists of 257 users in a single country.

Our second dataset, MovieLens, consists of a trace from a movie recommendation system[2]. It contains a set of movies, each associated with a vector of ratings (1 to 5 integers) by a subset of the users, and a set of n pairs, each consisting of a tag and a real-valued relevance score. The rating $R_u(m)$ expresses the interest of a user u in movie m, while the relevance $r_m(t)$ score expresses the importance of a tag t for a given movie m. Based on this information, we compute the interest score u_t of a user u for a tag t as follows.

$$u_t = \frac{1}{n} \sum_{m=1}^{n} (r_m(t) * R_u(m)) \tag{2}$$

Since we want to evaluate Mignon's ability to estimate the aggregation of a score value, we consider a synthetic set of new "videos", whose profile only comprises a single tag taken from the dataset. For each such video v, we first select the set of users in its KNN and RPS views, and then compute its affinity with these users. We use this sample of affinity values to produce an estimate (noted $\hat{a}_v$) of the video's aggregated affinity with all the users in the system (which we note a_v). To assess the performance of different estimation techniques, we define an estimation ratio: $\mathrm{ER}_v = \frac{\hat{a}_v}{a_v}$. We evaluate ER_v in a variety of configurations

---

[1] http://www.alexa.com/siteinfo/youtube.com.
[2] www.movielens.org.

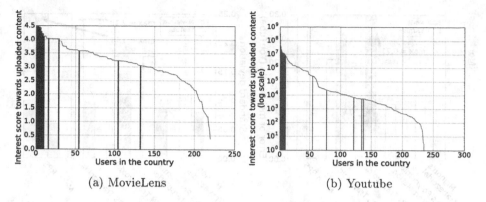

(a) MovieLens (b) Youtube

Fig. 6. Interest curve for MovieLens(a) and YouTube(b) datasets. Black vertical lines represent KNN and RPS samples.

on each of our datasets. Let n be the number of tags in a dataset (and hence of synthetic videos), we present the distribution of ER_v, its mean $\overline{\mathrm{ER}} = \frac{1}{n}\sum_{i=1}^{n}\mathrm{ER}_{v_i}$, as well as its standard deviation $\sqrt{\overline{\mathrm{ER}^2} - \overline{\mathrm{ER}}^2}$.

Figure 6 exemplifies the affinity score distribution of particular tags (interpreted as videos) in each of the two dataset. The curve depicts the affinity score of each user for the tag in decreasing order, while the vertical bars represent the data available in the KNN and RPS views.

4.1 Accuracy Comparison

We start our evaluation by comparing the results obtained by Mignon with those obtained by three baseline approaches that exploit either the KNN or the RPS views but not both. For Mignon, we consider the two estimation techniques presented in Sect. 3.2 (the *Trapezoidal* and *Polynomial* interpolations). For the baselines, we tested both these techniques as well as linear and quadratic regression and selected the three that obtained the best performance. Specifically, **KNN-Trapezoid** applies the trapezoid rule on a KNN view without using the RPS, **RPS-Trapezoid** also applies the trapezoid rule but on an RPS view with no KNN, while **RPS-Mean** simply computes the average similarity of the nodes in the RPS view and multiplies it by the size of the network. We configured our techniques to use a KNN view size of 15 and an RPS size of 10, while all the baselines use a single view (RPS or KNN) of size 25.

Figure 7 shows the results on both of our datasets. Figure 7a depicts the error on the mean estimation ratio, that is $|\overline{\mathrm{ER}} - 1|$, and shows that combining the KNN and the RPS views allows Mignon to adapt to multiple data sets. Specifically, both the Trapezoidal rule and Polynomial interpolation obtain very good estimates on both datasets with an error on the mean ratio respectively of 0.06 (6 %) and 0.01 (1 %) on MovieLens and of 0.143 (14.3 %) and 0.114 (11.4 %) on YouTube. The baselines, on the other hand, can achieve good performance on

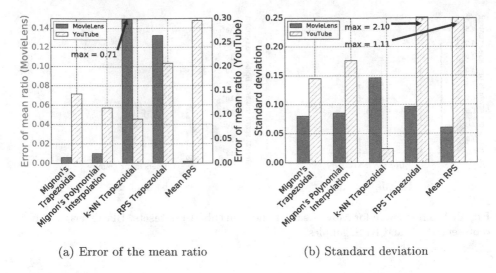

(a) Error of the mean ratio   (b) Standard deviation

Fig. 7. Evaluation of the error and the standard deviation for both datasets MovieLens and YouTube

one of the datasets but not on both. KNN-Trapezoid achieves a very low error of 0.09 (9 %) on YouTube, but a very high error of 0.7 (70 %) on MovieLens. RPS-Mean achieves a very low error of 0.02 (2 %) on MovieLens but a high error of 0.30 (30 %) on YouTube, while RPS-Trapezoid achieves errors of 0.13 (13 %) on MovieLens and of 0.21 (21 %) on YouTube, worse than both of Mignon's approaches on both datasets.

Figure 7b completes the picture by showing the standard deviation of the estimation ratio. Again, Mignon obtains low standard deviations on both data sets, contrary to RPS-Trapezoid and RPS-Mean. KNN-Trapezoid also achieves good standard deviations on both dataset, but with a very high mean error on MovieLens (Fig. 7a).

4.2   Sensitivity Analysis

Now that we have shown the effectiveness of Mignon's estimation approach on multiple datasets, we analyze how the KNN and RPS views impact its performance. We present our results in the form of whisker plots in Figs. 8 and 9. Each box in the plot covers the values between the lower and the upper quartiles; the point in the box represents the mean, while the line the median. The endpoints of the whiskers represent the lowest datum still within $1.5 * $ InterQuartile Range (IQR) of the lower quartile, and the highest datum still within $1.5 * $ IQR of the upper quartile, while the points outside the whiskers represent outliers.

Trapezoidal Rule. Figure 8 shows how the effectiveness of the trapezoid rule varies when we vary the sizes of the KNN and RPS views. For fairness we maintain a total view size of 25 and vary the proportion of nodes in the two views from |KNN|=2 |RPS|=23 to |KNN|=23 |RPS|=2. Figure 8a shows that larger KNN views slightly tend to overestimate the total affinity, while large RPS views slightly tend to underestimate it, with the best performance being achieved with a KNN view of 15 and an RPS view of 10. Additional tests (results not shown for space reason) showed that this results primarily from the size of the RPS view. Varying the KNN size with a constant RPS size has almost no impact, while varying the RPS size with a constant KNN size results in overestimation with few RPS nodes and in underestimation with too many RPS nodes.

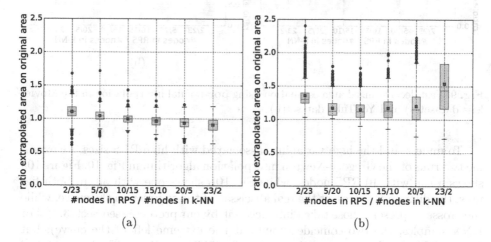

(a)   (b)

Fig. 8. Fast decentralized area estimation using the trapezoid rule in the Movielens dataset(a) and YouTube dataset(b).

Figure 8b complements the above results with the performance of the Trapezoid rule on the YouTube dataset. Again, we obtain the best performance with a KNN-to-RPS ratio of 3/2. With a KNN view of 15 and an RPS view of 10, the mean estimation ratio settles at 1.14. Moreover, slightly smaller or slightly larger KNN-to-RPS ratios impact this result only to a limited extent. In our tests, we observed that this results from the fact that when one view remains constant, performance consistently improves when increasing the size of the other.

Polynomial Interpolation. Next, we evaluate the effectiveness of Mignon using polynomial interpolation. To this end, we used the Gregory-Newton interpolation algorithm as implemented in SciPy. Figure 9 shows the results. Both datasets exhibit similar behaviors. For low RPS sizes, results resemble those obtained with the trapezoid rule, with the best performance being achieved with an RPS of 10 and a KNN of 15. However, results start diverging as soon as the RPS size goes beyond 15. We experimentally verified that this also occurs when increasing the RPS size with a constant KNN size, but not when increasing the KNN size with a constant RPS size.

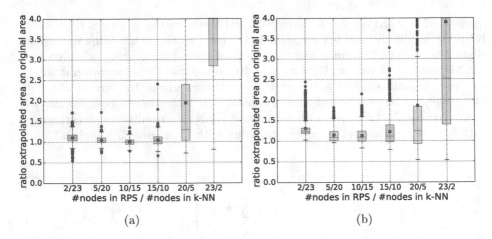

Fig. 9. Fast decentralized area estimation using polynomial interpolation in the Movielens dataset(a) and YouTube dataset(b).

To understand the high variability associated with high RPS sizes, we examine two runs of the Gregory-Newton interpolation algorithm in Fig. 10. Figure 10a shows a run with 10 RPS nodes, while Fig. 10b shows one with 30. In both figures, the diamonds represent the real abscissas of the samples on the curve, while the crosses represent those taken into account by our protocol (see Sect. 3.2). For KNN samples, the two coincide (points at the extreme left of the curve), but for the RPS the difference can be very large. This, together with the numerical instability of the Gregory-Newton's method causes oscillations at the right end of the curve. Some oscillations are visible even with an RPS of 10. But with an RPS of 30, they completely disrupt the estimation.

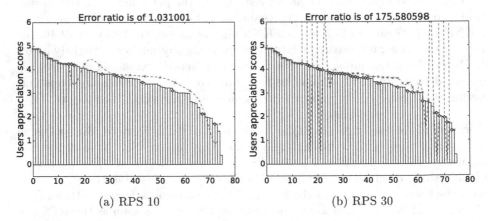

Fig. 10. Details of the Gregory-Newton interpolation with different RPS sizes in the Movielens dataset.

Table 2. Mean error percentage for various size-estimation errors, for Polynomial interpolation(a) and Trapezoidal rule(b).

Error	0%	+10%	-10%	Error	0%	+10%	-10%
MovieLens	-0.8%	+8.8%	-11%	MovieLens	-0.6%	+8.9%	-11.1%
YouTube	+12.4%	+14.9%	+8.7%	YouTube	+14.3%	+10.4%	+17%
	(a)				(b)		

4.3 Influence of Sample & Collide

We now assess the impact of errors on the network-size estimation. As previously stated, nodes do not need to recompute the size of the network for every new upload as we assume the network to be relatively stable. Nonetheless, it is possible to limit the cost of size estimation by means of protocols like Sample & Collide [26]. Such a protocol yields an estimate with a 10 % error at a very limited network cost. We estimate the impact of this error in Table 2 where we shows the absolute value of the error on the mean estimation ratio for both Mignon's approaches in the presence of a positive or negative error on the estimation size. The data shows that the error on the network size has almost no impact on YouTube, and a relatively low one on MovieLens.

4.4 Convergence Speed

We conclude by evaluating the time required to compute the estimate using Mignon. First, let us consider a baseline system that would simply compute the sum of the affinities of the uploaded video with all the other nodes in the country. Such a system would either require the uploading node to contact each other node in the country to compute its affinity, or it would have to disseminate the video's profile so that other nodes could evaluate the video's affinity with them. Both of these approaches would clearly be difficult to scale to large numbers of nodes and their convergence time would be comparable, if not worse, than that required by a KNN protocol to converge from a completely random configuration.

Mignon, on the other hand, takes advantage of the presence of an already converged KNN protocol. This overlay allows the uploading node to quickly reach its closest neighbors. To evaluate this difference, we counted the number of gossip cycles required by a KNN protocol to reach convergence from scratch with 6000 nodes. In each cycle, a node contacts one other node, and is, on average, contacted by another one. We then added one random node, and counted the cycles it took to reach convergence again. Convergence from scratch took between 150 and 190 gossip cycles, while convergence after adding a node to an already converged network took an order of magnitude less (10–20).

5 Conclusion

In this paper, we have proposed *Mignon*, a new protocol to rapidly estimate the aggregate affinity of a newly uploaded video in a community of users in a fully decentralized manner. Our proposal avoids an explicit and costly aggregation by relying on the properties of similarity-based self-organizing overlay networks, and can be used to decide where to place videos in a decentralized UGC system. By eschewing the need for a central support infrastructure, our approach hints at the possibility of fast reactive aggregate analytics in decentralized systems. This may be useful both to promote alternatives to the cloud-centered model of current UGC video services, but also to improve hybrid P2P/cloud architectures [23,38] by offloading complex adaptive tasks to the P2P part of a hybrid system.

References

1. Global internet phenomena report: 2h 2013. Technical report, Sandvine Incorporated (2013)
2. Androutsellis-Theotokis, S., Spinellis, D.: A survey of peer-to-peer content distribution technologies. ACM Comput. Surv. **36**(4), 335–371 (2004)
3. Bai, X., Bertier, M., Guerraoui, R., Kermarrec, A.-M., Leroy, V.: Gossiping personalized queries. In: EDBT (2010)
4. Baraglia, R., Dazzi, P., Mordacchini, M., Ricci, L.: A peer-to-peer recommender system for self-emerging user communities based on gossip overlays. J. Comput. Syst. Sci. **79**(2), 291–308 (2013)
5. Bertier, M., Frey, D., Guerraoui, R., Kermarrec, A.-M., Leroy, V.: The gossple anonymous social network. In: Gupta, I., Mascolo, C. (eds.) Middleware 2010. LNCS, vol. 6452, pp. 191–211. Springer, Heidelberg (2010)
6. Boutet, A., Frey, D., Guerraoui, R., Jégou, A., Kermarrec, A.-M.: WhatsUp decentralized instant news recommender. In: IPDPS (2013)
7. Brodersen, A., Scellato, S., Wattenhofer, M.: YouTube around the world: geographic popularity of videos. In: WWW (2012)
8. Cha, M., Kwak, H., Rodriguez, P., Ahn, Y.-Y., Moon, S.: I tube, you tube, everybody tubes: analyzing the world's largest user generated content video system. In: IMC (2007)
9. Crespo, A., Garcia-Molina, H.: Routing indices for peer-to-peer systems. In: ICDCS (2002)
10. Delbruel, S., Frey, D., Taïani, F.: Exploring the geography of tags in youtube views. Research report RT-0461, IRISA, Inria Rennes, April 2015
11. Delbruel, S., Frey, D., Taïani, F.: Exploring the use of tags for georeplicated content placement. In: IC2E (2016)
12. El Dick, M., Pacitti, E., Kemme, B.: Flower-cdn: a hybrid p2p overlay for efficient query processing in cdn. In: EDBT 2009, pp. 427–438. ACM (2009)
13. Frey, D., Goessens, M., Kermarrec, A.-M.: Behave: behavioral cache for web content. In: Magoutis, K., Pietzuch, P. (eds.) DAIS 2014. LNCS, vol. 8460, pp. 89–103. Springer, Heidelberg (2014)
14. Frey, D., Guerraoui, R., Kermarrec, A.-M., Koldehofe, B., Mogensen, M., Monod, M., Quéma, V.: Heterogeneous gossip. In: Bacon, J.M., Cooper, B.F. (eds.) Middleware 2009. LNCS, vol. 5896, pp. 42–61. Springer, Heidelberg (2009)
15. Geisler, G., Burns, S.: Tagging video: conventions and strategies of the youtube community. In: ACM/IEEE-CS Joint Conference on Digital Libraries (2007)
16. Google Inc.: Google peering and content delivery. https://peering.google.com/about/ggc.html. Accessed 5 Feb 2015

17. Greenaway, S., Thelwall, M., Ding, Y.: Tagging youtube - a classification of tagging practice on youtube. In: International Conference on Sciento- & Informetrics (2009)
18. Huguenin, K., Kermarrec, A.-M., Kloudas, K., Taïani, F.: Content and geographical locality in user-generated content sharing systems. In: NOSSDAV (2012)
19. Idreos, S., Koubarakis, M., Tryfonopoulos, C.: P2P-diet: an extensible P2P service that unifies ad-hoc and continuous querying in super-peer networks. In: SIGMOD, pp. 933–934. ACM (2004)
20. Jelasity, M., Montresor, A.: Epidemic-style proactive aggregation in large overlay networks (2004)
21. Jelasity, M., Montresor, A., Babaoglu, O.: T-man: gossip-based fast overlay topology construction. Comput. Netw. **53**(13), 2321–2339 (2009)
22. Jelasity, M., Voulgaris, S., Guerraoui, R., Kermarrec, A.-M., van Steen, M.: Gossip-based peer sampling. ACM TOCS **25**, 8 (2007)
23. Kreitz, G., Niemelä, F.: Spotify - large scale, low latency, P2P music-on-demand streaming. In: P2P (2010)
24. Kubiatowicz, J., Bindel, D., Chen, Y., Czerwinski, S., Eaton, P., Geels, D., Gummadi, R., Rhea, S., Weatherspoon, H., Weimer, W., et al.: Oceanstore: an architecture for global-scale persistent storage. ACM Sigplan Not. **35**(11), 190–201 (2000)
25. Le Merrer, E., Kermarrec, A.-M., Massoulie, L.: Peer to peer size estimation in large, dynamic networks: a comparative study. In: HPDC (2006)
26. Massoulié, L., Le Merrer, E., Kermarrec, A.-M., Ganesh, A.: Peer counting, sampling in overlay networks: random walk methods. In: PODC (2006)
27. Montresor, A., Jelasity, M., Babaoglu, O.: Robust aggregation protocols for large-scale overlay networks. In: DSN (2004)
28. Pujol, J.M., Erramilli, V., Siganos, G., Yang, X., Laoutaris, N., Chhabra, P., Rodriguez, P.: The little engine(s) that could: scaling online social networks. In: SIGCOMM (2010)
29. Ratnasamy, S., Francis, P., Handley, M., Karp, R., Shenker, S.: A scalable content-addressable network. In: SIGCOMM (2001)
30. Rowstron, A., Druschel, P.: Pastry: scalable, decentralized object location, and routing for large-scale peer-to-peer systems. In: Guerraoui, R. (ed.) Middleware 2001. LNCS, vol. 2218, p. 329. Springer, Heidelberg (2001)
31. Saroiu, S., Gummadi, K.P., Gribble, S.D.: Measuring and analyzing the characteristics of napster and gnutella hosts. Multimed. Syst. **9**(2), 170–184 (2003)
32. Sastry, N., Yoneki, E., Crowcroft, J.: Buzztraq: predicting geographical access patterns of social cascades using social networks. In: SNS (2009)
33. Scellato, S., Mascolo, C., Musolesi, M., Crowcroft, J.: Track globally, deliver locally: improving content delivery networks by tracking geographic social cascades. In: WWW (2011)
34. Stoica, I., Morris, R., Karger, D., Kaashoek, M.F., Balakrishnan, H.: Chord: a scalable peer-to-peer lookup service for internet applications. In: SIGCOMM 2001, pp. 149–160 (2001)
35. Voulgaris, S., Gavidia, D., van Steen, M.: Cyclon: inexpensive membership management for unstructured p2p overlays. J. Netw. Syst. Manage. **13**(2), 197–217 (2005)
36. Voulgaris, S., van Steen, M.: Epidemic-style management of semantic overlays for content-based searching. In: Cunha, J.C., Medeiros, P.D. (eds.) Euro-Par 2005. LNCS, vol. 3648, pp. 1143–1152. Springer, Heidelberg (2005)

37. Youtube, LCC: Statistics, viewership. http://www.youtube.com/yt/press/statistics.html. Accessed 5 Feb 2015
38. Zhao, M., Aditya, P., Chen, A., Lin, Y., Haeberlen, A., Druschel, P., Maggs, B., Wishon, B., Ponec, M.: Peer-assisted content distribution in Akamai NetSession. In: IMC (2013)

Privacy-Preserving Data Allocation in Decentralized Online Social Networks

Andrea De Salve[1,2]([✉]), Paolo Mori[2], Laura Ricci[1], Raed Al-Aaridhi[3], and Kalman Graffi[3]

[1] Department of Computer Science, University of Pisa,
Largo B. Pontecorvo, Pisa, Italy
{desalve,laura.ricci}@di.unipi.it
[2] IIT-CNR, via G. Moruzzi 1, Pisa, Italy
paolo.mori@iit.cnr.it
[3] Heinrich Heine Universität Düsseldorf, Universitätsstr. 1, Düsseldorf, Germany
{alaaridhi,graffi}@hhu.de

Abstract. Distributed Online Social Networks (DOSNs) have been recently proposed as an alternative to centralized solutions to allow a major control of the users over their own data. Since there is no centralized service provider which decides the term of service, the DOSNs infrastructure exploits users' devices to take on the online social network services. In this paper, we propose a data allocation strategy for DOSNs which exploits the privacy policies of the users to increase the availability of the users' contents without diverging from their privacy preferences. A set of replicas of the profile's content of a user U are stored on the devices of other users who are entitled to access the profile according to U's privacy policies. The experimental results obtained from the simulations on traces taken from a real social network show the effectiveness of our approach.

Keywords: Decentralized online social network · Data availability · Privacy policy · Peer-to-peer

1 Introduction

A Distributed Online Social Network (DOSN) [7] is an Online Social Network (OSN) implemented in a distributed and decentralized way. Hence, instead of being based on a single provider which manages the whole system by storing and controlling the data representing users' profiles, a DOSN consists of a (dynamic) set of nodes, such as a network of trusted servers, a P2P system or an opportunistic network, which collaborate to implement the social network services. Therefore, DOSNs shift the control over users' profiles data to the peers that build up the DOSN (i.e., to the users these peers belong to), thus solving some, but introducing new security issues, such as the ones concerning the privacy, integrity and availability of user data.

© IFIP International Federation for Information Processing 2016
Published by Springer International Publishing Switzerland 2016. All Rights Reserved
M. Jelasity and E. Kalyvianaki (Eds.): DAIS 2016, LNCS 9687, pp. 47–60, 2016.
DOI: 10.1007/978-3-319-39577-7_4

The privacy of the contents published in users' profiles is one of the main issues in DOSNs because, being personal data, these contents must be properly protected. In particular, DOSN users should be enabled to define their privacy policies, and the DOSN framework is responsible for properly enforcing these policies in order to disclose the users' contents only to authorized friends. On the other hand, DOSNs are also responsible for data availability [13], because the contents published in the profile of a user must be kept available even when the owner (i.e., the corresponding peer) is disconnected from the network. Different solutions may be exploited to guarantee data availability in DOSNs, for instance profiles may be saved on a Distributed Hash Table (DHT) [3] or directly on the peers of the users' friends. Most of the current DOSNs ensure data availability by exploiting a DHT. This implies that contents are stored on untrusted peers and that cryptographic mechanisms are used in order to prevent undesired disclosure of the users data to the owners of the peers storing their profiles. To achieve fine-grained access control, every time a user u wants to share a content c with a group of n users (according to the privacy policy defined for c), u encrypts c with a new symmetric key before being stored and, in turn, that symmetric key is encrypted separately with the individual public keys of the n users. Finally, the encrypted symmetric keys are distributed to the n authorized users or directly attached to the content c (see, e.g. [2, 11, 14]). However, this kind of scheme is not scalable because the number of asymmetric encryption operations and the storage cost of encrypted data depend on the number of users n allowed to read the content c, which is clearly a performance issue because the number of such users can be quite big and can be changed quite often (e.g. addition or removal of friends). As a matter of fact, users tend to have a significantly large number of friends in their networks (e.g. 27 % of 18–29 year old Facebook users have more than 500 friend[1]). Recent studies [4, 14] have investigated the overhead introduced by encryption schemes used in current DOSNs in terms of storage and computational cost by highlighting the impact they have on performance and user experience.

This paper proposes an alternative approach for preserving the privacy of the users' contents and increasing their availability by avoiding the use of data encryption. The approach consists in modelling the contents belonging to the profile of user u using a hierarchical data structure, i.e. a tree, and adopting a proper strategy for allocating the nodes of the tree on the peers of online friends of u. The idea is to allocate a copy of each content c of the tree on another peer that is currently online, and whose user v is allowed to access c according to u's privacy policy. In this way, there is no need of employing encryption mechanisms to protect the confidentiality of u's data once stored on v's peer, because v is entitled to access these data according to u's privacy policy. In fact, v cannot collect additional information about u by directly inspecting the contents of u allocated on its devices (e.g., by browsing the files stored in its file systems), because v would find only the contents that is already allowed to access.

The rest of the paper is structured as follows. Section 2 describes how user's profile is modelled through a tree. In Sect. 3 we introduce our content replication

---

[1] Statistics of Facebook are available at http://pewrsr.ch/1dm5NmJ.

strategy. Section 4 describes the general system architecture, while Sect. 5 introduces the main algorithms. Section 6 evaluate the effectiveness of the proposed data allocation strategy on a real data set taken from a Facebook application. Section 7 discusses related work, while Sect. 8 reports the conclusions and discusses future works.

2   Modelling Social Profiles

In our system, the social profile P_u of a user u is hierarchically modelled by a tree whose nodes correspond to the contents belonging to P_u. Since we have a one to one mapping between the nodes of the tree P_u and the user's contents, we use interchangeably the terms node or content to refer them. Furthermore, we suppose that an unique identifier is assigned to each node of the user's content tree. The root of the tree is considered as an entry point for all the contents related to a profile owner, such as personal information, interests, friendship information, private communication, posts, images, comments, etc. Each node of the profile tree embeds information about the identifiers of the children and parent nodes and is paired with privacy preferences chosen by the owner. Since we model the profile as a tree, the privileges on each content can be expressed in terms of operations on the tree, such as insertion/removal of a children node and reading/changing the content. Therefore, we can define, for each type of content, four different privileges corresponding to the operations available on the tree: *readData*, *editData*, *appendChild*, and *removeChild*. The readData privilege corresponds to a read operation, while the other ones correspond to updates of the content or of the tree structure. For instance, a user may exploit the appendChild operation to add comments to a post or to a photo published by the profile's owner. The profile owner specifies the privacy preferences for each node of the profile tree, i.e. the privileges granted to the other users in term of the previous operations. Since we model each user's profile as a tree of contents, a privacy policy that permit readData privilege to a content in the hierarchy implies that the same privilege is also permitted to ancestor nodes. In fact, a property of the hierarchical profile structure is that read permission on one node depends on the privacy policies of the parent nodes. Specifically, the sequence of the privacy policies on a hierarchy of contents can only limit the intended audience In fact, for each node, the user can only specify a privacy policy that restrict the privileges already granted to the ancestor nodes. On the other hand, a privacy policy that permit readData privilege to a node in the hierarchy does not imply that readData privilege is also granted to the descendant nodes in the hierarchy. An example of a user's tree structured profile annotated with the corresponding policies is shown if Fig. 1(a). Since user Charlie can not access the Image1 content, then he can not access the comments, likes and tags of the Image1.

Privacy policies paired with profile's content may exploit different aspects (or attributes) derived from the OSN knowledge. Attributes are used to model interesting properties of users or contents (such as the tagged users, creation date of a content or user's birthday) – as well as the kind of operations performed on resources (such as read or write of contents).

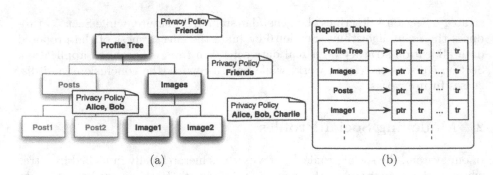

Fig. 1. (a) shows the general profile tree data structure which contains posts and images of the user U. The root of the profile tree and the *Images* node are intended to be shared with the entire circle of U's friends. Finally, the privacy policies specified by U for the contents *Image1* and *Image2* allow access to the set of users {*Alice*, *Bob*} and {*Alice*, *Bob*, *Charlie*}, respectively. While (b) shows the replicas table for the profile tree of U where names of the nodes are used as content ids. A primary trusted replica (*ptr*) and a set of further replicas (*tr*) are defined for each node.

3   Privacy Preserving Content Replication

DOSNs should guarantee that contents of a user's profile are available at any time in the system. In order to ensure higher data availability, contents of a profile tree are replicated on k peers of the DOSN, called trusted replicas, where k is an input parameter of the system. The idea behind our approach is to exploit the privacy policies paired with the contents of the user's profile to define a privacy-preserving allocation of the profile tree to the available peers of the DOSN. In particular, our approach allocates a content c of the user's u profile tree P_u to the peers who are already allowed to read c according to the privacy policy defined by u. In order to select the trusted replicas where the contents of the profile tree P_u could be copied, the privacy policy specified for the content c is evaluated by using the authorization component of the privacy-preserving framework and by simulating an access to the content. To this aim, we exploit the privacy-preserving framework we have proposed in [9] to support users in the management of their privacy preferences. The framework: *(i)* allows users to define flexible privacy policies to regulate the accesses to the content they have shared by means of a proper Privacy Policy Language, *(ii)* evaluates the privacy policy and returns the corresponding authorization decision that indicates whether or not a user can access the content of another user.

For each content, our framework defines a primary trusted replica (*ptr*) and a set of further replicas (*tr*). When the user is on-line, it acts as primary replica of its content and it enforces the privacy policies on the content of the profile tree by its own. If the user crashes abruptly or voluntary leaves the social network, the availability of its profile is guaranteed by the other replicas. In this case, the authorization framework is exploited also by the replicas peers to enforce the privacy policy on the users' contents stored on their device. Specifically, when a user v requests access to the content c of P_u, the replica storing c evaluates the privacy policies of u (linked to the profile P_u) in order to decide whether to permit or deny the access to c. From a performance point of view, every time a user u wants to share a content c with a group of n users (according to the privacy policy defined for c), our approach avoids a number of encryption operations proportional to n (which, depending on the choosen policy, is typically of the order of number of u's friends or even Friends of Friends). We do not focus in this paper on the problem of ensuring integrity and authenticity of the profiles' contents. To this aim, well-established solutions [1,5,6] could be adopted.

4   The System Model

In this section we describe the general architecture of the system we propose to support the privacy-aware allocation of the user's contents. In the following, we assume a one-to-one mapping between users and their peers and we use interchangeably the terms peer or user to indicate them.

Each user u is bind to its user descriptor D_u which contains information about the IP address of the corresponding peer, the online/offline status of the peer, the identifier of the root of its profile tree and the current replicas available for all contents of the profile. Since the descriptor D_u must be available to all the peers which are going to access the profile of u when it is offline, it is stored on a DHT and may be retrieved by exploiting the identifier of the u. Note that the DHT is exploited not only to keep track of the content replicas, but it is also indispensable for peer bootstrapping, addressing and for supporting the search of new friends.

4.1   The Replication Framework

When a content is created, the user who created it specifies the privacy policy for that node of the profile tree that best matches its needs. Such policies are statements of the privacy policy language that specify who has access to the content in terms of a set of features encoded by attributes.

The association between the contents of a profile tree P_u and the trusted replica peers where they are stored are maintained in the *replicas table* R_u (see Fig. 1(b)) which is located in the user's descriptor D_u of the profile owner. The replicas table R_u contains, for each content c of P_u, the trusted replica list $R_u(c) = \{ptr, tr_1 \ldots, tr_{k-1}\}$, where ptr is the primary trusted replica, while $tr_1 \ldots, tr_{k-1}\}$ are the other replicas of the content. For maintaining replication transparency, the trusted replica lists are managed according to a *passive replication model* [10] where every user communicates only with ptr, the *primary trusted replica*.

When the peer of the profile owner is online, it becomes primary trusted replica of their contents. Primary trusted replica peers are responsible for the availability of the contents, for enforcing privacy policies every time a user tries to access a content and for the selection of the new trusted replicas. Only the primary replica can elect new replicas for the content and it can add them at the end of the trusted replica list. The selection of a new trusted replica for a content c of user profile P_u can be performed: *(i)* actively by the content owner u during the online periods since it acts as primary replicas for their contents or *(ii)* by the current primary trusted replica of c, when the owner is not online.

Let us denote by $tr(c)$ and $ptr(c)$ respectively, the set of trusted replicas and the primary trusted replica for the content c and assume that user t wants to read a content c of the profile P_u of a user u which is offline. t navigates through the profile of u starting from the root of the profile tree, whose reference is stored in the descriptor D_u (we recall that D_u contains a reference to the replica owning the root of the profile). Recall that each node (content) of the profile stores the identifier of its children in the tree. The access to a content c thus requires a sequence of recursive accesses to the descriptor stored on the DHT to obtain the references to the replicas storing the nodes on the path from the root of the DHT to the requested content. When the content c has been located, t accesses the replicas table R_u for that content stored in D_u, and locates the trusted replicas of c (see Fig. 1(b)). If a primary trusted replica is available, t sends an access request to it. The primary replica checks whether t is authorized (according to u's privacy policy) to read the content c and if the case, it send back to t the requested content. Robustness against peers failure and involuntary disconnections of replica peer may be ensured through periodical exchanges of heartbeat messages between the primary trusted replica and the trusted replicas.

5   The Algorithms

In this section we describe the algorithms executed by the peers in order to realize the contents allocation strategies described above. Initially, we assume that each user is online and connected to the system. When a peer u leaves the DOSN, it executes Algorithm 1. Initially, u retrieves its user descriptor D_u from the DHT and notifies its status to the other peers by updating its availability information (line [2–3]). At the moment of disconnection, u has to update the trusted replica list tr of each content c it stores, by removing its contact information (line [5–9]), regardless of the user n to which the content c belongs. In this way, u will no longer be considered trusted replica for the contents while the replica at the first position of the in the list tr (if any) will act as the primary trusted replica for the content. For availability purposes, the trusted replica u which is going to disconnect from the network, must keep a copy of each stored content c until its reconnection. Finally, u can leave the underlying DHT network (line 11).

Algorithm 2 specifies the steps performed by a user's peer u who wants to join the network. Initially, u retrieves its user descriptor D_u and updates its status information in order to inform other peers about its presence (line [2–3]). By using the user descriptor D_u, u will be able to get its replica table R_u and to have information about their contents and the replicas available for each of them. It may happen that the peer u that joins the system is an old trusted replica peer that reconnects to the DOSN and has old contents stored on its

---

Algorithm 1. User u leaves the network

1: **procedure** LEAVE
2:      D_u=getUserDescriptor(u);
3:      $D_u.status = OFFLINE$;
4:      **for all** c stored in local memory **do**
5:          n=owner(c);
6:          D_n=getUserDescriptor(n);
7:          R_n=getReplicaTable(D_n);
8:          $tr(c)$=getTrustedReplicas(R_n,c);
9:          $tr(c) = tr(c) -\{u\}$;
10:     **end for**
11:     leaveDHT();
12: **end procedure**

---

local memory. For each content c of a generic user n stored in the local memory of user u two different scenarios may occur. When there are trusted replicas available for the content c (line 9), then the peer u has to synchronize the local copy of the content with those currently available in the system by sending c to the current primary replica $ptr(c)$ (line 10). In the case where u is the owner of c, u becomes the primary trusted replica of c otherwise it can remove the local copy content (line [11–13]). When there are no trusted replicas for the content c, the user u will act as primary trusted replica for c and provides a (possibly) outdated copy of c in the system (line [14–16]). When a user's peer decides to behave as a trusted replica for a content c of the profile P_n, it needs to modify the replica table R_n by adding the contact information of the new trusted replicas (line 12 and 15). It is worh noting that after the execution of the Algorithm 2 all the contents stored on the local memory of u have been either updated or provided by u.

At the end of the join procedure, a periodic *dataAvailability* operation is initiated.

When a peer u becomes a primary trusted replica for a content c, it has to periodically check if new trusted replicas are needed and, in this case, it has to find another peer who is currently online and is allowed to access c according to u's privacy policy. Algorithm 3 describes the periodic steps performed by primary trusted replicas in order to ensure that at least k trusted replicas are available for each content they store. Every $interval_A$ time unit, a primary trusted replica u selects a content c of the profile P_n stored on its local memory and checks whether the number of available trusted replicas for c is less then k (line 3–7). In this case, u executes an election procedure which selects a new trusted replica for c. User u gets the set of online users F having a friendship relation with n (the owner of the content) and then use the authorization module of the privacy preserving framework to evaluate whether a friend $f \in F$ is authorized to read the content c of n (line 8–15). The privacy policy of c is evaluated for each user f in the set of neighbours by simulating an access request on a user's content c and it may only return permit or deny (line 11). The set of feasible trusted

---

Algorithm 2. User u join the network

1: **procedure** JOIN
2:     D_u=getUserDescriptor(u);
3:     $D_u.status = ONLINE$;
4:     **for all** c stored in local memory **do**
5:         n=owner(c);
6:         D_n=getUserDescriptor(n);
7:         R_n=getReplicaTable(D_n);
8:         ptr=getPrimaryTrustedReplica(R_n,c);
9:         **if** $ptr \neq null$ **then**
10:            synchronizes(c, $ptr(c)$);
11:            **if** $n = u$ **then**
12:                $ptr(c) = u$
13:            **end if**
14:         **else**   ▷ u becomes primary trusted replica of c
15:            $ptr(c) = u$
16:         **end if**
17:     **end for**
18:     start dataAvailability(u,D_u);
19: **end procedure**

---

replica peers where the unencrypted user content c could be copied is composed of the users who have obtained a permit authorization decision (line 12–14). Finally, the data availability procedure chooses a trusted replica peer, among those available, that meets specific performance objectives (line 16). If such user exists, the content c is copied in clear on its local memory, which is considered a trusted replica (line 17).

6 Experimental Results

With the aim of evaluating the feasibility of our approach, we have developed a set of simulations of our system using the P2P PeerfactSim.KOM[2] simulator, a highly scalable simulator written in java. We have also implemented a Facebook application, called *SocialCircles!*[3] which exploits the Facebook API to retrieve the following sets of information: *(i)* the friendships and profile information of registered users and *(ii)* we sampled the Facebook chat status of registered users and their friends every 8 min for 10 consecutive days (from Tuesday 3 June 2014 to Friday 13 June) in order to derive the average session length of the users [8].

We exploit some reference policies to evaluate our framework. Although the enforceable privacy policies are expressed by using proper Privacy Policy Language [12], for the sake of clarity, we express the policy examples in natural language. We use policy's attributes to model friendships, common friends number, geographic location, common interests and the strength of the relationship

---

[2] Available at www.peerfactsim.com/.

[3] Available at http://www.socialcircles.eu/.

Algorithm 3. Periodic actions performed by primary trusted replicas u

---

Require: k - max number of trusted replicas
1: **procedure** DATAAVAILABILITY(u,k)
2:     **while** $interval_A$ **do**
3:         get $c \in$ Local memory $| ptr(c) = u$;
4:         n=owner(c);
5:         D_n =getUserDescriptor(n);
6:         tr=getTrustedReplicas(c);
7:         **if** $tr < k$ **then**   ▷ looks for new trusted replica
8:             F =getOnlinePeer(D_n);
9:             $candidates = \emptyset$;
10:            **for** $f \in F$ **do**
11:                $result$=evaluateAccess($c,READ,f$);
12:                **if** $result = $ PERMIT **then**
13:                    $candidates = candidates \cup \{f\}$;
14:                **end if**
15:            **end for**
16:            r=selectTrustedReplica($candidates$);
17:            $tr(c) = tr(c) \cdot r$;   ▷ trusted replica selection
18:        **end if**
19:    **end while**
20: **end procedure**

---

in terms of Dunbar circles, which is a representation of the intensity of the relationship between two users which can be approximated by using the number of interactions occurred between users [8]. Consider the user Alice and a content c of her profile. In the experiments, we consider the following reference policies:

Policy 1. Only users who have a friendship relationship with Alice can read c.
Policy 2. Only users who have a friendship relationship with Alice and at least k common friends with Alice and can read c.
Policy 3. Users who have a friendship relationship with Alice can read c provided that they are in a specific Dunbar circle C.
Policy 4. Only users who have a friendship relationship with Alice and common school information can read c
Policy 5. Only users who have a friendship relationship with Alice and a home location which is far at most d km from Alice's home can read c.

The experiment size is set to 3000 peers and contains a subset of the Social-Circle! Facebook dataset. From minutes 1 to $t_0 = 200$, the simulation is initiated, each peer joins the DHT and then loads its attribute values. Those users which represent a user registered to our Facebook application start to create and publish an empty profile which can be used by their friends to access Posts and Images of the profile. In our simulation 35 users in total publish their profiles, in this phase. Afterwards, user churn is activated and around 50 % of the peers leave the network (see Fig. 2(a)). We used a exponential churn models (which simulates the temporal absence of hosts) based on the realistic measurements

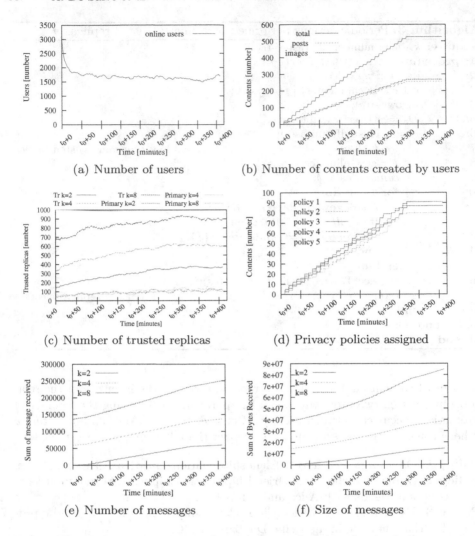

Fig. 2. Contents and trusted replicas created during the simulation.

obtained from our dataset [13] while the network layer is implemented by the Global Network Positioning (GNP) module based on measurements from the PingER project.

At the time t_0 the set-up phase is finished and those peers which represent a user registered to the Facebook application start to publish either Posts or Images with a probability of 0.5. Furthermore, the data availability protocol (Algorithm 3) is started. In Fig. 2(b) we present the number of user's contents created during the simulation. A total of 600 data objects were created during the simulation. The number of profiles in the DOSN is constant and equal to the number of registered users, while Posts and Images are generated with equal probability and do not exceed the number of 300 contents. A the moment of the creation of a content, user assign to the generated content a privacy policy randomly chosen among those previously defined, namely: *(i)* Policy 1, *(ii)* Policy 2 with a number of common friends (k) equal to 8, *(iii)* Policy 3 with Dunbar circle C randomly chosen, *(v)* Policy 4 and *(vi)* Policy 5 with distance d equal to 5 km. The Fig. 2(d) shows the number of contents assigned to each privacy policy.

During the simulation, users publish their contents and select at most k trusted replicas to increase the availability of each content. We investigated the availability provided by our approach by selecting the maximum number of replicas k for each content equals to 2, 4 and 8. In Fig. 2(c) we present the total number of online trusted replicas available during the simulation. As we use a passive replication model where the copies of each content are managed by a primary trusted replicas, we differentiate primary trusted replicas (Primary) from other trusted replicas (Tr). The number of primary replicas created during the simulation is almost 100 and the same for all values of k, while the total number of online trusted replicas depends on the value of k.

Furthermore, we focus on the costs of the data availability service in terms of message consumption and network traffic and for diffent values of maximum number of replicas k. Figure 2(e) and (f) present the amount of system messages and the number of bytes generated by the proposed algorithm. The total number of messages exchanged in a given time-interval is proportional to the number of online users in the systems. In order to investigate the rate of available contents in

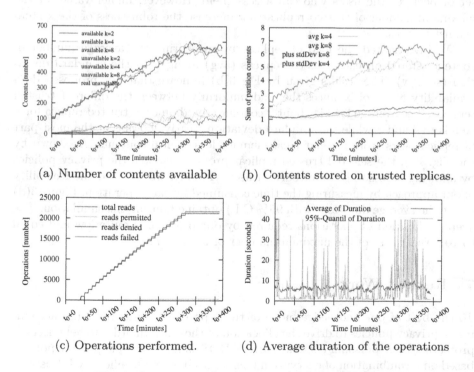

(a) Number of contents available   (b) Contents stored on trusted replicas.

(c) Operations performed.   (d) Average duration of the operations

Fig. 3. Assessment of contents availability and load.

the network we start reads to the published profiles contents every 5 min. Access request to the contents may return permit (i.e. user can read the content) or deny (user can not read the content). Figure 3(c) shows the number of reads operation performed by online peers. On the basis of the privacy policy defined for the requested content, the applicant could have or not the right to access it. In order to assess the availability of our approach, we compute the number of contents available in the system through trusted replicas by counting the number of times a content is replicated at least on one online trusted replica. The Fig. 3(a) shows the number of available/unavailable contents for different values of maximun number of replica k. It is important to note that our approach guarantees the availability of the most part of the contents present in the system by selecting as replicas the peers which can store unencrypted copy of the contents. During the simulation, an average number of 100 contents (out of 600) are not available in the system. Since the contents of a profile tree can be accessible only by authorized user (if any), we have measured the fraction of unavailable contents that can be accessed by at least one online user in the system. This metric (named real unavailale) is almost the same for all the values of k and it proves that the real amount of unavailable contents that can be accessed by online users is at most 10. As shown by the graph in Fig. 3(a), the maximun number of trusted replica k selected for each content does not strongly affect the availability of the system because, over time, contents are incrementally replicated on the set of peers of the users who can access them. However, higher values of the maximum number of trusted replicates k increase the robustness of the system against failures.

We investigated the load of replicas by measuring the average number of contents stored on each trusted replicas (avg) along with the standard deviation (stdDev). The results given by Fig. 3(b) indicate that our proposed data availability protocol balances the load uniformly between the different trusted replicas. The average load is about 2 content stored on each trusted replica for k equals to 4 and 8 while the standard deviation clearly shows that the most part of replica peers store in their local memory less then 6 contents. As shown by the Fig. 3(c), the selected trusted replicas properly enforce the privacy policies by allowing access only to authorized users. Finally, we assessed the feasibility of our approach by measuring the time consumed by each operation. Figure 3(d) shows the average duration (with 95 % C.I.) obtained during the simulation. The average duration of operations required by our protocol is quite low and equal to 10 s, regardless of the maximun number of replicas k.

7 Related Work

To the best of our knowledge, none of these previous works take into account users' privacy policies to drive the allocation of the data. In order to help users in protecting their personal content, current DOSNs adopt simple privacy policies based on a combination of encryption techniques, namely Public Key Infrastructure (PKI) and Attribute Based Encryption (ABE). In Diaspora[4] users may agree to act as a local server in order to keep complete control of their data, or choose to use an existing server. The Diaspora server grants its administrator read and write access to unencrypted users' information hosted by its device. Users rely on the server's owner to maintain the security, integrity, and reliability of their data. In Safebook [6] users associate a particular trust level with their friends and this level is used to select closely related contacts that primarily will store the user's data. The trust level of the nodes is directly specified by the users without taking into account their privacy policies. The user's data are allocated by using an access control scheme based symmetric and asymmetric encryption. PeerSoN [5] exploits local users devices to store their data securely. Users data are encrypted with the public keys of the users who have access to it. LotusNet [1] relies on structured architectures where users' data could be stored and replicated securely by combining symmetric and asymmetric encryption. In Super-Nova [15] users' data are kept available by exploiting stranger or users' friends peers. The user's data on stranger peers (or on friend peers) are encrypted by using a threshold-based secret sharing approach. In LifeSocial.KOM [11] users' data could be stored and replicated on different peers arranged according to a DHT. Any data is first encrypted with a new symmetric key, then, this symmetric key is encrypted individually with the public key of the users able to access the data and attached to the user's content.

In Cachet [14] users' data are securely stored and replicated on the peers of a DHT by using a cryptographic hybrid structure which leverages Attribute Based Encryption (ABE) and symmetric key. Only users that meet the policy can decrypt the private key used to encrypt the content.

Persona [2] leverages a hybrid architecture where users store their data either on their local storage device or on external storage services provided by others parties. Private user data in Persona is always encrypted with a symmetric key. In turn, the symmetric key is encrypted with an ABE key or with a traditional public key.

8   Conclusion and Future Works

This paper proposes a content allocation strategy supporting contents availability in a Distributed Online Social Network. The main feature of this allocation strategy is that it tries to replicate the content of user u without encrypting it on the peers which are considered trusted, i.e., the peers belonging to users who can access the content of u according to u's privacy policy. The experimental results performed on real data traces show that the proposed approach ensures high availability of the profiles' contents.

We plan to extend our system in several directions. The partitioning of the tree can be optimized in order to store contents belonging to sub-paths of the tree on the same replica so that the number of DHT accesses during the visit of a profile is minimized. Finally, even if our approach guarantees an high degree

---

[4] https://joindiaspora.com/.

of availability, we are working on a mechanism to store a content on the DHT when there are no available trusted replicas.

References

1. Aiello, L.M., Ruffo, G.: LotusNet: tunable privacy for distributed online social network services. Comput. Commun. **35**(1), 75–88 (2012)
2. Baden, R., Bender, A., Spring, N., Bhattacharjee, B., Starin, D.: Persona: an online social network with user-defined privacy. ACM SIGCOMM Comput. Commun. Rev. **39**(4), 135–146 (2009)
3. Balakrishnan, H., Kaashoek, M.F., Karger, D., Morris, R., Stoica, I.: Looking up data in p2p systems. Commun. ACM **46**(2), 43–48 (2003)
4. Bodriagov, O., Buchegger, S.: Encryption for Peer-to-Peer Social Networks. Springer, New York (2013)
5. Buchegger, S., Schiöberg, D., Vu, L.H., Datta, A.: Peerson: p2p social networking: early experiences and insights. In: Proceedings of the Second ACM EuroSys Workshop on Social Network Systems, pp. 46–52. ACM (2009)
6. Cutillo, L.A., Molva, R., Strufe, T.: Safebook: a privacy-preserving online social network leveraging on real-life trust. IEEE Commun. Mag. **47**(12), 94–101 (2009)
7. Datta, A., Buchegger, S., Vu, L.H., Strufe, T., Rzadca, K.: Decentralized online social networks. In: Furht, B. (ed.) Handbook of Social Network Technologies and Applications, pp. 349–378. Springer, New York (2010)
8. De Salve, A., Dondio, M., Guidi, B., Ricci, L.: The impact of users availability on on-line ego networks: a Facebook analysis. Comput. Commun. **73**, 211–218 (2015)
9. De Salve, A., Mori, P., Ricci, L.: A privacy-aware framework for decentralized online social networks. In: Chen, Q., Hameurlain, A., Toumani, F., Wagner, R., Decker, H. (eds.) DEXA 2015. LNCS, vol. 9262, pp. 479–490. Springer, Heidelberg (2015)
10. Ghosh, S.: Distributed Systems: An Algorithmic Approach. CRC Press, Boca Raton (2014)
11. Graffi, K., Gross, C., Stingl, D., Hartung, D., Kovacevic, A., Steinmetz, R.: Lifesocial. KOM: a secure and p2p-based solution for online social networks. In: 2011 IEEE Consumer Communications and Networking Conference, pp. 554–558. IEEE (2011)
12. Kumaraguru, P., Cranor, L., Lobo, J., Calo, S.: A survey of privacy policy languages. In: ACM Workshop on Usable IT Security Management (USM 2007), Proceedings of the 3rd Symposium on Usable Privacy and Security. Citeseer (2007)
13. Mega, G., Montresor, A., Picco, G.P.: On churn and communication delays in social overlays. In: 2012 IEEE 12th International Conference on Peer-to-Peer Computing (P2P), pp. 214–224. IEEE (2012)
14. Nilizadeh, S., Jahid, S., Mittal, P., Borisov, N., Kapadia, A.: Cachet: a decentralized architecture for privacy preserving social networking with caching. In: Proceedings of the 8th International Conference on Emerging Networking Experiments and Technologies, pp. 337–348. ACM (2012)
15. Sharma, R., Datta, A.: Supernova: super-peers based architecture for decentralized online social networks. In: Fourth International Conference on Communication Systems and Networks, pp. 1–10. IEEE (2012)

An RDMA Middleware for Asynchronous Multi-stage Shuffling in Analytical Processing

Rui C. Gonçalves[1](✉), José Pereira[1], and Ricardo Jiménez-Peris[2]

[1] HASLab, INESC TEC & U. Minho, Braga, Portugal
{rgoncalves,jop}@di.uminho.pt
[2] Univ. Politécnica de Madrid & LeanXcale, Madrid, Spain
rjimenez@leanxcale.com

Abstract. A key component in large scale distributed analytical processing is *shuffling*, the distribution of data to multiple nodes such that the computation can be done in parallel. In this paper we describe the design and implementation of a communication middleware to support data shuffling for executing multi-stage analytical processing operations in parallel. The middleware relies on RDMA (Remote Direct Memory Access) to provide basic operations to asynchronously exchange data among multiple machines. Experimental results show that the RDMA-based middleware developed can provide a 75 % reduction of the costs of communication operations on parallel analytical processing tasks, when compared with a sockets middleware.

Keywords: Distributed databases · OLAP · Middleware · RDMA

1 Introduction

The proliferation of web platforms supporting user generated content and of a variety of connected devices, together with the decreasing cost of storage, lead to a significant growth on data being generated and collected every day. This explosion of data brings new opportunities for businesses that overcome the challenge of storing and processing it in a scalable and cost-effective way. It has thus sparked the emergence of NoSQL database systems and processing solutions based on the MapReduce [2] programming model as alternatives to the traditional Relational Database Management Systems (RDBMS) for large scale data processing.

Briefly, in a MapReduce job, a *map* function converts arbitrary input data to key-value pairs. For instance, in the classical word count example, for each input text file, *map* outputs each word found as a key and its number of occurrences as the value. A *reduce* function computes an output value from all values attached to the same key. For instance, in the word count example, *reduce* sums all values for each key to obtain the global count for each word. Both these operations can easily be executed in parallel across a large number of servers with minimal coordination: Multiple mappers work on different input files, and multiple reducers work on different keys.

© IFIP International Federation for Information Processing 2016
Published by Springer International Publishing Switzerland 2016. All Rights Reserved
M. Jelasity and E. Kalyvianaki (Eds.): DAIS 2016, LNCS 9687, pp. 61–74, 2016.
DOI: 10.1007/978-3-319-39577-7_5

The key element of a MapReduce implementation, which needs distributed coordination, is the *shuffling* step between map and reduce operations. It gathers all data elements with the same key on the same server such that they can be processed together. In classical MapReduce, this is a synchronous step: All map tasks have to finish before reduce tasks can be started. This impacts the latency of MapReduce jobs, in particular as multiple map and reduce stages are often needed to perform data processing operations. Therefore, it restricts the usefulness of systems based on MapReduce to batch processing, even if, as in Hive [15], they offer a high-level SQL-like interface.

There has thus been a growing demand for NoSQL solutions that combine the scalability of MapReduce with the interactive performance of traditional RDBMS for on-line analytical processing (OLAP). For instance, Impala [6] offers the same interface as Hive but avoids MapReduce to improve interactive performance. Again, a key element in these data processing systems is the ability to perform shuffling efficiently over the network. In detail, the shuffling has to be asynchronous, to allow successive data processing tasks to execute in parallel, and multi-stage, to allow an arbitrarily long composition of individual tasks in a complex data processing job. Being the component that involves distributed communication and synchronization, shuffling is the key component for the performance and scalability of the system.

This paper presents an asynchronous and multi-stage shuffling implementation that exploits the Remote Direct Memory Access (RDMA) networking interface to add analytical processing capabilities to an existing Distributed Query Engine (DQE) [7]. The DQE provides a standard SQL interface and full transactional support, while scaling to hundreds of nodes. Whereas the scalability for on-line transactional processing (OLTP) workloads is obtained executing multiple transactions (typically short lived) concurrently on multiple DQE instances, for OLAP workloads it is also important to have multiple machines and DQE instances computing a single query in parallel. That is, as OLAP queries have longer response times, it is often worth considering intra-query parallelism to reduce queries response time [8].

The parallel implementation of the DQE for OLAP queries follows the *single program multiple data* (SPMD) [1] model, where multiple symmetric *workers* (threads) on different DQE instances execute the same query, but each of them deals with different portions of the data. The parallelization of stateful operators requires shuffling rows, so that the same worker processes the related rows. Shuffling is done using a communication middleware that provides all-to-all asynchronous data transfers, which was initially implemented using non-blocking Java sockets. In this paper we describe an RDMA-based implementation of the middleware, which was developed as an alternative to reduce the communication overheads associated with parallel execution of OLAP queries, and we discuss aspects considered while redesigning the middleware to leverage from RDMA technologies.

Our middleware implementation relies on the RDMA Verbs programming interface, and uses one-sided write operations for data transfers, and send/receive operations for coordination messages. For improved performance, it makes heavy use of pre-allocated and lock-free data structures to operate. Moreover, it uses batching to make a more efficient use of network. Experimental results show that our RDMA-based middleware implementation can provide a 75 % reduction on communication costs, when compared with a sockets implementation.

The rest of this paper is structured as follows: In Sect. 2, we describe the requirements for supporting shuffling and the functionality offered by RDMA networking. Section 3 describes the proposed solution. Section 4 compares the proposed solution to a sockets-based middleware and Sect. 5 contrasts it to alternative proposals. Finally, Sect. 6 concludes the paper.

2   Background

2.1   Shuffling

In the DQE, shuffle operators are used when parallelizing stateful operators to redirect rows to a certain worker based on a hash-code (computed from the attributes used as key by the stateful operator being parallelized). Shuffle operators are also used to redirect all results to the master worker at the end of the query, or to broadcast rows from sub-queries.

The communication middleware provides efficient intra-query synchronization and data exchange, and it is mainly used for exchanging rows in shuffle operators. A push-based approach is followed. When processing a row that should be handled by other worker, the sender immediately tries to transfer it. Each receiver maintains *shuffle queues* (Fig. 1), which are used to asynchronously receive the rows. The shuffle queues abstract a set of queues used by a worker to receive rows from the other workers, and they contain an incoming and an outgoing buffer per each other worker, which are used to temporarily store rows being exchanged. That is, the rows are initially serialized to the appropriate outgoing buffer (on the sender side), and then the serialized data is transferred to the matching incoming buffer of the receiver worker, using the communication middleware. An optimization is made for the case where the receiver worker is running on the same DQE instance of the sender. In those cases, the shared session state is used to allow the sender to directly move the rows to the shuffle queues of the receiver.

Multiple shuffle operators may be required by a parallel query plan, thus the need for multi-stage shuffling. To reduce the memory cost associated to buffers – which increases quadratically with the number of workers – there is a single incoming and a single outgoing buffer shared by all shuffle operators (multiplexing is used to logically separate data from multiple shuffle operators).

The communication middleware was initially implemented using Java sockets. For this implementation, a communication end-point is created when initializing a worker, which means to start a server socket and bind it to the IP address of the machine. Then a non-blocking socket channel is opened between each pair of workers running on different DQE instances, and the associated incoming/outgoing buffers are allocated.

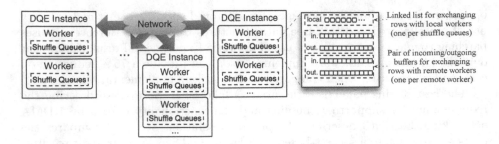

Fig. 1. DQE architecture and shuffle queues structure.

When a row is requested by a shuffle operator, the operator starts by polling its shuffle queues, where it may have received rows from other workers. The polling process of shuffle queues comprises the following steps:

- Check if there is a row received from a worker from the same DQE instance.
- If no row is available:
  - Read (copy) data available on socket channels to incoming buffers.
  - Poll the incoming buffers for available rows for the current shuffle operator.

If a row is obtained, it is returned by the shuffle operator. However, polling shuffle queues may return no rows. In that case, the shuffle operator obtains a local row from its child task/operator (as defined in the query plan). The row is hashed to determine the worker that should process it. If it is a row for the current worker, it is returned by the shuffle operator. Otherwise it is sent to the appropriate worker, which implies serializing the row to an outgoing buffer, and writing the data available to the socket channel. As the shuffle operator still does not have a row to return, it goes back to the polling process and it tries again to obtain a row for itself. As long as the shuffle operator has local rows to process from its child operator, it does not block polling the shuffle queues. After processing all those rows, the worker blocks if polling the shuffle queues returns no rows. It will poll the shuffle queues again as soon as new data is received. The only other situation where the worker may block is when there is no free space on an outgoing buffer when sending a row to a remote worker.

In summary, the push-based asynchronous shuffling approach followed by the DQE requires the following key functionalities from the communication middleware [5]: ability to send and queue rows on remote workers; ability to retrieve the rows queued; ability to block a worker when there are no rows to process (and to wake it up when new rows are received); and ability to block a worker when a row cannot be immediately copied to a buffer (and to wake it up when space becomes available).

2.2 RDMA Verbs

RDMA protocols [12] provide efficient and reliable mechanisms to read/write data directly from the main memory of remote machines, without the involvement of the remote machine CPU, enabling data transfers with lower latency and higher throughput. By providing applications with direct access to network hardware, RDMA also bypasses typical complex network stacks and operating system, reducing memory copies and CPU usage. The RDMA Verbs is the basic programming interface to use RDMA protocols, and it supports data transfers using either one-sided read/write operations, or two-sided send/receive operations. Additionally, there is the *write with immediate data* operation, which is a one-sided write operation that also triggers a receive operation.

The API is asynchronous, that is, *queue pairs* – comprised of a send and a receive queue – are used to queue operation requests for each connection. The application may choose to receive *completion events* when requests are finished, which are posted into a *completion queue* associated with the queue pair. To avoid active polling, the application may request to be notified when a completion event is added to the completion queue (these notifications are sent to a *completion channel*).

In our work, we used the jVerbs library [13], a Java implementation of the RDMA Verbs interface available on the IBM JRE. Besides providing an RDMA Verbs API for Java, jVerbs relies on modifications of the IBM JVM to reduce memory copies.

3   Middleware Design and Implementation

In this section we first present the design of the RDMA communication middleware developed, and we then discuss in detail the implementation decisions critical to the performance of our solution.

3.1   Design Overview

The RDMA middleware relies on one-sided RDMA write operations to transfer rows' data directly between Java memory buffers, and send/receive operations for coordination.

When initializing workers for a parallel connection, on each DQE instance running workers, an RDMA server connection is created and bound to the machine IP address. Then all DQEs are connected with each other, which requires (i) to pre-allocate and initialize memory buffers, queue pairs, completion channel, and completion queue; (ii) to start a new thread (the network thread), which will handle the work completion events; (iii) to start RDMA connections with all other DQE instances; and (iv) to pre-allocate and initialize the data structures needed to execute the network requests.

These steps are performed when opening a database connection, where it is specified the level of parallelism – number of workers to use – for queries executed using that connection. In this way, the overheads of preparing the network are avoided during the execution of queries. On the other hand, the resources remain allocated even if the connection is not being used to run queries.

As described before, when executing a shuffle operator, workers send and receive rows asynchronously through shuffle queues, which use buffers to serialize and temporarily store those rows until they are polled on the receiving side. However, when using the RDMA middleware, the sender uses an RDMA write request to transfer the serialized data from one of its outgoing buffers to a remote incoming buffer. Then, after the network thread receives a work completion event confirming the execution of the RDMA write request, the receiving side is notified, and the tail of the local outgoing buffer is updated, to release the space occupied by the data transferred during the request. The sending side takes into account the tail position of the remote buffer to determine the free space available. When there is no space available on the remote buffer, the data transfer can only occur after the network thread receives a notification updating the tail of the remote buffer (i.e., releasing space on the remote buffer), thus the network thread assumes the task of posting the RDMA write request, and the worker proceeds with its operation, unless the local outgoing buffer is also full. In this case, instead of spilling data to disk – as it is done in some MapReduce implementations, for example –, we chose to block the worker, until space is released.

When workers want a new row to consume, they follow the polling process described in Sect. 2.1. However, as now data is transferred using RDMA write operations, some changes are required. Firstly, the workers do not have to copy data from the channels to their incoming buffers, as the data is transferred directly to those buffers. Moreover, as the data is transferred without the intervention of the receiving side, the network thread uses the notifications previously described to keep track of buffers with data available for each worker, and it wakes up blocked workers when it receives notifications.

3.2   Implementation Decisions

Network and Worker Threads. We use a thread dedicated to track completion of operations (the network thread). To reduce CPU consumption, this thread blocks waiting for completion events, and it is in charge of operations that follow a completion event of a network operation. This includes to process the completion of RDMA write requests (sending the needed notifications, and updating outgoing buffer states), as well as processing received notifications (possibly waking up blocked worker threads). As this thread blocks waiting for completion events, we decided to not use this thread to post the RDMA write requests, as the requests would not be posted until the network thread wakes up. Worker threads are in charge of performing the RDMA write requests to transfer rows, with one exception: In case there is an ongoing RDMA write request, the new request is delayed until the previous one completes. As it is the network thread that tracks the completion of the requests, it is also this thread that will post the RDMA write requests in those cases. As after returning from the sending operation workers may want to reuse the memory space that contains the row to send, the sending operation always serializes the row to the outgoing buffer (even if it does not perform the RDMA write request). Therefore, if this buffer is full the worker blocks. The alternative would imply to copy the row to a temporary buffer, or to spill data to disk, as we mentioned previously. As typically there are many other threads to keep the system busy, we choose this option that avoids wasting CPU time.

RDMA Connections. A single connection/queue pair is used per pair of machines, which means that multiple workers share the same connection/queue pair. In this way, if we have m machines with n workers each, we require $m - 1$ connections per machine. If we used a connection for each pair of workers, we would require $n \times n \times (m - 1)$ connections per machine (i.e., for each of the n workers on a machine, there would be a connection to each of the n workers on every other $m - 1$ machines). We followed this approach to reduce the needs of on-chip memory of the network card, which can compromise the scalability of the communications [3]. Regarding memory buffers, we use a single contiguous memory region per pair of machines, which is later divided in multiple buffers, to be used by the different pairs of workers.

Notifications. To detect the availability of new received data, we decided to use send/receive requests to notify the receiving side. The main goal was to avoid active polling on all incoming buffers, which results in scalability problems. As receivers are notified when data is written/received, they can easily keep track of the list of buffers with data available. An alternative would be to use an *RDMA write with immediate data*, but this operation is not provided by the jVerbs API. Moreover, the notifications are also used to notify the sending side that data was read from a buffer, which is essential to determine when data can be transferred. To reduce the number of read notifications, they are only sent after reading a configurable amount of data (an approach similar to the one followed by [3]). That is, the sender does not have knowledge of the released space immediately. Although this could make workers block more often when sending rows, our experiments showed that workers rarely block in these situations.

Batching. In the initial implementation, the middleware was prepared to transfer data as soon as it was available, in order to reduce latency. However, due to the small size of the rows being transferred, we noticed that this could result in significant communication overheads, particularly when using an RDMA software implementation such as Soft-iWARP [17]. Due to the asynchronous nature of the DQE, the latency is not critical. Therefore, the middleware provides the ability to define a minimum threshold of data, that is, the data transfer request is delayed until a certain amount of data to transfer is available (or a *flush* operation is performed). This threshold may be adjusted, namely to take into account the network hardware characteristics (i.e., we can use lower thresholds when using network hardware with support for RDMA). Moreover, notifications are also sent in batches. That is, when performing actions that originate multiple notifications, the notifications are initially queued, and at the end they are sent in a batch.

Lock-free Pre-initialized Data-structures. For increased performance, the middleware makes use of lock-free data structures, allowing worker threads to operate without blocking, until they have no work to process. The network thread blocks waiting for completion events, but the middleware is designed so that worker threads are not prevented from progress in this case. The incoming and outgoing buffers are implemented using *circular buffers* on top of direct byte buffers (i.e., this memory is outside of the Java garbage-collected heap). These circular buffers are designed to support a write and a read operation concurrently without using locks, to avoid contention when serializing rows. Moreover, the main data structures needed are initialized during connection, and are reused for all queries executed with the connection. To reduce overheads associated to JNI serialization when jVerbs makes RDMA verbs calls to lower level libraries, jVerbs provides *stateful verbs methods (SVM)*, which cache the serialized state of the call, enabling this state to be reused in later calls without additional serialization overheads. By making use of this mechanism, and by initializing the SVM objects during connection, we keep these overheads outside the execution of queries.

RDMA Writes vs Send/Receive. We decided to use RDMA writes to transfer data. Regarding performance, RDMA write requests usually provide better latencies and lower CPU usage on the passive side [11]. Even though the latency is not critical, the lower CPU usage is important to leave more resources for the worker threads. Moreover, RDMA write requests also simplify the communication process, as a single connection is used to transfer data between multiple pairs of buffers. That is, the receiver does not know in advance where the received data should be placed. Whereas with RDMA write operations it is the sender that determines where the data is placed on the receiving side, with send/receive operations this is determined by the receiver. Therefore, to use send/receive requests the sender would need to tell the receiver in advance the buffer to use to receive the data. The receiver would then post a receive request with the appropriate buffer, and tell the sender it could send the actual data (or tell the sender it cannot send data if there is no buffer space on the receiving side). This increases the number of requests to transfer data, and it forces the data transfer operations to be posted one at a time, to make sure that data is placed on the right buffer on the receiving side, whereas our current solution allows for multiple posted RDMA write requests pending completion. To avoid this, we would have to either use a single buffer per pair of DQE instances (instead of a single buffer per pair of workers), or an RDMA connection per pair of workers. The former solution would impose contention among workers when serializing and deserializing rows. The latter would increase the number of connections needed, which would compromise scalability, as we discussed previously in this section.

4   Evaluation

To evaluate the solution developed we conducted performance experiments, which we report in this section. First we compare the RDMA middleware with the original sockets middleware in a synthetic benchmark, which simulates the use of the middleware to execute queries, but that removes all the computation related with the actual query execution, leaving only the shuffle operators. Then we compare both middleware implementations executing real analytical queries with the DQE.

The evaluation was conducted using a cluster of 9 servers. All servers have Intel Core i3 CPUs, with 2 physical cores (4 threads), 8GB of RAM, SATA HDD (7200 rpm), and GigaBit Ethernet. As the servers do not have network hardware supporting RDMA, we used Soft-iWARP [17].

4.1 Synthetic Benchmark

In this section we compare the performance of the middleware implementations using an application that simulates the execution of shuffle operators in real queries, but without operators that do the actual query computation. That is, each worker thread of the application executes a "query plan" that essentially contains two shuffle operators (see Fig. 2). The "rows" are integers generated sequentially (node Int Generator on Fig. 2), and between the two shuffle operators a simple transformation is applied to the integers received from the previous operator to make sure that most of them will be sent to a different worker in the next shuffle operator.

For these experiments we used a setup with 4 servers running one application process each, and another setup with 8 servers running one application process each. The tests were conducted using IBM JRE 8.0-1.10. The size of the buffers used by the communication middleware was set to 64 KB (the default value). Each application process generates 5M integers, which are shuffled twice (i.e., the shuffle operators of each process handle 10M integers in total).

We measured the execution time with different numbers of workers on each process, both using the sockets and the RDMA middleware. The execution times (averages of 8 executions) are reported on Fig. 3. Considering the fastest times for each middleware in the two setups tested, we can observe that the RDMA middleware resulted in a reduction of around 75 % of the execution time.

We also used this synthetic application to illustrate the impact of batching multiple rows before transferring them, as described in Sect. 3.2. Figure 4

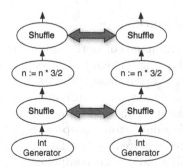

Fig. 2. Plan used for the synthetic benchmark.

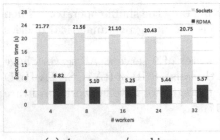

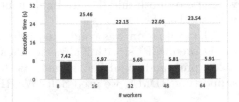

(a) 4 processes/machines.   (b) 8 processes/machines.

Fig. 3. Execution times of the synthetic application for the sockets and RDMA middleware, when varying the number of DQE instances and the number of workers.

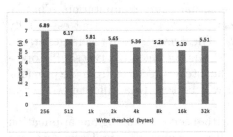

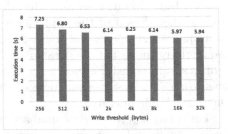

(a) 4 processes/machines, 2 workers per process.

(b) 8 processes/machines, 2 workers per process.

Fig. 4. Execution times of the synthetic application with different thresholds for write requests batching.

shows the execution times using different minimum thresholds for transferring data, when using 4 processes and 8 processes (in both cases 2 worker threads per process were used). As we can observe, when using the RDMA middleware adjusting this threshold can lead to variations on the execution time higher than 25 %. With the used hardware we observed a good performance with a threshold of 16 KB, which is the value we used in the other tests reported in this section.

4.2   Application Benchmark

We also compared the performance of both middleware implementations using the DQE to run analytical queries. These tests were conducted using 3 analytical queries, executed over a TPC-C database [16]. Listing 1.1 shows the queries used, which expose different combinations of common operators of analytical queries.

For this experiment we used the following setups: 4 servers running DQE instances and the key-value data store component (HBase), and 1 server running the remaining services required by the DQE; and 8 servers running DQE instances and the key-value data store component, and 1 server running the remaining services required by the DQE. The tests were conducted using HBase 0.98.6, running on Oracle JRE 1.7.0_80-b15, and the DQEs were running on IBM

JRE 8.0-1.10. The size of the buffers used by the communication middleware was set to 64 KB (the default value).

```
-- Query 1
select ol_o_id, ol_w_id, ol_d_id, sum(ol_amount) as revenue, o_entry_d
    from order_line, orders, new_order, customer
    where c_id = o_c_id and c_w_id = o_w_id and c_d_id = o_d_id
        and no_w_id = o_w_id and no_d_id = o_d_id and no_o_id = o_id
        and ol_w_id = o_w_id and ol_d_id = o_d_id and ol_o_id = o_id
        and c_state like 'A%' and o_entry_d > timestamp('2013-07-01-00.00.00.000000')
    group by ol_o_id, ol_w_id, ol_d_id, o_entry_d
    having sum(ol_amount) > 80000.00
    order by revenue desc, o_entry_d;

-- Query 2
select 100.00 * sum(case when i_data like 'a%' then ol_amount else 0 end) /
    (1+sum(ol_amount)) as promo_revenue
    from order_line, item
    where ol_i_id = i_id
        and ol_delivery_d >= timestamp('2013-06-01 00:00:00.000')
        and ol_delivery_d < timestamp('2013-08-01 00:00:00.000');

-- Query 3
select ol_number, sum(ol_quantity) as sum_qty, sum(cast(ol_amount as decimal(10,2))) as
    sum_amount, sum(ol_quantity) / count(*) as avg_qty, sum(ol_amount) / count(*) as
    avg_amount, count(*) as count_order
    from order_line
    where ol_delivery_d > timestamp('2013-07-01 00:00:00.000')
    group by ol_number order by sum(ol_quantity) desc;
```

Listing 1.1. Evaluation Queries.

We measured the execution time of the queries previously presented, running both without parallelization and with parallelization (with different numbers of workers), over TPC-C databases with a scale factor of either 15 (for the setup with $4+1$ servers) or 30 (for the setup with $8+1$ servers). The parallel times were obtained both for the sockets middleware and for the RDMA middleware. For each different setup, the queries were run 5 times, and the average of the last 4 runs was considered, to account for cache warm-ups.

Figure 5 shows the executions times obtained for the different setups. As we can observe from the results obtained, when using 4 DQE instances, the RDMA middleware resulted in improvements on the maximum speedup between 2.0 % (from 5.97x to 6.09x, in Query 2) and 16.2 % (from 6.44x to 7.49x, in Query 3), when compared with the sockets middleware. When using 8 DQE instances, the RDMA middleware resulted in improvements on the maximum speedups between 6.1 % (from 13.52x to 14.35x, in Query 3) and 14.3 % (from 10.34x to 11.83x, in Query 1).

As it would be expectable, significant improvements were obtained with Query 1, which is the query that involves more shuffle operators to be parallelized (thus, more communications). That is, the RDMA middleware is particularly important to the parallelization of more complex queries. On the other hand, Query 2 obtained lower benefits from the RDMA middleware, as it performs less communication. Load balancing issues affecting this query also contribute to the lower benefits obtained from using the RDMA middleware.

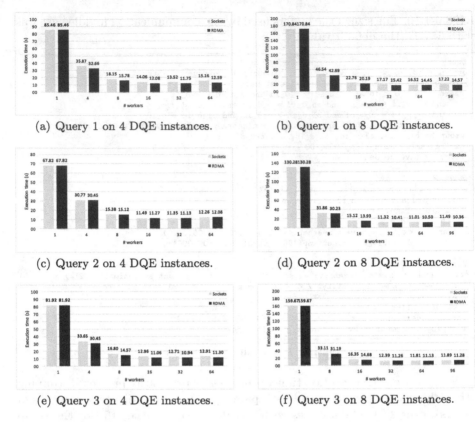

(a) Query 1 on 4 DQE instances.

(b) Query 1 on 8 DQE instances.

(c) Query 2 on 4 DQE instances.

(d) Query 2 on 8 DQE instances.

(e) Query 3 on 4 DQE instances.

(f) Query 3 on 8 DQE instances.

Fig. 5. Execution times of the analytical queries for the sockets and RDMA middleware, when varying the number of DQE instances and the number of workers.

5   Related Work

Different works explored previously the use of RDMA technologies (and the RDMA Verbs interface) to improve performance of communications in parallel/distributed systems. Liu *et al.* [9] proposed an implementation for MPI [4] (the *de facto* standard for communication in the high-performance computing field) based on RDMA writes. Similar to our approach, they use a pool of preallocated buffers, and there is also a match between buffers on sender and receiver sides, so that the state of the receiver buffer can be "predicted" on the sender side. Whereas we use a single pair of matching circular buffers, they use a pool of buffers organized as a ring. Moreover, they rely on active polling to detect incoming data, which limits scalability. Therefore, they limit RDMA communication to sub-sets of processes, and use send/receive requests for the remaining communications. Sur *et al.* [14] proposed a different approach. They use a *rendezvous protocol*, where the transfer of data is first negotiated through send/receive requests, and then RDMA read requests are used to transfer data. This approach is not appropriate to our case, where we have multiple threads communicating concurrently through the same connection. We choose to use matching buffers on sender and receiver, together with notifications of read (processed) data on the receiver, to simplify the coordination between sender and receiver side, which is particularly important to reduce contention when multiple threads may try to send data concurrently (an issue not discussed by [14]).

RDMA was used to implement FaRM [3], a distributed computing platform which exposes the memory of multiple machines of a cluster as a shared address space. FaRM design has similarities with the solution we propose: It also relies on circular buffers and RDMA write requests to transfer data, for example. However, it uses active polling to detect received data, and RDMA writes to notify the sender of data removed from the buffer by the receiver side. Moreover, FaRM is designed for minimal latency, whereas in our case we take advantage of the asynchronous nature of the application using the middleware to batch multiple messages, increasing latency, but reducing communication overheads, and improving the overall application performance.

In the recent years, RDMA was also explored to improve different components of well-known software stacks for distributed computing. Wang *et al.* [18,19] provide an alternative shuffling protocol for Hadoop implemented using RDMA, which uses send/receive requests to request data, and then RDMA write requests to transfer the data. Lu *et al.* [10] also used RDMA to improve the performance of the Hadoop RPC communication.

6   Conclusions

In this paper we presented an RDMA-based communication middleware to support asynchronous shuffling in parallel execution of analytical queries, discussing the alternatives considered and the insights acquired with its implementation. When compared with a previous sockets-based middleware implementation, experimental results show that our new RDMA implementation enables a reduction of communication costs of 75 % on a synthetic benchmark, and a reduction of as much as 14 % on the total execution time of analytical queries, even when using a software implementation of the RDMA protocol, showing that redesigning communications to follow an RDMA approach can provide considerable benefits.

Acknowledgements. This research has been partially funded by the European Commission under projects CoherentPaaS and LeanBigData (grants FP7-611068, FP7-619606), the Madrid Regional Council, FSE and FEDER, project Cloud4BigData (grant S2013TIC-2894), the Spanish Research Agency MICIN project BigDataPaaS (grant TIN2013-46883), and the ERDF – European Regional Development Fund through the Operational Programme for Competitiveness and Internationalisation – COMPETE 2020 Programme and by National Funds through the FCT – Fundação para a Ciência e a Tecnologia (Portuguese Foundation for Science and Technology) within project POCI-01-0145-FEDER-006961.

References

1. Darema, F.: The SPMD model: past, present and future. In: Cotronis, Y., Dongarra, J. (eds.) PVM/MPI 2001. LNCS, vol. 2131, p. 1. Springer, Heidelberg (2001)
2. Dean, J., Ghemawat, S.: MapReduce: simplified data processing on large clusters. Commun. ACM **51**(1), 107–113 (2008)
3. Dragojević, A., Narayanan, D., Castro, M., Hodson, O.: FaRM: fast remote memory. In: USENIX Symposium on Networked Systems Design and Implementation, pp. 401–414 (2014)
4. Forum, M.P.I.: MPI: A message-passing interface standard. University of Tennessee, Technical report (1994)
5. Gonçalves, R.C., Pereira, J., Jimenez-Peris, R.: Design of an RDMA communication middleware for asynchronous shuffling in analytical processing. In: CLOSER - CoherentPaaS/LeanBigData Projects Workshop (to appear)
6. Apache Impala project. http://impala.io
7. Jimenez-Peris, R., Patino-Martinez, M., Kemme, B., Brondino, I., Pereira, J., Vilaça, R., Cruz, F., Oliveira, R., Ahmad, Y.: CumuloNimbo: a cloud scalable multi-tier SQL database. Data Eng. **38**(1), 73–83 (2015)
8. Kossmann, D.: The state of the art in distributed query processing. ACM Comput. Surv. **32**(4), 422–469 (2000)
9. Liu, J., Wu, J., Panda, D.K.: High performance RDMA-based MPI implementation over InfiniBand. Int. J. Parallel Program. **32**(3), 167–198 (2004)
10. Lu, X., Islam, N.S., Wasi-Ur-Rahman, M., Jose, J., Subramoni, H., Wang, H., Panda, D.K.: High-performance design of Hadoop RPC with RDMA over Infini-Band. In: International Conference on Parallel Processing, pp. 641–650 (2013)
11. MacArthur, P., Russell, R.D.: A performance study to guide RDMA programming decisions. In: ACM International Conference on High Performance Computing and Communication & IEEE International Conference on Embedded Software and Systems, pp. 778–785 (2012)
12. Mellanox Technologies: RDMA Aware Networks Programming User Manual (2015)
13. Stuedi, P., Metzler, B., Trivedi, A.: jVerbs: ultra-low latency for data center applications. In: 4th Annual Symposium on Cloud Computing, pp. 10:1–10:14 (2013)
14. Sur, S., Jin, H.W., Chai, L., Panda, D.K.: RDMA read based rendezvous protocol for MPI over InfiniBand: design alternatives and benefits. In: ACM SIGPLAN Symposium on Principles and Practice of Parallel Programming, pp. 32–39 (2006)
15. Thusoo, A., Sarma, J.S., Jain, N., Shao, Z., Chakka, P., Anthony, S., Liu, H., Wyckoff, P., Murthy, R.: Hive: a warehousing solution over a map-reduce framework. Proc. VLDB Endow. **2**(2), 1626–1629 (2009)
16. Transaction Processing Performance Council: TPC Benchmark C Standard Specification, Revision 5.11 (2010)
17. Trivedi, A., Metzler, B., Stuedi, P.: A case for RDMA in clouds: turning supercomputer networking into commodity. In: Asia-Pacific Workshop on Systems (2011)
18. Wang, Y., Que, X., Yu, W., Goldenberg, D., Sehgal, D.: Hadoop acceleration through network levitated merge. In: International Conference for High Performance Computing, Networking, Storage and Analysis, pp. 57:1–57:10 (2011)
19. Wang, Y., Xu, C., Li, X., Yu, W.: JVM-bypass for efficient Hadoop shuffling. In: International Symposium on Parallel and Distributed Processing, pp. 569–578 (2013)

Holistic Shuffler for the Parallel Processing of SQL Window Functions

Fábio Coelho[(✉)], José Pereira, Ricardo Vilaça, and Rui Oliveira

INESC TEC & Universidade do Minho, Braga, Portugal
facoelho@inesctec.pt, {jop,rmvilaca,rco}@di.uminho.pt

Abstract. Window functions are a sub-class of analytical operators that allow data to be handled in a derived view of a given relation, while taking into account their neighboring tuples. Currently, systems bypass parallelization opportunities which become especially relevant when considering Big Data as data is naturally partitioned. We present a shuffling technique to improve the parallel execution of window functions when data is naturally partitioned when the query holds a partitioning clause that does not match the natural partitioning of the relation. We evaluated this technique with a non-cumulative ranking function and we were able to reduce data transfer among parallel workers in 85 % when compared to a naive approach.

1 Introduction

Window functions (WF) are a sub-group of analytical functions that allow to easily formulate analytical queries over a derived view of a given relation R. They allow operations like ranking, cumulative averages or time series to be computed over a given data partition. Listing 1.1 presents one window function that is expressed in SQL by the operator OVER, together with a partition by (PC) and an order by (OC).

Listing 1.1. Window Function example.

```
select rank() OVER(Partition By A Order By B) from R
```

The growing Big Data trend is shifting the processing of these functions to cloud environments deploying computation to a distributed mesh of computing nodes, where data and processing are naturally partitioned. The distributed execution of queries leverages on data partitioning as a way to attain gains associated with parallel execution. Nevertheless, the partitioning strategies are typically governed by a primary table key, which only benefits the cases where the partitioning of a query matches that same key as depicted in Fig. 1. When the query has to partition data according to a different attribute in a relation, it becomes likely that the members of each partition will not all reside in the same node, which compromises the final result for a subgroup of non-cumulative analytical operators, such as **rank**, since all members of a distinct partition need to be handled by a single entity, in order not to incur in unnecessary sorting steps, which is the most costly operation [3].

© IFIP International Federation for Information Processing 2016
Published by Springer International Publishing Switzerland 2016. All Rights Reserved
M. Jelasity and E. Kalyvianaki (Eds.): DAIS 2016, LNCS 9687, pp. 75–81, 2016.
DOI: 10.1007/978-3-319-39577-7_6

select rank() OVER (partition by PK) from table

PK	A	B
1	1	1
1	1	2
1	2	1
1	3	1

node #1

PK	A	B
2	1	1
2	2	3
2	2	3
2	3	1

node #2

PK	A	B
3	2	1
3	2	1
3	2	3
3	2	3

node #3

Fig. 1. Data partitioning according to the primary key (PK).

In this paper we propose an Holistic shuffler which according to the partitioning considered by the ongoing window function will instruct workers to handle specific partitions according to the data sizes they hold, minimizing data transfer among workers. We present the design and action of the shuffler which is based on prior knowledge of the data size distribution of each column in the relation, reflecting the data size held in each partition rather than considering the actual data value as seen in common use of database indexes. The preliminary evaluation of our mechanism shows that our approach is able reduce data transfer by 85 % when compared with a naive approach.

Roadmap: In the remainder of this paper, Sect. 2 introduces the distribution considered and Sect. 3 presents the design and architecture of the Holistic Shuffler we propose. Section 4 accesses our approach. Section 5 briefly reviews related work and overviews our contributions.

2 Data Transfer Statistics

The use of indexes [5], histograms [6] and other heuristics are now a staple feature in modern database systems, as they allow to expedite operations, avoiding full scan operations over relations. More recently, these strategies started to be present in cloud infrastructures [4], allowing for processing on primary and secondary attributes.

key	PK	A	B
1	4	2	3
2	0	1	1
3	0	1	0

(a) (p1)

key	PK	A	B
1	0	1	2
2	4	2	0
3	0	1	2

(b) (p2)

key	PK	A	B
1	0	0	2
2	0	4	0
3	4	0	2

(c) (p3)

key	PK	A	B
1	p1	p1	p1
2	p2	p3	p1
3	p3	p1 / p2	p2 / p3

(d) Global

Fig. 2. Partition and Global Histogram construction.

Histograms are commonly used by query optimizers as they provide a fairly accurate estimate on the data distribution, which is crucial for a query planner. An histogram allows to map keys to their observed frequencies. Database systems use these structures to measure the cardinality of keys or key ranges. Without histograms, the query planner would have to assume uniform distribution of data, leading to incorrect partitioning, particularly with skewed data [7], a common characteristic of non synthetic workloads.

When a query engine has to generate parallel query execution plans to be dispatched to distinct workers, each one holding a partition of data; having histograms like the aforementioned ones is an asset, but it does not completely present an heuristic that could be used to enhance how parallel workers would share preliminary and final results. This is so as such histograms only introduce and insight about the cardinality of each partition key. In order to improve bandwidth usage, thus reducing the amount of traded information, the histogram also needs to reflect the volume of data existing in each node, instead of just considering the row cardinality.

2.1   Histogram Construction

The cornerstone of the contribution we present is based on merging the knowledge for row cardinality and average row size for each partition. Both could be seen as global metrics that a given query engine may be able to produce and maintain, as this type of information is already used for similar purposes. The cadence at which the histogram should be updated was left outside of the scope of this paper due to space constraints. Nevertheless we note it as a relevant topic, since the optimal performance of any heuristic based approach is entirely connected with its own representativity. Figure 1 presents the result of hash partitioning a relation in 3 workers, according to key PK. The histogram to be built will consider the cardinality of each value in each attribute of the relation for each single partition. Since the construction of the histogram should not be done during query planning time, it cannot know beforehand the partitioning clauses induced by queries. As such, we consider all distinct groups of values in each attribute. Each partition will contribute to the histogram with the same number of attributes as the original relation, plus a key, reflecting the data in that partition. Afterwards, each worker should be able to share its partial histogram with the remainder workers in order to produce the global histogram.

Algorithm 1. Histogram Construction in Partition n

1: **procedure** COUNT_DISTINCT_KEYS($attr$)
2:     *foreach key : attr*
3:         *count ← count(distinct)*
4:         *size ← size(key)*
5:         *hist_P_n(key, attr) ← (count, size)*
6:     P_n ← [$attr_1, attr_2, attr_n$]
7:     *hist_P_n* ← [$key, attr_1, attr_2, attr_n$]
8: **function** GLOBAL HISTOGRAM(P_n)
9:     *for each attr : P_n*
10:         COUNT_DISTINCT_KEYS($attr$)

Algorithm 1 governs how each partition histogram ($hist\_P_n$) should be built. Briefly, each attribute ($attr$) is traversed and for each key, the total number of distinct occurrences of that key is computed, together with its size. The pair of values is then added to the histogram. The tables in Fig. 2(a), (b) and (c) present the resulting histograms for each partition according to Fig. 1.

When all workers have completed computing the histogram regarding its own physical partition, they need to share it with a designated worker, so that the global histogram is also computed. The global histogram will traverse each physical partition histogram and evaluate, for each key, which is the physical partition that holds the largest volume (in size, evaluating the *cardinality* × *average_row_size*). The table in Fig. 2(d) depicts the final result of the global histogram. The global histogram will have the same number of attributes of each partition histogram. Please note that the keys for both the physical partition and the global histograms are not the primary keys of the relation, but rather the distinct values found in each attribute during the construction of each partition histogram. Therefore, we provide a brief example on how to read this histogram. Consider that a given query requires data to be partitioned according to attribute A. Then, the histogram informs that key 1 and 2 have the largest volume of data respectively in partitions $p1,p3$ and, and regarding key 3, partitions $p2$ and $p3$ both hold the same volume.

3   Holistic Shuffler

The Holistic Shuffler leverages on the data distribution data collected by the Global Histogram in order to expedite shuffling operations. The Shuffle operator can be translated into a $SEND$ primitive that forwards a bounded piece of data to a given destination, considering the underlying network to be reliable. During the workflow for processing a window operator, there are two different moments where data needs to be shuffled. The first moment occurs immediately after the operator starts, and its goal is to reunite partitions, thus fulfilling the locality requirement. The second moment occurs in the end of the operator and it is intended to reconcile partial results in order to produce the final result.

Both operators define distinct goals regarding the destinations that need to be chosen for each forwarding operation. Therefore, we establish two shuffle operators, the local shuffle and the global shuffle contemplating each set of requirements. The Local Shuffle will dispatch rows of a given partition to the worker responsible for that partition as dictated by the Global histogram. Algorithm 2 depicts the behavior of the operator. As each row is read from scanning the partition, the value contained in that row for the attribute that dictates the partition clause is collected (*partition*). This value is then used together with the partitioning attribute to obtain the destination worker from the global histogram. If this row is not meant to be handled by the ongoing worker, then it is forwarded to the correct worker.

Algorithm 2. Local Shuffle Operation	**Algorithm 3.** Global Shuffle Operation
1: $worker\_id$	1: $worker\_id$
2: $row \leftarrow [key, attr_1, attr_n]$	2: $master\_worker \leftarrow hist\_P_n$
3: $hist\_P_n \leftarrow [key, row]$	3: **function** GSHUFFLE($aggregated\_data$)
4: $partition\_by \leftarrow attr_1$	4: $foreach\ row : aggregated\_data$
5: **function** LSHUFFLE($local\_partition$)	5:
6: $for\ each\ row : local\_partition$	6: **if** $worker\_id \neq master\_worker$ **then**
7: $partition \leftarrow row[attr_1]$	7: $SEND(master\_worker, row)$
8: $destination \leftarrow hist\_p_n[partition, attr_1]$	
9:	
10: **if** $worker\_id \neq destination$ **then**	
11: $SEND(destination, row)$	

The Global Shuffle will forward all aggregated rows to the worker that will hold the overall largest data volume, which will from now on designate as master worker. By instructing the workers that hold the least volume of data, we are promoting the minimal usage of bandwidth possible. Algorithm 3 reflects the behavior for the Global Shuffle operator. The input data considered by the Global Shuffler is composed by the ordered and aggregated rows, both produced by earlier stages of the worker work flow. Such rows will now have to be reconciled by a common node, which for this case will be dictated by the master node, as previously stated. Upon start, the Global Shuffle operator will interrogate the histogram regarding the identity of the master node. Afterwards, as each aggregated row is handled by the operator, it is forwarded to the master worker, if the master node is not the current one.

4   Evaluation

Along the current Section, we present the preliminary evaluation for the contributions we propose. In order to evaluate our contribution, we used RX-Java [2] to simulate the parallel execution of the window operator in several workers. This framework establishes bindings to the Java language, enabling it to use the semantics of Reactive Programming [1]. We selected this framework as it allows to establish a series of data streams, mimicking the window operator data flow. Throughout the evaluation, we employed a single ranking query (Listing 4) holding a window function over a synthetically-generated relation as in TPC-C's Order Line relation, holding 10 distinct attributes. The values considered for each of these attributes were distributed according to TPC-C's specification. The generated data composes 100 distinct partitions, each one with 500 rows. Globally, the Order Line relation held 500 K tuples.

```
select rank() OVER (partition by OL_D_ID order by OL_NUMBER)
    from Order Line
```

The experiments were performed on a system with an Intel i3-2100-3.1 GHz 64 bit processor with 2 physical cores (4 virtual), 8 GB of RAM memory and SATA II (3.0 Gbit/s) hard drives, running Ubuntu 12.04 LTS as the operating system.

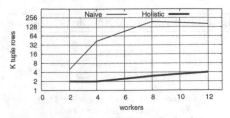 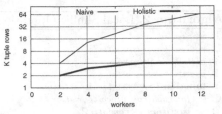

(a) Average Forwarded Rows for both stages   (b) Forwarded Rows for the Shuffle Local

Fig. 3. Comparison results between the Naive and Holistic approach.

For comparison purposes, we report the results by using a naive approach and our Holistic Shuffler. The naive approach, instead of using any knowledge to forward data, disseminates all data among all participating workers. The results in both pictures are depicted according to a logarithmic scale, in the average of 5 independent tests for each configuration.

The Holistic technique we propose required in average only 14.7 % of the rows required for the Naive approach to reunite all the partition in each computing node, as depicted in Fig. 3(a). The large difference is justified by the fact that the naive approach reunites partitions by forwarding data among all participating nodes, which intrinsically creates duplicates in each node, growing in proportion to the number of nodes. The Local Shuffling stage is depicted in Fig. 3(b), in which we varied the number of computing nodes that participate in the computation of the ranking query, verifying the number of rows that were forwarded according to each technique.

5   Related Work and Conclusion

Despite its relevance, optimizations considering this operator are scarce in the literature. The work by [3] or [8] are some of the exceptions. Respectively, the first overcomes optimization challenges related with having multiple window functions in the same query, while the second presents a more broad use of window functions, showing that it is possible to use them as a way to avoid sub-queries and reducing execution time down from quadratic time.

In this paper we proposed an Holistic Shuffler, tailored to be used for the efficient parallel processing of queries with non-cumulative window functions. The design is based on a statistical method that can be used to reduce the amount of data transfered among computing nodes of a distributed query engine, where data is naturally partitioned. Moreover, the preliminary evaluation we present shows that by applying this methodology we were to reduce in average 85 % of data transferred among computing nodes. As future work, we plan to translate this approach to a real query engine.

Acknowledgments. This work was part-funded by project LeanBigData: Ultra-Scalable and Ultra-Efficient Integrated and Visual Big Data Analytics (FP7-619606), and by the ERDF – European Regional Development Fund through the Operational Programme for Competitiveness and Internationalisation - COMPETE 2020 Programme within project ≪POCI-01-0145-FEDER-006961≫, and by National Funds through the FCT – Fundação para a Ciência e a Tecnologia (Portuguese Foundation for Science and Technology) as part of project UID/EEA/50014/2013.

References

1. Reactive programming (2015). http://reactivex.io
2. Reactive programming for java (2015). https://github.com/ReactiveX/RxJava
3. Cao, Y., Chan, C.Y., Li, J., Tan, K.L.: Optimization of analytic window functions. Proc. VLDB Endowment **5**(11), 1244–1255 (2012)
4. Chen, G., Vo, H.T., Wu, S., Ooi, B.C., Özsu, M.T.: A framework for supporting DBMS-like indexes in the cloud. Proc. VLDB Endowment **4**(11), 702–713 (2011)
5. Garcia-Molina, H.: Database Systems: The Complete Book. Pearson Education, India (2008)
6. Poosala, V., Ganti, V., Ioannidis, Y.E.: Approximate query answering using histograms. IEEE Data Eng. Bull. **22**(4), 5–14 (1999)
7. Poosala, V., Haas, P.J., Ioannidis, Y.E., Shekita, E.J.: Improved histograms for selectivity estimation of range predicates. ACM SIGMOD Record **25**, 294–305 (1996). ACM
8. Zuzarte, C., Pirahesh, H., Ma, W., Cheng, Q., Liu, L., Wong, K.: Winmagic: subquery elimination using window aggregation. In: Proceedings of the 2003 ACM SIGMOD International Conference on Management of Data, pp. 652–656. ACM (2003)

Providing CUDA Acceleration to KVM Virtual Machines in InfiniBand Clusters with rCUDA

Ferran Pérez, Carlos Reaño$^{(\boxtimes)}$, and Federico Silla

DISCA, Universitat Politècnica de València, 46022 Valencia, Spain
ferpelo@upv.es, carregon@gap.upv.es, fsilla@disca.upv.es

Abstract. There is a trend towards using graphics processing units (GPUs) not only for graphics visualization, but also for accelerating scientific applications. But their use for this purpose is not without disadvantages: GPUs increase costs and energy consumption. Furthermore, GPUs are generally underutilized. Using virtual machines could be a possible solution to address these problems, however, current solutions for providing GPU acceleration to virtual machines environments, such as KVM or Xen, present some issues. In this paper we propose the use of remote GPUs to accelerate scientific applications running inside KVM virtual machines. Our analysis shows that this approach could be a possible solution, with low overhead when used over InfiniBand networks.

Keywords: CUDA · KVM · Virtualization · InfiniBand · HPC

1 Introduction

Virtual machine (VM) technologies such as KVM [1], Xen [7], VMware [6], and VirtualBox [3] appeared several years ago in order to address some of the concerns present in computing. One of the issues addressed by VMs was data and/or process isolation. That is, without the use of VMs, in a computing cluster providing service to different institutions and companies, each of the nodes of the cluster should only host processes from a single owner if data or process isolation is a requirement. This guarantee for data security, in addition to some other concerns, led in general to low CPU and system utilization, presenting the additional indirect drawbacks of an unnecessarily increased power consumption as well as an increased hardware acquisition cost and higher space and cooling requirements. Virtualization technologies addressed all these concerns by creating virtual computers that are concurrently executed within a single cluster node thus sharing the CPU in that node as well as other subsystems and, therefore, increasing overall resource utilization. Acquisition and maintenance costs are also reduced because a smaller amount of computers are required to address the same workload, thus reducing also energy consumption needs. Finally, data isolation is expected because different VMs manage separate address spaces,

© IFIP International Federation for Information Processing 2016
Published by Springer International Publishing Switzerland 2016. All Rights Reserved
M. Jelasity and E. Kalyvianaki (Eds.): DAIS 2016, LNCS 9687, pp. 82–95, 2016.
DOI: 10.1007/978-3-319-39577-7_7

thus making not possible that a process being executed in one VM addresses memory belonging to other VM.

The importance that VMs have acquired in data centers can be understood just by considering all the support included for them in current mainstream multicore processors from Intel or AMD. Actually, although VMs were known in the past to noticeably reduce application performance with respect to executions in the native (or real) domain, the virtualization features included in current CPUs allow VMs to execute applications with a negligible overhead [15].

However, despite the many achievements accomplished in the field of VMs, they still do not efficiently support the current trend of using graphics processing units (GPUs). This trend allows that many high-performance computing (HPC) clusters deployed in current datacenters and other computing facilities benefit from server configurations that include several multicore CPU sockets and one or more GPUs. In this way, these heterogeneous configurations noticeably reduce the time required to execute applications from areas as different as data analysis (Big Data) [36], chemical physics [32], computational algebra [13], and finance [16], to name just a few. Unfortunately, the lack of efficient GPU support in current VMs makes that, when using these virtualization technologies, applications being executed in the virtualized domain cannot easily access GPUs in the native domain.

The reason why VMs cannot take advantage of the benefits of using GPUs is mainly due to the fact that current GPUs do not feature virtualization capabilities. Furthermore, in those cases where it is possible for applications within VMs to access real GPUs, by using the PCI passthrough mechanism [35], for example, accelerators cannot be efficiently shared among the several VMs concurrently running inside the same host computer. These limitations impede the deployment of GPGPU computing (general-purpose computing on GPUs) in the context of VMs. Fortunately, GPU virtualization solutions such as V-GPU [5], dOpenCL [22], DS-CUDA [30], rCUDA [14,31], vCUDA [33], GridCuda [26], SnuCL [23], GVirtuS [17], GViM [19], VOCL [37], and VCL [12] may be used in VM environments, such as KVM, VirtualBox, VMware, or Xen, in order to address their current concerns with respect to GPUs. These GPU virtualization frameworks detach GPUs from nodes, thus allowing applications to access virtualized GPUs independently from the exact computer they are being executed at. In this regard, the detaching features of remote GPU virtualization frameworks may turn them into an easy and efficient way to overcome the current limitations of VM environments regarding the use of GPUs.

In this paper we explore the use of remote GPU virtualization in order to provide CUDA acceleration to applications running inside KVM VMs. The aim of this study is to analyze which is the overhead that these applications experience when accessing GPUs outside their VM. For this study we make use of the rCUDA remote GPU virtualization framework because it was the only solution that was able to run the tested applications.

The rest of the paper is organized as follows. Section 2 thoroughly reviews previous efforts to provide GPU acceleration to applications being executed inside VMs and further motivates the use of general GPU virtualization frameworks to provide acceleration features to VMs. Later, Sect. 3 introduces in more detail rCUDA, the remote GPU virtualization framework used in this study. Next, Sect. 4 addresses the main goal of this paper: studying the performance of real GPU-accelerated applications when executed within KVM VMs. Finally, Sect. 5 summarizes the main conclusions of our work.

2   Remote GPU Virtualization Solutions

Providing acceleration services to VMs is, basically, the same problem as sharing a GPU among the VMs concurrently running in the host computer or, in a more general perspective, sharing a GPU among several computers.

Sharing accelerators among several computers has been addressed both with hardware and software approaches. On the hardware side, maybe the most prominent solution was NextIO's N2800-ICA [2], based on PCIe virtualization [24]. This solution allowed to share a GPU among eight different servers in a rack within a two-meter distance. Nevertheless, this solution lacked the required flexibility because a GPU could only be used by a single server at a time, thus preventing the concurrent sharing of GPUs. Furthermore, this solution was expensive, what maybe was one of the reasons for NextIO going out of business in August 2013. GPU manufacturers have also tried to tackle the problem with virtualization enabled accelerators, but so far this GPUs are oriented towards the graphics acceleration usage, not compute. Nvidia GRID[1] only supports CUDA enabled VMs under Citrix XenServer and even in this case, the GPU resources are not shared between the VMs, each one has a reserved disjoint segment of the accelerator. The AMD FirePro S-series[2] solution is more flexible, but it only supports OpenCL and it is still oriented towards graphics.

A cheaper and more flexible solution for sharing accelerators, in the context of a server hosting several VMs, is PCI passthrough [35,38]. This mechanism is based on the use of the virtualization extensions widely available in current HPC servers, which allow to install several GPUs in a box and assign each of them, in an exclusive way, to one of the VMs running at the host. Furthermore, when making use of this mechanism, the performance attained by accelerators is very close to that obtained when using the GPU in a native domain. Unfortunately, as this approach assigns GPUs to VMs in an exclusive way, it does not allow to simultaneously share GPUs among the several VMs being concurrently executed at the same host. In order to address this concern, there have been several attempts, like the one proposed in [21], which dynamically changes on demand the GPUs assigned to VMs. However, these techniques present a high time overhead given that, in the best case, two seconds are required to change the assignment between GPUs and VMs.

As a flexible alternative to hardware approaches, several software-based GPU sharing mechanisms have appeared, such as V-GPU, dOpenCL, DS-CUDA, rCUDA, SnuCL, VOCL, VCL, vCUDA, and GridCuda, for example. Basically,

---

[1] http://www.nvidia.com/object/nvidia-grid.html.
[2] http://www.amd.com/en-us/solutions/professional/virtualization.

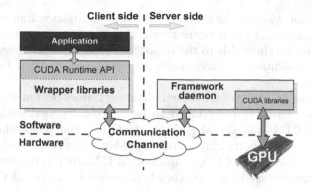

Fig. 1. Architecture usually deployed by GPU virtualization frameworks.

these software proposals share a GPU by virtualizing it, so that they provide applications (or VMs) with virtual instances of the real device, which can therefore be concurrently shared. Usually, these GPU sharing solutions place the virtualization boundary at the API level (Application Programming Interface), which can either be OpenCL [18] or CUDA [29] in the GPGPU field. Nevertheless, we will focus on CUDA-based solutions because CUDA is more widely used. In general, CUDA-based virtualization frameworks aim to offer the same API as the NVIDIA CUDA Runtime API [10] does.

Figure 1 depicts the architecture usually deployed by these virtualization solutions, which follow a distributed client-server approach. The client part of the middleware is installed in the computer (either native or virtual) executing the application requesting GPU services, whereas the server side runs in the native domain owning the actual GPU. Communication between client and server sides may be implemented by means of shared-memory mechanisms if both ends are located at the same physical computer or by using the network fabric if they are placed at different computers. The architecture depicted in Fig. 1 is used in the following way: the client middleware receives a CUDA request from the accelerated application and appropriately processes and forwards it to the server. There, the middleware receives the request and interprets and forwards it to the GPU, which completes the execution of the request and returns the execution results to the server middleware. Finally, the server sends back the results to the client middleware, which forwards them to the accelerated application. Notice that remote GPU virtualization frameworks provide GPU services in a transparent way and, therefore, applications are not aware that their requests are actually serviced by a remote GPU instead of by a local one.

CUDA-based GPU virtualization frameworks may be classified into two types: (1) those intended to be used in the context of VMs and (2) those devised as general purpose virtualization frameworks to be used in native domains, although the client part of these latter solutions may also be used within VMs. Frameworks in the first category usually make use of shared-memory mechanisms in order to transfer data from main memory inside the VM to the GPU in the native domain, whereas the general purpose virtualization frameworks in the second type make use of the network fabric in the cluster to transfer data from main memory in the client side to the remote GPU located in the server. This is why these latter solutions are commonly known as remote GPU virtualization frameworks.

Regarding the first type of GPU virtualization frameworks mentioned above, several solutions have been developed to be specifically used within VMs, as for example vCUDA [33], GViM [19], gVirtuS [17], and Shadowfax [28]. The vCUDA technology supports only an old CUDA version (v3.2) and implements an unspecified subset of the CUDA Runtime API. Moreover, its communication protocol presents a considerable overhead, because of the cost of the encoding and decoding stages, which causes a noticeable drop in overall performance. GViM is based on the obsolete CUDA version 1.1 and, in principle, does not implement the entire CUDA Runtime API. gVirtuS is based on the old CUDA version 2.3 and implements only a small portion of its API. For example, in the case of the memory management module, it implements only 17 out of 37 functions. Furthermore, despite it being designed for KVM VMs, it requires a modified version of KVM. Nevertheless, although it is mainly intended to be used in VMs, granting them access to the real GPU located in the same node, it also provides TCP/IP communications for remote GPU virtualization, thus allowing applications in a non-virtualized environment to access GPUs located in other nodes. Regarding Shadowfax, this solution allows Xen VMs to access the GPUs located at the same node, although it may also be used to access GPUs at other nodes of the cluster. It supports the obsolete CUDA version 1.1 and, additionally, neither the source code nor the binaries are available in order to evaluate its performance.

In the second type of virtualization framework mentioned above, which provide general purpose GPU virtualization, one can find rCUDA [14,31], V-GPU [5], GridCuda [26], DS-CUDA [30], and Shadowfax II [4]. rCUDA, further described in Sect. 3, features CUDA 7.0 and provides specific communication support for TCP/IP compatible networks as well as for InfiniBand fabrics. V-GPU is a recent tool supporting CUDA 4.0. Unfortunately, the information provided by the V-GPU authors is unclear and there is no publicly available version that can be used for testing and comparison. GridCuda also offers access to remote GPUs in a cluster, but supporting an old CUDA version (v2.3). Although its authors mention that their proposal overcomes some of the limitations of the early versions of rCUDA, they later do not provide any insight about the supposedly enhanced features. Moreover, there is currently no publicly available version of GridCuda that can be used for testing. Regarding DS-CUDA, it integrates a more recent version of CUDA (4.1) and includes specific communication support for InfiniBand. However, DS-CUDA presents several strong limitations, such as not allowing data transfers with pinned memory. Finally, Shadowfax II is still under development, not presenting a stable version yet and its public information is not updated to reflect the current code status.

It is important to notice that although remote GPU virtualization has traditionally introduced a non-negligible overhead, given that applications do not

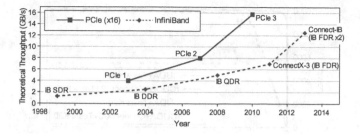

Fig. 2. Comparison between the theoretical bandwidth of different versions of PCI Express x16 and those of commercialized InfiniBand fabrics and network adapters.

access GPUs attached to the local PCI Express (PCIe) link but rather access devices that are installed in other nodes of the cluster (traversing a network fabric with a lower bandwidth), this performance overhead has significantly been reduced thanks to the recent advances in networking technologies. For example, as depicted in Fig. 2, the theoretical bandwidth of the InfiniBand network is 12.5 GB/s when using the Mellanox Connect-IB dual-port adapters [8]. This bandwidth is very close to the 15.75 GB/s of PCIe 3.0 × 16. This makes that the bandwidth achieved by InfiniBand Connect-IB network adapters and that of the NVIDIA Tesla K40 GPU are very close. Moreover, the previous generation of these technologies (NVIDIA Tesla K20 GPU and InfiniBand ConnectX-3 network adapter), provides performance figures that are also very close: the Tesla K20 GPU used PCIe 2.0, which achieves a theoretical bandwidth of 8 GB/s, whereas InfiniBand ConnectX-3 (which uses PCIe 3.0 × 8) provides 7 GB/s. As a result, when using remote GPU virtualization solutions in both hardware generations (Tesla K40 & Connect-IB and Tesla K20 & ConnectX-3), the path communicating the main memory in the computer executing the application and the remote accelerator presents a similar bandwidth in all of its stages. This bandwidth is very close to the one initially attained by the traditional approach using local GPUs, as shown in Fig. 3. These small differences in bandwidth cause that the initial non-negligible performance overhead of remote GPU virtualization solutions is now noticeably reduced, thus boosting the performance of GPU virtualizing frameworks. Furthermore, when remote GPU virtualization solutions are considered at the cluster level, it has been shown in [20] that they provide a noticeable reduction on the execution time of a given workload composed of a set of computing jobs. Moreover, important reductions in the total energy required to execute such workloads are also achieved [9]. All these aspects have definitively turned remote GPU virtualization frameworks into an appealing option, hence motivating the use of such frameworks in order to provide GPU services to applications being executed inside VMs. As mentioned before, we will make use of the rCUDA framework in our study because it was the sole solution being able to run the tested applications. In next section we present additional information on rCUDA relevant to the work presented in this paper.

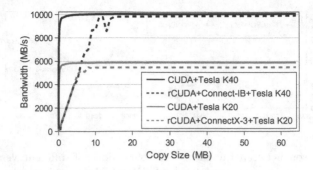

Fig. 3. Bandwidth test for copies between pinned host memory and GPU memory, using CUDA and a remote GPU virtualization framework (rCUDA) over InfiniBand employing different cards: ConnectX-3 single port and Connect-IB dual port. Both cards employ PCIe 3.0. The former makes use of 8 PCIe lanes whereas the latter uses 16 PCIe lanes. The CUDA accelerators used in the plot are an NVIDIA Tesla K20 (PCIe 2.0 × 16) and an NVIDIA Tesla K40 (PCIe 3.0 × 16). Notice that the Tesla K20 GPU and the ConnectX-3 network adapter went into the market at the same time, approximately. The same holds for the Tesla K40 GPU and the Connect-IB network adapter.

3   rCUDA: Remote CUDA

The rCUDA middleware supports version 7.0 of CUDA, being binary compatible with it, which means that CUDA programs using rCUDA do not need to be modified. Furthermore, it implements the entire CUDA Runtime API (except for graphics functions) and also provides support for the libraries included within CUDA, such as cuFFT, cuBLAS, or cuSPARSE. Furthermore, the rCUDA middleware allows a single rCUDA server to concurrently deal with several remote clients that simultaneously request GPU services. This is achieved by creating independent GPU contexts, each of them being assigned to a different client [31].

rCUDA additionally provides specific support for different interconnects [31]. Support for different underlying network fabrics is achieved by making use of a set of runtime-loadable, network-specific communication modules, which have been specifically implemented and tuned in order to obtain as much performance as possible from the underlying interconnect. Currently, two modules are available: one intended for TCP/IP compatible networks and another one specifically designed for InfiniBand.

Regarding the InfiniBand communications module, as explained by the rCUDA developers in [31], it is based on the InfiniBand Verbs (IBV) API. This API offers two communication mechanisms: the channel semantics and the memory semantics. The former refers to the standard send/receive operations typically available in any networking library, while the latter offers RDMA operations where the initiator of the operation specifies both the source and destination of a data transfer, resulting in zero-copy transfers with minimum involvement of the CPUs. rCUDA employs both IBV mechanisms, selecting one or the other depending on the exact communication to be carried out [31].

Moreover, independently from the exact network used, data exchange between rCUDA clients and remote GPUs located in rCUDA servers is pipelined so that higher bandwidth is achieved, as explained in [31]. Internal pipeline buffers within rCUDA use preallocated pinned memory given the higher throughput of this type of memory.

4 Impact of KVM Virtual Machines on Real Applications

In order to gather performance figures, we have used a testbed composed of two 1027GR-TRF Supermicro nodes running the CentOS 6.4 operating system. Each of the servers includes two Intel Xeon E5-2620 v2 processors (six cores with Ivy Bridge architecture) operating at 2.1 GHz and 32 GB of DDR3 SDRAM memory at 1600 MHz. They also own a Mellanox ConnectX-3 VPI single-port InfiniBand adapter[3], which uses a Mellanox Switch SX6025 (InfiniBand FDR compatible) to exchange data at a maximum rate of 56 Gb/s. The Mellanox OFED 2.4-1.0.4 (InfiniBand drivers and administrative tools) was used at both servers. Furthermore, the node executing the rCUDA server includes an NVIDIA Tesla K20 GPU (which makes use of a PCIe 2.0 × 16 link) with CUDA 7.0 and NVIDIA driver 340.46. On the other side, at the client node, the OFED has been configured in order to provide 2 virtual instances (virtual functions) of the InfiniBand adapter. One of these virtual functions will be used in the tests, for comparison purposes, by applications being executed at the native domain of the node whereas the other virtual function will be provided to a VM by using the PCI passthrough mechanism in order to assign it to the virtualized computer in an exclusive way. In addition to the use of virtual functions (virtual instances), we will also make use, for comparison purposes, of the original non-virtualized InfiniBand adapter, which will be referred to as physical function in the experiments. On the other hand, the VM has been created using qemu-kvm version 0.12.1.2, installed from the official CentOS repositories and has later been configured to have 16 cores and 16 GB of RAM memory.

Figure 4 graphically depicts the configurations to be used in the experiments presented in this section. First, the configuration where an accelerated application running in the native domain of the client machine communicates with the remote node using a non-virtualized InfiniBand adapter will be denoted in the performance plots as *PF-Rem* (*P*hysical *F*unction to *Rem*ote node). In a similar way, a configuration where the application is being executed in the native domain of the client node but makes use of the virtual copy (virtual function) of the InfiniBand adapter will be labeled as *VF-Rem* (*V*irtual *F*unction to *Rem*ote node). Finally, when the application is being executed inside the KVM VM, we will refer to this configuration as *VM-Rem* (*V*irtual *M*achine to *Rem*ote

---

[3] Notice that the new Mellanox InfiniBand Connect-IB network adapters are already available. These adapters feature a PCIe 3.0 × 16 connector, that, in addition to their dual-port configuration, provides an aggregated bandwidth larger than 12 GB/s. Nevertheless, the Mellanox driver is not ready yet to provide support for VMs. This is why in this work we use the previous ConnectX-3 adapters.

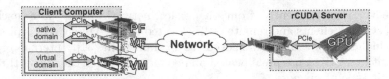

Fig. 4. Testbed used in the experiments presented in this paper. The client node, hosting the KVM VM, owns an InfiniBand ConnectX-3 network adapter, which has been virtualized. The server node also owns an InfiniBand ConnectX-3 network adapter. Notice that the tests in this paper will always use the real instance of this latter adapter, which has not been virtualized.

node). In all the three configurations, the remote node used a non-virtualized InfiniBand card.

The applications analyzed in this section are CUDASW++, GPU-BLAST and LAMMPS, all of them listed in the NVIDIA Popular GPU-Accelerated Applications Catalog [11].

CUDASW++ [27] is a bioinformatics software for Smith-Waterman protein database searches that takes advantage of the massively parallel CUDA architecture of NVIDIA Tesla GPUs to perform sequence searches. In particular, we have used its latest release, version 3.0, for our study, along with the latest Swiss-Prot database and the example query sequences available in the application website[4].

GPU-BLAST [34] has been designed to accelerate the gapped and ungapped protein sequence alignment algorithms of the NCBI-BLAST[5] implementation using GPUs. It is integrated into the NCBI-BLAST code and produces identical results. We use release 1.1 in our experiments, where we have followed the installation instructions for sorting a database and creating a GPU database. To search the database, we then use the query sequences that come with the application package.

LAMMPS [25] is a classic molecular dynamics simulator that can be used to model atoms or, more generically, as a parallel particle simulator at the atomic, mesoscopic, or continuum scale. For the tests below, we use the release from Feb. 1, 2014, and benchmarks `in.eam` and `in.lj` installed with the application. We run the benchmarks with one processor, scaling by a factor of 5 in all three dimensions (i.e., a problem size of 4 million atoms).

Figure 5 shows the execution times for these three applications when run in the four different scenarios under analysis: execution with CUDA with a local GPU in a native domain (label *CUDA*) and with rCUDA in the three remote scenarios (labels *rCUDA PF-Rem*, *rCUDA VF-Rem*, and *rCUDA VM-Rem*). Additionally, the performance of these applications when executed within the VM, using the GPU of the host by leveraging the PCI passthrough mechanism, is also analyzed (label *CUDA VM-PT*). Every experiment has been performed ten times, so that the figures show the averaged results. For the experiments involving executions in the native domain, the VM was shut off in order to avoid interferences.

---

[4] http://cudasw.sourceforge.net.
[5] http://www.ncbi.nlm.nih.gov.

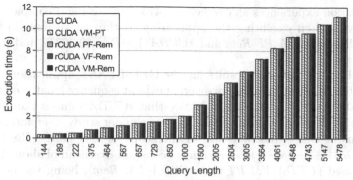

(a) Execution time of CUDASW++ application.

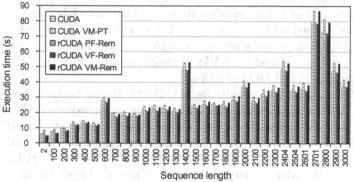

(b) Execution time of GPU-BLAST application.

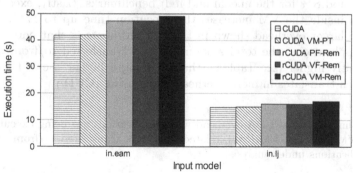

(c) Execution time of LAMMPS application.

Fig. 5. Execution time with respect to CUDA of the several applications when executed in different local and remote scenarios.

Regarding CUDASW++, Fig. 5(a) shows that execution times of this application in the different scenarios considered are very similar. As expected, executing the application within the VM using a remote GPU (*rCUDA VM-Rem*) introduces the larger overhead with respect to CUDA, 0.804 % on average. When the PCI passthrough mechanism is used from inside the VM (*CUDA VM-PT*), the application experiences an overhead (0.475 % on average) comparable to the one achieved when executing the application in the native domain using the remote GPU (*rCUDA PF-Rem* and *rCUDA VF-Rem*, 0.323 % and 0.358 % on average, respectively).

Next, Fig. 5(b) presents results for the GPU-BLAST application. It can be seen that this application presents several peaks at sequence lengths equal to 600, 1400, 2000, 2404, 2701, and 2800. Notice that rCUDA mimics the behavior of CUDA for all of these peaks in all the scenarios under study, therefore, analyzing the reasons of this behavior is out of the scope of this paper. Regarding the overhead, in this case we can see an almost constant overhead of about 10 % when VMs are used (*CUDA VM-PT* and *rCUDA VM-Rem*), being the later a little inferior. Surprisingly, in the case of executions using the rCUDA framework from the native domain, the application is slightly accelerated, 0.451 % on average. A deeper analysis of these experiments shows that KVM is introducing some overhead not related with the use of rCUDA or the InfiniBand network. In this way, the application presents periods of time in which the GPU is not used and the overhead is introduced by KVM in tasks not involving the GPU, such as CPU computations and I/O operations.

Finally, Fig. 5(c) shows results for LAMMPS. It can be seen that the lower execution time is achieved in the native domain, as expected. Furthermore, executing the application from the inside of the VM using the GPU in the host (*CUDA VM-PT*) introduces a negligible overhead of 0.3 % and 1.1 % for the in.eam and in.lj input models, respectively. The use of the rCUDA framework, however, introduces a larger overhead. When used from the native domain (*rCUDA PF-Rem* and *rCUDA VF-Rem*) execution time increases, respectively, up to 13 % and 8 % for the in.eam and in.lj benchmarks. Lastly, executing this application inside the VM increases the execution time up to 17 %. The reason for the larger overhead shown in these experiments is that here, unlike in previous applications, the total amount of data transferred to/from the GPU is significantly higher (see Table 1), thus meaning a higher use of the network fabric, which translates in more overhead when using rCUDA.

Table 1. Summary of rCUDA overhead when applications are being executed inside the KVM VM (*rCUDA VM-Rem*), related with data transferred to/from the GPUs, for the applications under analysis.

Application	rCUDA VM-Rem overhead	Total amount of data transfers to/from GPU
CUDASW++	0.804 %	0.20 GB
GPU-BLAST	2.835 %	1.76 GB
LAMMPS	16.68 %	5.00 GB

As a summary, in Table 1 we present rCUDA overhead when applications are being executed inside the KVM VM (labeled as *rCUDA VM-Rem* in previous figures). As we can observe, the overhead is directly related with total amount of data transferred to/from the GPUs. Thus, we can conclude that the more data transfers, the more overhead.

5 Conclusions

In this paper we have analyzed the use of the remote GPU virtualization mechanism in order to provide acceleration services to scientific applications running inside KVM virtual machines in InfiniBand clusters. This approach overcomes the issues of other methods, such as the PCI passthrough mechanism, allowing the concurrent sharing of GPUs by multiple virtual machines.

The main conclusion from the paper is that remote GPU virtualization frameworks could be a feasible option to provide acceleration services to KVM virtual machines. In this manner, our experiments have shown that the performance experienced by GPU-accelerated applications, running inside a virtual machine and accessing a remote GPU, mainly depends on data transferred to/from the remote GPU: the more data the application transfers to the remote GPU, the more overhead it will show with respect to using a local GPU.

Acknowledgment. This work was funded by Generalitat Valenciana under Grant PROMETEOII/2013/009 of the PROMETEO program phase II. The authors are grateful for the generous support provided by Mellanox Technologies and the equipment donated by NVIDIA Corporation.

References

1. Kernel-based Virtual Machine. http://www.linux-kvm.org. Accessed: Jan 2016
2. NextIO, N2800-ICA — Flexible and manageable I/O expansion and virtualization. http://www.nextio.com/. Accessed: Mar 2012
3. Oracle VM VirtualBox. http://www.virtualbox.org/. Accessed: Jan 2016
4. Shadowfax II - scalable implementation of GPGPU assemblies. http://keeneland.gatech.edu/software/keeneland/kidron. Accessed: Jan 2016
5. V-GPU: GPU virtualization. http://www.zillians.com/products/vgpu-gpu-virtualization/. Accessed: Jan 2016
6. VMware virtualization. http://www.vmware.com/. Accessed: Jan 2016
7. Xen Project. http://www.xenproject.org/. Accessed: Jan 2016
8. Mellanox, Connect-IB Single and Dual QSFP+ Port PCI Express Gen3x16 Adapter Card User Manual (2013). http://www.mellanox.com/related-docs/user_manuals/Connect-IB_Single_and_Dual_QSFP+_Port_PCI_Express_Gen3_x16_Adapter_Card_User_Manual.pdf
9. rCUDA: Virtualizing GPUs to reduce cost and improve performance (2014). http://www.rcuda.net
10. CUDA API Reference Manual 7.0 (2015). https://developer.nvidia.com/cuda-toolkit
11. NVIDIA Popular GPU-Accelerated Applications Catalog (2015). http://www.nvidia.es/content/tesla/pdf/gpu-accelerated-applications-for-hpc.pdf

12. Barak, A., Ben-Nun, T., Levy, E., Shiloh, A.: A package for OpenCL based heterogeneous computing on clusters with many GPU devices. In: 2010 IEEE International Conference on Cluster Computing Workshops and Posters (CLUSTER WORKSHOPS), pp. 1–7. IEEE (2010)

13. Barrachina, S., Castillo, M., Igual, F.D., Mayo, R., Quintana-Ortí, E.S., Quintana-Ortí, G.: Exploiting the capabilities of modern GPUs for dense matrix computations. Concurrency Comput.: Pract. Experience 21(18), 2457–2477 (2009)

14. Duato, José, Igual, Francisco D., Mayo, Rafael, Peña, Antonio J., Quintana-Ortí, Enrique S., Silla, Federico: An efficient implementation of GPU virtualization in high performance clusters. In: Lin, Hai-Xiang, Alexander, Michael, Forsell, Martti, Knüpfer, Andreas, Prodan, Radu, Sousa, Leonel, Streit, Achim (eds.) Euro-Par 2009. LNCS, vol. 6043, pp. 385–394. Springer, Heidelberg (2010)

15. Felter, W.: An updated performance comparison of virtual machines and linux containers. IBM Research Report (2014)

16. Gaikwad, A., Toke, I.M.: GPU based sparse grid technique for solving multidimensional options pricing PDEs. In: Proceedings of the 2nd Workshop on High Performance Computational Finance, WHPCF 2009, pp. 6: 1–6: 9. ACM, New York (2009)

17. Giunta, G., Montella, R., Agrillo, G., Coviello, G.: A GPGPU transparent virtualization component for high performance computing clouds. In: D'Ambra, P., Guarracino, M., Talia, D. (eds.) Euro-Par 2010, Part I. LNCS, vol. 6271, pp. 379–391. Springer, Heidelberg (2010)

18. Group, K.O.W: OpenCL 1.2 Specification (2011)

19. Gupta, V., Gavrilovska, A., Schwan, K., Kharche, H., Tolia, N., Talwar, V., Ranganathan, P.: GViM: GPU-accelerated virtual machines. In: Proceedings of the 3rd ACM Workshop on System-level Virtualization for High Performance Computing, pp. 17–24. ACM (2009)

20. Iserte, S., Gimeno, A.C., Mayo, R., Quintana-Ortí, E.S., Silla, F., Duato, J., Reaño, C., Prades, J.: SLURM support for remote GPU virtualization: Implementation and performance study. In: 26th IEEE International Symposium on Computer Architecture and High Performance Computing, SBAC-PAD 2014, Paris, France, 22–24 October, pp. 318–325 (2014)

21. Jo, H., Jeong, J., Lee, M., Choi, D.H.: Exploiting GPUs in virtual machine for BioCloud. BioMed Res. Int. 2013, 1–11 (2013)

22. Kegel, P., Steuwer, M., Gorlatch, S.: dopencl: Towards a uniform programming approach for distributed heterogeneous multi-many-core systems. In: 2012 IEEE 26th International Parallel and Distributed Processing Symposium Workshops PhD Forum (IPDPSW), pp. 174–186, May 2012

23. Kim, J., Seo, S., Lee, J., Nah, J., Jo, G., Lee, J.: SnuCL: An OpenCL framework for heterogeneous CPU/GPU clusters. In: Proceedings of the 26th ACM International Conference on Supercomputing, ICS 2012, pp. 341–352. ACM, New York (2012)

24. Krishnan, V.: Towards an integrated IO and clustering solution using PCI express. In: 2007 IEEE International Conference on Cluster Computing, pp. 259–266. IEEE (2007)

25. Laboratories, S.N.: LAMMPS Molecular Dynamics Simulator (2013). http://lammps.sandia.gov/

26. Liang, T.Y., Chang, Y.W.: GridCuda: a grid-enabled CUDA programming toolkit. In: 2011 IEEE Workshops of International Conference on Advanced Information Networking and Applications (WAINA), pp. 141–146. IEEE (2011)

27. Liu, Y., Wirawan, A., Schmidt, B.: CUDASW++ 3.0: accelerating Smith-Waterman protein database search by coupling CPU and GPU SIMD instructions. BMC Bioinform. **14**(1), 1–10 (2013)

28. Merritt, A.M., Gupta, V., Verma, A., Gavrilovska, A., Schwan, K.: Shadowfax: scaling in heterogeneous cluster systems via GPGPU assemblies. In: Proceedings of the 5th International Workshop on Virtualization Technologies in Distributed Computing, VTDC 2011, pp. 3–10. ACM, New York (2011)

29. NVIDIA: CUDA C Programming Guide 7.0 (2015)

30. Oikawa, M., Kawai, A., Nomura, K., Yasuoka, K., Yoshikawa, K., Narumi, T.: DS-CUDA: a middleware to use many GPUs in the cloud environment. In: Proceedings of the 2012 SC Companion: High Performance Computing, Networking Storage and Analysis, SCC 2012, pp. 1207–1214. IEEE Computer Society, Washington, DC (2012)

31. Peña, A.J., Reaño, C., Silla, F., Mayo, R., Quintana-Ortí, E.S., Duato, J.: A complete and efficient CUDA-sharing solution for HPC clusters. Parallel Comput. **40**(10), 574–588 (2014)

32. Playne, D.P., Hawick, K.A.: Data parallel three-dimensional cahn-hilliard field equation simulation on GPUs with CUDA. In: PDPTA, pp. 104–110 (2009)

33. Shi, L., Chen, H., Sun, J.: vCUDA: GPU accelerated high performance computing in virtual machines. In: IEEE International Symposium on Parallel and Distributed Processing, IPDPS 2009, pp. 1–11. IEEE (2009)

34. Vouzis, P.D., Sahinidis, N.V.: Gpu-blast: Using graphics processors to accelerate protein sequence alignment. Bioinformatics **27**(2), 182–188 (2010)

35. Walters, J.P., Younge, A.J., Kang, D.I., Yao, K.T., Kang, M., Crago, S.P., Fox, G.C.: GPU-Passthrough performance: a comparison of KVM, Xen, VMWare ESXi, and LXC for CUDA and OpenCL applications. In: 7th IEEE International Conference on Cloud Computing (CLOUD 2014) (2014)

36. Wu, H., Diamos, G., Sheard, T., Aref, M., Baxter, S., Garland, M., Yalamanchili, S.: Red fox: an execution environment for relational query processing on GPUs. In: Proceedings of Annual IEEE/ACM International Symposium on Code Generation and Optimization, CGO 2014, pp. 44: 44–44: 54. ACM, New York (2014)

37. Xiao, S., Balaji, P., Zhu, Q., Thakur, R., Coghlan, S., Lin, H.,Wen, G., Hong, J., Chun Feng, W.: Vocl: An optimized environment for transparentvirtualization of graphics processing units. In: Proceedings of the 1st Innovative Parallel Computing (InPar) (2012)

38. Yang, C.T., Wang, H.Y., Ou, W.S., Liu, Y.T., Hsu, C.H.: On implementation of GPU virtualization using PCI pass-through. In: 2012 IEEE 4th International Conference on Cloud Computing Technology and Science (CloudCom), pp. 711–716. IEEE (2012)

Benchmarking Wireless Protocols for Feasibility in Supporting Crowdsourced Mobile Computing

João Rodrigues[1], Joaquim Silva[1], Rolando Martins[1(✉)], Luís Lopes[1],
Utsav Drolia[2], Priya Narasimhan[2], and Fernando Silva[1]

[1] CRACS/INESC-TEC, Faculty of Science, University of Porto, Porto, Portugal
{joao.rodrigues,joaquim.silva,rmartins,lblopes,fds}@dcc.fc.up.pt
[2] ECE, Carnegie Mellon University, Pittsburgh, USA
udrolia@andrew.cmu.edu, priya@cs.cmu.edu

Abstract. Recent advances in mobile device technology have triggered research on using their aggregate computational and/or storage resources to form edge-clouds. Whilst traditionally viewed as simple clients, smartphones and tablets today have hardware resources that allow more sophisticated software to be installed, and can be used as thick clients or even thin servers. Simultaneously, new standards and protocols, such as Wi-Fi Direct and Wi-Fi TDLS (Tunneled Direct Link Setup), have been established that allow mobile devices to talk directly with each other, as opposed to over the Internet or across Wi-Fi access points. This can, potentially, lead to ubiquitous, low-latency, device-to-device (D2D) communication. In this paper, we study whether D2D protocols can support mobile-edge clouds by benchmarking different protocols and configurations for a specific application. The results show that decentralized device-to-device techniques can be used to efficiently disseminate multimedia contents while diminishing contention in the wireless infrastructure, allowing for up to 65 % traffic reduction at the access points.

1 Introduction and Motivation

Mobile devices are now ubiquitous [1]. The increase in the sheer number of devices has also led to the increase in the density of devices, i.e. more often than not, there will be multiple mobile devices in proximity of each other. Moreover, these devices are now equipped with multi-core processors, multi-GB memory and multiple communication interfaces. This trend has been leveraged by a new class of systems, *mobile edge-clouds* [2–8]. These systems aggregate computation and storage resources across nearby mobile devices to enable resource-efficient applications.

Simultaneously, new standards and protocols, such as Wi-Fi Direct and Wi-Fi TDLS (Tunneled Direct Link Setup), have been established that allow mobile devices to talk directly with each other, as opposed to over the Internet or across Wi-Fi access points. This can, potentially, lead to ubiquitous, low-latency, device-to-device (D2D) communication.

M. Jelasity and E. Kalyvianaki (Eds.): DAIS 2016, LNCS 9687, pp. 96–108, 2016.
DOI: 10.1007/978-3-319-39577-7_8

We believe that these new D2D protocols can boost the efficiency of mobile edge-clouds. Since these systems are meant for scenarios where devices are in proximity of each other, D2D communication seems like a natural fit. For example, let us consider the following scenario: watching video replays on mobile devices at live events, e.g. soccer match. There is a growing market of apps that provide users within (and outside) the venue with almost real-time statistics and multimedia contents like the number of kilometers a player has run or video replays for goals or interesting events [9,10]. If a fan chooses to watch a video replay, the content is downloaded from the central servers through stadium installed access points (Wi-Fi or cellular), and then played on the device. If, however, the venue is crowded, the large number of requests can stress the infrastructure [11,12].

One way to solve this problem is to use mobile edge-clouds. In this way, you and your neighbours may form a local cache for the server contents - users of the service can be encouraged to share in several ways, e.g., sweepstakes of team merchandise or lower rates for the service. For example, before asking the server for a video replay, your app might ask the other phones in the mobile network whether they have a copy of the video. If a copy of the replay is located, your app can retrieve it directly from a neighboring device. Our first hypothesis is that such retrievals can be accelerated through D2D protocols. Moreover, if the retrievals in mobile edge-clouds are done over infrastructural access points, the access points would be congested in-turn leading to high-latency downloads and an overall bad user-experience. Our second hypothesis is that D2D protocols can alleviate such infrastructural stress.

In this paper, we study whether D2D protocols can support mobile-edge clouds by benchmarking different protocols and configurations for a specific application. The results suggest that decentralized, device-to-device techniques can be used to efficiently disseminate multimedia contents while diminishing contention in the wireless infrastructure, e.g., central servers and access points, namely through the use of TDLS and WiFi-Direct.

The remainder of this paper is structured as follows. Section 2 describes the scenarios we are interested in exploring and the experimental setup. Section 3 describes the application we developed to perform the experiments. Sections 2 and 4 describe the experimental setup, the results obtained and discusses their implications. Section 5 overviews related research work and, finally, Sect. 6 ends the paper with the conclusions and future work.

2   Assumptions and Scenarios

We make the following assumptions: (a) all the devices are non-rooted since we are interested in improvements that can be readily implemented in current infrastructures and do not rely on invasive procedures for the devices; (b) we do not control the usage of the radio channels and the choice of the radio band, 2.4 GHz or 5 GHz, for communication; (c) all devices are within radio range and can make requests and transfer contents using direct connections or using an

AP or a hot-spot as an intermediate; (d) there is no application-level routing or discovery mechanisms, we only use what is provided by the underlying wireless protocols; (e) in the scenarios that involve mobile servers, the latter have all the files that will be requested by the clients, and that would otherwise be present at the central server in a traditional infrastructure, and; (f) clients know the location of the servers from the start.

We define a set of content dissemination scenarios for downloading video replays from a soccer game in a stadium (Fig. 1). In all scenarios we assume WiFi is used for communication. In the case of pure WiFi, all scenarios include a traditional, dedicated, access point that the devices use for communication. When using WiFi with TDLS, the access point is used only for the initial contact between the nodes. In the case of WiFi-Direct, this role is performed by a mobile device known as the "group owner".

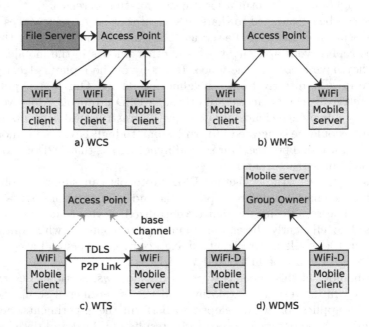

Fig. 1. (a) WCS - central server, access point, mobile clients, using WiFi. (b) WMS - access point, mobile servers, mobile clients, using WiFi. (c) WTS - access point, mobile servers, mobile clients, using WiFi/TDLS. (d) WDMS - group owner, mobile server, mobile clients, using WiFi-Direct.

In the first scenario (WCS - WiFi Central Server) we have a main server, part of the infrastructure of the stadium, acting as the source of the video replays. The server is connected to access points in the stadium via high-speed Ethernet links. Each access point handles tens of devices in the part of the venue it provides coverage [12]. All mobile devices are clients.

In the second scenario (WMS - WiFi Mobile Server) we remove the main server, and just stick with the access point. Part of the mobile devices in the venue will act as servers (servers only) for the multimedia contents, thus providing the same content as the central server in the previous scenario.

In the third scenario (WTMS - WiFi TDLS Mobile Server) we use the access point only for the first contact between the devices. TDLS then allows the devices to communicate directly and transfer data. Again, part of the devices in the venue will act as the servers for the video replays. As in the previous scenario, mobile servers are not also clients and contain all the content that might be provided by the central server.

In the fourth scenario (WDMS - WiFi Direct Mobile Server) the configuration is similar to WMS with the access point replaced by one of the devices acting as a hot-spot, known as "group owner". All communication between mobile servers and clients must go through the group owner.

We identified an additional scenario, similar to WTS, in which the access point is replaced with the group owner. Here, however, we use TDLS to allow servers and clients to communicate directly (mostly) without the intervention of the group owner. We did not experiment with this last configuration. We were not able to form networks of more than 5 or 6 devices using WiFi-Direct and thus present only preliminary results for the WDMS scenario. This difficulty arises not only from the fact that we are using non-rooted devices, and thus cannot fully control operating system configurations, but mostly because most network card drivers/firmware are proprietary software.

3   Test Application

We developed Java/Android applications to implement the clients and servers in the aforementioned scenarios. The servers, both fixed, in the first scenario, and mobile, in the others, follow the standard client-server architecture. The server waits for a connection from a client; when one is received, they launch a new thread that examines the request and transfers the requested file. The mobile clients are tailored to be used with the Android Debug Bridge (ADB) tool. We developed a template from which all client behaviours could be implemented by extending a base class. This class has three main methods that are overridable for different scenarios, namely: `startApp`, `transferFiles` and `endApp`. `startApp` executes a sequence of checks to ensure that a client will run correctly, e.g., if the device is connected to the correct WiFi network. It also initializes a logger in order to record information about the run, and fills a work queue with the file requests, a permutation of the file names, to be downloaded by the device. Each file is mapped to a set of predefined servers that can provide it. The clients choose one of these for each download. After that, method `transferFiles` is called to download the files, which are transfered, one by one, after selecting appropriate servers. Once a transfer finishes, the next file on the queue begins to be downloaded. When all files are downloaded, the application calls the `endApp` method to perform all the necessary cleanup.

The execution of the application by the devices starts simultaneously thanks to a barrier implemented (a shared file is used for this) at the end of the `startApp` method. The devices also synchronize before ending, again by using a barrier at the beginning of the endApp method. We used a set of shell scripts to automate the execution of the application and to control the devices through the Android Debug Bridge (ADB). The adb command line tool allows to execute ordinary Linux shell commands remotely on Android devices, e.g., ls, cp. This allows, for example, uploading all log files from the devices to a server for processing and commanding all experiments using simple scripts.

Algorithm 1 Execution cycle

    function RUN(n, m, l)
        $devices$ ← GET_DEVICES(n)
        $servers$ ← GET_SERVERS_LIST(m)
        $clients$ ← GET_CLIENTS_LIST($n - m$)
        run ← 0
        while $run < l$ **do**
            REBOOT($devices$)
            RUNSERVERS($servers$)
            RUNCLIENTS($clients$)
            run ← $run + 1$
        end while
        COPY_LOGS($devices$)
    end function

Fig. 2. Algorithm for running the experiments.

For better control, we decided to use ADB through the USB interface (instead of WiFi), with all devices connected to the control computer through an USB hub. Figure 2 shows the basic procedure for running the experiments. The procedure takes three arguments: n, the number of devices, m, the number of servers and, l, the number of times the experiment is to be repeated. We start each run by rebooting the mobile devices to ensure that all devices are in similar circumstances and that there are no extra processes running that could interfere with the results. Afterwards, the RUNSERVERS procedure sends a command to all the server devices to start the local server application. Next, RUNCLIENTS starts the local client application at each client device, that in turn calls the startApp entry point. Once all the runs are performed, the logs are copied from the devices to a desktop computer for analysis.

4   Experiments and Results

Our experimental setup is composed of the following hardware: 1 Asus RT-AC56U router (AP), 20 non-rooted HTC Nexus 9 tablets, 2 Trust USB hubs (10 ports each) and 1 desktop computer. The layout of the deployment can be seen in Fig. 3. The devices were placed on top of a table, side-by-side, in a 4×5 pattern, as in a typical of stadium seats arrangement. They all run Android Lollipop 5.1.1 (API level 22) on top of which our test software was executed. The devices were connected to a control desktop computer via the Android Debug Bridge.

The experiments were setup in such a way that we guarantee that all the content requested by the clients during the runs exists in all servers. In each experiment, clients must download 20 video files, each 3 Mbytes in size from the servers. This size represents a video clip with 10 s duration and encoded with H264 video codec using 480×270 (width × height) as the frame size, a typical format used by mobile apps. Before starting the transfer, each client computes a random permutation of the 20 file names using a uniform distribution, to even out the requests for each individual file during an experiment. Accesses are also performed randomly in time, as each client waits a random time interval, within given bounds, before requesting the next file of the sequence. For each scenario, we run a set of experiments with a varying number of mobile servers/clients. Each experiment was repeated 8 times to smooth out statistic flukes.

The average download time for each video is represented in the graphs in the next sections, together with the bars for the 95 % confidence intervals. The values for power dissipation are given as the average per download, as measured using the Android API (`android.os.BatteryManager`) The instantaneous current intensity and the voltage (mostly constant) are read periodically to compute the dissipated power which is then integrated over the complete experiment to get the total energy spent per download.

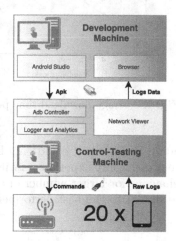

To characterize the radio environment, we performed a WiFi analysis on our campus and detected that the 2.4 Ghz band was extensively utilized by various services, while the 5Ghz band usage was minimal. All the experiments were

Fig. 3. The experimental setup.

performed using the 802.11n for packets exchanged between the AP and the devices; 802.11ac was used whenever packets were exchanged device-to-device[1].

4.1   Single Server

We start by restricting the experiments to only one server (infrastructural or mobile), and experiment with four scenarios: WCS, WMS, WTMS, and WDMS. The results for WiFi-Direct (WDMS) are just preliminary. We vary the number of mobile clients downloading videos from 1 to 16. Figure 4 shows the average download time per file. Figure 5 shows the total traffic processed by the AP, in the WCS, WMS and WTMS scenarios. For Fig. 5, given that the amount of traffic for WCS is exactly the same amount as in the case of WMS (we only accounted for outgoing traffic), we decided not to show it for clarity. Note the small 95 % confidence interval error bars.

In Fig. 4 WMS is clearly the worst performer, taking almost twice as much time comparing to the other scenarios. This is due to the presence of two wireless hops in the communication path, more specifically, from the mobile client device to the AP and then from the AP to the mobile server device. WCS wins as a result of the much faster link between the central server and the AP. As we

---

[1] As a note, Android TDLS implementation switches automatically between the 2.4 and 5 GHz bands and this is neither controlable and observable from the API.

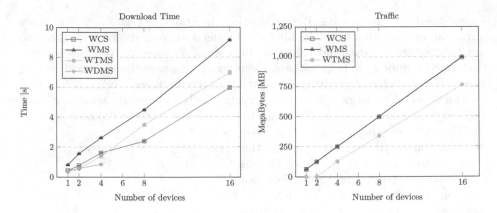

Fig. 4. Average download time per file.   **Fig. 5.** Traffic handled by the AP.

stated, WiFi-Direct could only be used up to 5 devices - 4 clients and 1 server. We present only experiments with 1, 2 and 4 clients. It is hard to extrapolate the behaviour for larger number of clients but for low numbers of clients the results are similar to the best performer (WCS).

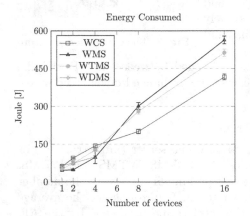

Fig. 6. Average energy consumed per experiment.

The behaviour of WTMS is more subtle. While the 802.11z [13] specification extension allows for a peer to have multiple links to different base stations, in practice only 2 channels were available from the server at any given time, leading us to conclude that only one channel is available per radio (since our test devices, Nexus 9, have 2 radios), and thus no multiplexing is performed. This is visible in Fig. 5, where no traffic is routed through the AP up to 2 clients. The introduction of additional clients only shows limited savings on the traffic being routed through the AP. This is due to the 802.11z's mandatory periodical switch-over to the base channel (the regular AP's WiFi communication channel) to process buffered messages (by the AP).

Given this, if there are only two clients then the two radios can be used to setup TDLS channels. Adding more clients will result in the traffic being routed through the AP, that in turn, will lead to the server device to spend more airtime on one of the available channels to communicate with the AP. This will effectively only allow for 1 offloading channel to be available.

Figure 6 shows the energy consumed per experiment. The figure shows some similarity to Fig. 4 which is expected since our application uses almost exclusively the WiFi hardware to send/receive replays; it does not play the videos on arrival, it just stores them. Hence, download time is an excellent proxy for energy consumption. We observed this correspondence for the other experiments we performed and therefore will not present more graphs on energy consumption in this paper. In absolute value, the energy spent in the downloads is rather small. For example, given the 25.5 Wh specification of the battery from the Nexus 9, this is equivalent to about 91000 J. The energy spent per download in, e.g., the WCS scenario, with 1 server and 1 client, is about 50 J/20 downloads = 2.5 J, corresponding to 0.002 % of the total charge; this value grows to 0.02 % when using 16 clients.

4.2 Multiple Servers

We extended our experiments to examine the impact of introducing multiple mobile servers in the mobile scenarios WMS and WTMS. Figures 7 and 8 show the results obtained. In WTMS we introduced an extra level of refinement. In one case we let the clients choose a random server for each file to be downloaded from a predefined set - this is shown as $WTMS^D$ in the graphs. The alternative process is to statically map each file to a specific server from the start, potentially decreasing competition between clients - this is shown as $WTMS^S$. We increase the number of servers, from 1 to 8, while using a fixed number of clients (12).

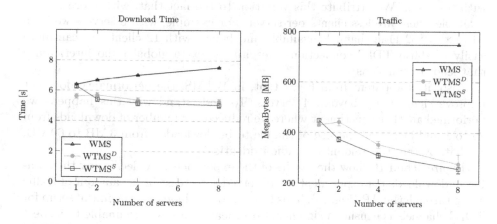

Fig. 7. Average download time per file.   **Fig. 8.** Traffic handled by AP.

Figure 7 shows the average download time with an increasing number of servers. The introduction of TDLS clearly decreases the download time, with the static assignment performing slightly better than the random assignment. This is due to the better client distribution that the static approach provides, decreasing the possibility of clients overloading a subset of the servers. The results show a slight increase of 20 % in the download time with WTMS scenarios from 4 servers relative to the WCS scenario (for 12 clients) (c.f. Fig. 4). This, however, is compensated by a 65 % decrease in the traffic handled by the AP under WTMS with 8 servers (note that, in WMS as in WCS all traffic goes through the AP). Relative to the WMS scenario we also observe a 33 % decrease in the download time.

We resorted to simulation using ns-3 to better understand the behaviour of TDLS, namely, how the number of successful TDLS links varied with the number of available servers in the WTMS (static) scenario. Since there is no native support in ns-3 for TDLS, we had to implement our own code to mimic the behaviour of the radio interfaces. Based on the available documentation and on our empirical experience we deduced that the Nexus 9 allows the use of 2 simultaneous channels that can be any combination of 802.11n and 802.11ac. To simulate this behaviour, we implemented each ns-3 node with 3 network interfaces ($2 \times 802.11ac$, $1 \times 802.11n$), so that at any given time we can have 2 channels as in the Nexus 9. So, although the nodes have 3 software radio interfaces, if we have 1 or 2 clients connected to a server, the server node can only use 2 TDLS interfaces. If more than 2 clients are connected to a server, then we can only use 1 TDLS interface, and all the other connections are done via 802.11n (through the AP). An auxiliary class manages the TDLS connections, parametrized on the percentage of successfully established TDLS links.

We ran several simulations varying the percentage of TDLS connection success. The results show that, to explain the traffic values from Fig. 8, the percentage of successful TDLS links must vary from 50 % with 1 server to 60 %–65 % with 8 servers. We attribute this variation to the fact that, with more servers available, there are less clients per server. For example, with 8 servers we have 16 (2×8) 802.11ac channels available and hence, with 12 clients we can more easily establish TDLS connections, despite the extra global radio interference that leads to collisions.

Also, it is apparent from Fig. 7 that, in WTMS, the performance does not improve significantly beyond 4 servers. To understand why this happens we performed another experiment where we reduced the number of downloads from 20 to 1 and increased the size of the file to be dowloaded from 3 MB to 60 MB, so that, overall, the amount of traffic is identical.

Figures 9 and 10 show the results of the experiment. By decreasing the number of downloads per experiment, we observed a decrease in the amount of traffic going through the AP (Fig. 10). This lead us to conclude that the initial setup for TDLS channels is causing a significant overhead. Since we are unable to inspect the internal behaviour of the network driver, we infer that the creation of a TDLS channel requires multiple attempts, probably due to contention and interference, resulting in a performance degradation. By decreasing the number of downloads (and thus the number of TDLS tunnel negotiations), the expected behaviour was verified with the introduction of additional servers, namely, each server is able to support 2 distinct channels, with 1 being allocated to the AP base channel in the presence of 3 or more clients. For example, in the case of 4 servers, there were

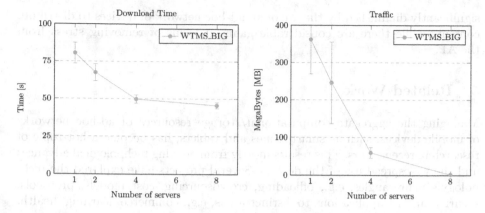

Fig. 9. Average download time while using a 60 MB file.

Fig. 10. Traffic handled by AP while using a 60 MB file.

3 clients statically allocated with each server (statically assigned, represented by WTMS^S), while with 8 servers, we had 4 servers assigned with 2 clients and 4 servers assigned with 1 client.

The download time and amount of traffic tend to lower with the introduction of additional servers, as depicted in Figs. 9 and 10. However, there is a substantial amount of variation on the results due to the negotiation process of the TDLS links. As stated in 802.11z, if during the setup of a direct link the driver detects a beacon then the negotiation is aborted; or if the amount of traffic on a channel is high enough then the TDLS link could be renegotiated to a different channel, with the traffic between the two peers being redirected through the AP during that time.

4.3 Discussion

The fastest download time is achieved by the traditional infrastructure, mostly because it uses a very fast wired 1Gbit/s network between the server and the AP, and also because the AP did not reach saturation in our experiments, even with the highest number (16) of clients. However, the use of multiple servers in an ad-hoc network of devices, all within radio reach, allowed significant removal of traffic from the AP, up to a maximum of 65 % less traffic using 8 servers. The corresponding download time for files is 20 % higher than the one observed for the traditional server/AP infrastructure, which, in absolute figures, for 3MB files, results in a delay of $\approx$ 1 s. Energy-wise, the cost of transfer is small for the Nexus 9, with a nominal battery capacity of about 91000 J, amounting to 0.02 % with the maximum number of clients competing for the files. Smartphone batteries have typical capacities an order of magnitude smaller and thus we would expect each download to require a few tenths of percent of the battery. Since each user individually is not expected to make many downloads during a game, battery shortage is, evidently, not a limitation. Thus, the user experience is not significantly diminished by the use of an ad-hoc network of devices to distribute contents while there are considerable gains in terms of removing stress from the AP.

5 Related Work

Managing the aggregate computational/storage resources of ad-hoc networks of mobile devices, such as smartphones and tablets, has become a hot topic of research in recent years. This results mostly from ongoing technological advances and the widespread use of the devices. Several projects have explored the technology's many angles, e.g., offloading, crowdsourcing, cost models, protocols, security, and its applications to distinct areas, e.g., commerce, learning, health, entertainment [14,15].

FireChat [6] is a proprietary mobile app, developed by Open Garden, that allows smartphones to organize into a wireless mesh network and exchange messages using available technologies such as Bluetooth or Wi-Fi. The iOS version uses Apple's Multipeer Connectivity Framework [16] that enables services to be advertised and discovered between nearby iOS devices using different wireless protocols. Services can be provided through personal area type-of networks using infrastructure WiFi, peer-to-peer WiFi and Bluetooth.

Bonjour [17] focus on three main areas: Addressing (allocating IPs to Devices), Naming (creating alias for each network device) and Service Discovery. The discovery works similarly to a publish-subscribe, where nodes advertise their services which then other nodes can use them. In order for devices in a network to be discovered, upon turning on the bonjour service, they send a announce themselves to the network. At the same time, other nodes in the network, already running a Bonjour Service, periodically ask the network what devices are available.

Alljoyn [18] is an, open source, agnostic network framework that allows different types of devices and apps to discover and communicate in an abstract way, hiding the complexity of distinct network protocols and hardware. Generically, it publishes APIs over the network through a general bus, which permits distinctive network technologies to be used, such as Wi-Fi, Wi-Fi Direct, Bluetooth, Ethernet and PowerLine. To the best of our knowledge only infrastructure WiFi is actually implemented. Regarding the network formation, Alljoyn, uses a super peer paradigm, mesh of stars network, where the leaf nodes are connected to router nodes and these act as bridges to the others router nodes.

Efforts to transform mobile networks into actual computational and/or storage resources have been the subject of fundamental work. In [19,20] Hadoop was successfully ported into mobile devices connected though WiFi to perform map reduce computations. The goal was to identify the problems that might arise from porting a system developed for full-fledged cloud servers to a resource-starved cloud of devices. Doolan et al. [3] try a different approach by adapting the well established Message Passing Interface (MPI) for mobile systems, with the goal of performing parallel processing over these platforms.

In [21] the authors study the trade-offs between offloading computation to an infrastructure cloud versus retaining the computation within a mobile edge-cloud. They present two diverse workloads for mobile edge-clouds based on the distribution of data and motivate the use of edge-clouds for one of them, specifically when data is inherently distributed in the edge-cloud it is better (in terms of latency and power consumption) to process them in an in-situ manner as opposed to transferring them to the infrastructural-cloud for processing.

6   Conclusions

In this paper, we study whether D2D protocols can be used to efficiently disseminate multimedia contents in networks of mobile devices. We do this by benchmarking different protocols and configurations for a specific application. Our first hypothesis, that the download speed would be improved with D2D protocols was not vindicated, although the number of devices we used (and had available) was really not enough to take the AP close to saturation, in which case we would expect such improvements. The observed difference and corresponding extra energy usage is small and does not degrade user experience. On the other hand, the experiments suggest that our second hypothesis, that the use of D2D protocols could significantly remove load from the AP, is valid for we observed a decrease in traffic up to 65 % for a multiple server configuration.

Thus we conclude that D2D protocols that take advantage of existing wireless technologies can indeed be used to efficiently disseminate multimedia contents and, especially, to diminish the load in the traditional wireless infrastructure, a critical problem for service providers in large sports venues, while maintaining a good user experience.

We plan to expand this line of work to include network overlays in order to create a fully decentralized and self organizing mesh that leverages the different underlying wireless protocols.

Acknowledgment. This work has been sponsored by projects HYRAX (CMUP-ERI/FIA/0048/2013), funded by FCT, and SMILES (NORTE-01-0145-FEDER-000020), funded by NORTE 2020, under PORTUGAL 2020, and through the ERDF fund.

References

1. Global mobile statistics 2013. http://mobiforge.com/. Accessed 19 Feb 2016
2. Drolia, U., Mickulicz, N., Gandhi, R., Narasimhan, P.: Krowd: A key-value store for crowded venues. In: Proceedings of the 10th International Workshop on Mobility in the Evolving Internet Architecture, MobiArch 2015, pp. 20–25. ACM (2015)
3. Doolan, D.C., Tabirca, S., Yang, L.T.: MMPI a message passing interface for the mobile environment. In: Proceedings of the 6th International Conference on Advances in Mobile Computing and Multimedia, MoMM 2008, pp. 317–321. ACM, New York (2008)

4. Marinelli, E.E.: Hyrax: Cloud computing on mobile devices using mapreduce, Master's thesis, Master's Thesis, Carnegie Mellon University (2009)
5. Yan, T., Marzilli, M., Holmes, R., Ganesan, D., Corner, M.: mcrowd: A platform for mobile crowdsourcing. In: 7th ACM Conference on Embedded Networked Sensor Systems (SenSys 2009), pp. 347–348. ACM, New York (2009)
6. OpenGarden's FireChat App. http://opengarden.com/firechat/. Accessed 19 Feb 2016
7. A security, private internet and tactical cloud at the edge. Kurzweil News, August 2013
8. Wait, P.: Darpa creates cloud using smartphones, Information Week, August 2013
9. YinzCam. http://www.yinzcam.com/. Accessed 19 Feb 2016
10. Agile stadiums bring digital content to sports fans, June 2015. http://goo.gl/4BHxr6. Accessed 19 Feb 2016
11. Kapustka, P., Stoffel, C.: State of the Stadium Technology Survey, Technical report (2014)
12. Erman, J., Ramakrishnan, K.: Understanding the super-sized traffic of the super bowl. In: Proceedings of the 2013 Conference on Internet Measurement Conference, IMC 2013, pp. 353–360. ACM (2013)
13. 802.11z Amendment 7: Extensions to Direct-Link Setup. http://goo.gl/acQa0i
14. Fernando, N., Loke, S.W., Rahayu, W.: Mobile cloud computing: A survey. Future Gener. Comput. Syst. **29**(1), 84–106 (2013)
15. Dinh, H.T., Lee, C., Niyato, D., Wang, P.: A survey of mobile cloud computing: architecture, applications, and approaches. Wireless Commun. Mobile Comput. **13**(18), 1587–1611 (2013)
16. Apple's Multipeer Framework. https://goo.gl/332lwR. Accessed 19 Feb 2016
17. Apple's Implementation of Bonjour. https://www.apple.com/support/bonjour/. Accessed 19 Feb 2016
18. Alljoyn Framework. https://allseenalliance.org/framework. Accessed 19 Feb 2016
19. Marinelli, E.E.: Hyrax: cloud computing on mobile devices using mapreduce. Master's thesis, Carnegie Mellon University (2009)
20. Teo, C.L.V.: Hyrax: Crowdsourcing mobile devices to develop proximity-based mobile clouds. Ph.D. dissertation, Carnegie Mellon University (2012)
21. Drolia, U., Martins, R., Tan, J., Chheda, A., Sanghavi, M., Gandhi, R., Narasimhan, P.: Motivating mobile edge-clouds. In: 10th IEEE International Conference on Ubiquitous Intelligence and Computing (UIC 2013) (2013)

BFT-Dep: Automatic Deployment of Byzantine Fault-Tolerant Services in PaaS Cloud

Bijun Li[(✉)] and Rüdiger Kapitza[(✉)]

TU Braunschweig, Braunschweig, Germany
{bli,kapitza}@ibr.cs.tu-bs.de

Abstract. Cloud computing has been a massive trend over the recent years and eased the deployment of scalable distributed applications. While initially renting out virtual machines was the predominant form of cloud computing, nowadays Platform as a Service (PaaS) solutions are emerging. The main advantages of the latter are a faster and easier application deployment as well as built-in support for horizontal scalability. However, when it comes to services with more demanding dependability requirements, currently provided deployment mechanisms quickly become insufficient, forcing cloud customers to fall back into manual, self-made strategies.

In this paper, we present BFT-DEP, a framework for deploying Byzantine fault-tolerant (BFT) services in a PaaS cloud automatically. BFT-DEP leverages the existing PaaS functionality to address specific deployment requirements and provides tailored support to set up and manage replicated services. It flexibly integrates BFT protocols as an independent service layer, thereby alleviating the complexity that the deployment of such systems entails. An initial prototype of BFT-DEP has been implemented on top of the open-source PaaS platform Open-Shift and a first evaluation shows its practicability.

Keywords: Automatic application deployment · Platform as a Service (PaaS) cloud · Byzantine fault tolerance

1 Introduction

Cloud computing [22] offers a new form of resource provisioning, where services and applications are no longer hosted on local computing resources but on shared ones provided by remote infrastructures. Customers, i.e. software developers, are offered with services delivered over the Internet without having to manage and maintain the underlying hardware or system software that hosts these services.

B. Li—This research was supported by Siemens Rail Automation Graduate School (iRAGS). We would thank Torgen Hauschild, Marcel Kessler, Philipp Markiewka, Matthias Natho, Manuel Nieke, Mathias Rudnik for their contributions to this paper.

© IFIP International Federation for Information Processing 2016
Published by Springer International Publishing Switzerland 2016. All Rights Reserved
M. Jelasity and E. Kalyvianaki (Eds.): DAIS 2016, LNCS 9687, pp. 109–114, 2016.
DOI: 10.1007/978-3-319-39577-7_9

Although delivering virtual machines is the most common form of cloud offering, Platform as a Service (PaaS) clouds [7,12,13,16], are getting increasingly popular. PaaS clouds aim at helping customers to quickly deploy and run their applications without considering infrastructure management tasks. Contrary to lower-level cloud services, non-functional properties like horizontal scalability are often part of the built-in features of these platforms. This makes PaaS clouds particularly appealing for more critical applications. However, if the applications depend on state, current PaaS solutions fall short as they lack deployment strategies for dependable stateful services. When services need to be replicated for high availability, the deployment is not a question of configuring independent service instances anymore, but of setting up and coordinating collaborating and highly interconnected replicas. This becomes even more complex, if the systems are supposed to tolerate not only crash faults but also Byzantine faults. For all that, cloud customers have to implement and maintain custom solutions, contradicting the primary goal of an automatic deployment in PaaS clouds.

This paper presents BFT-DEP, a novel application deployment framework that automatically sets up Byzantine fault-tolerant (BFT) [6] applications in PaaS clouds. Based on state-machine replication [18], BFT is able to tolerate crashes as well as arbitrary faults. By encapsulating BFT replicas into PaaS conform services, BFT-DEP simplifies the deployment of replicated applications without requiring changes to the cloud itself, and handles coordination among replicas automatically. An initial realization of BFT-DEP has been implemented as an extension of the popular open-source PaaS cloud OpenShift [16] and by using BFT-SMaRt [3,4] to enable replication.

Research works, which integrate Byzantine fault-tolerance protocols into cloud infrastructures to tolerate Byzantine failures have been proposed [2,8,11,19]. Also at middleware level, BFT has been combined with multi-tier web services to guarantee their heterogeneous reliability requirements [15]. Unlike them, our work is targeting the automatic deployment of reliable applications as an enhancement and extension of PaaS cloud functionality thereby making BFT services easier to deploy and manage.

The remainder of the paper is organized as follows: Sect. 2 explains the system design of BFT-DEP, Sect. 3 shows an implementation of BFT-DEP on a popular open-source PaaS cloud with interim evaluation results, and Sect. 4 concludes the paper and indicates future works.

2   System Design

An integral part of replicated Byzantine fault-tolerant services is the agreement protocol. It is responsible for coordinating the order in which requests must be executed by the stateful replicas to ensure the consistency of non-faulty ones. Consequently, to enable an easy deployment of BFT systems, the agreement protocol has to be integrated into the PaaS platform. BFT-DEP achieves this by introducing a *BFT agreement layer* that is separated from the application replicas (see Fig. 1). The BFT agreement layer can be realized using a common

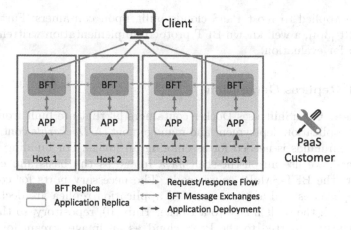

Fig. 1. Architecture of BFT-DEP

BFT protocol implementation [1,6,14]. In principle this follows separation of agreement and execution stages [21] and the typical assumptions for Byzantine fault-tolerant systems are made. A minimum of $3f + 1$ replicas are required to tolerate up to f Byzantine faults. Faulty replicas may crash or behave arbitrarily and maliciously. However, they are unable to break cryptographic techniques so that they cannot corrupt authenticated messages without being noticed. Note that enforcing fault tolerance of the cloud infrastructure itself is out of scope, as it is an orthogonal issue and has been addressed before [5].

We build the BFT agreement layer by containerizing a BFT protocol, e.g. using Docker [9], into the software stack of a PaaS platform as a built-in service. Thus a BFT replica can be deployed and operated in the same way as any other service instances of a PaaS cloud. This way, BFT-DEP is able to leverage as much as possible the existing PaaS cloud facilities and is to a large extent immune to cloud architecture changes. When deploying applications, BFT-DEP first creates and configures a set of BFT replicas to establish the BFT agreement layer and then instantiates replicas for the customer's application. BFT-DEP guarantees that the application replicas together with their associated BFT replicas are distributed over different hosts of the cloud for fault independence. Each BFT replica exposes an access entry point to the clients. Upon receiving requests, the replicas of the BFT agreement layer first order them and then forward the requests to the corresponding application replicas. To do so, each BFT replica needs to connect to the application replica that locates on the same host to keep communication latency low. Application replicas then generate replies and send them back to the client through the BFT agreement layer, and the client will eventually verify the replies.

3   Implementation

We chose OpenShift Origin v3 [17] to implement BFT-DEP. Since BFT-DEP assumes a container-based PaaS model, it is not bound to a specific platform but can be applied to most PaaS clouds built upon containers. Furthermore, BFT-SMaRt [3,4], a well-known BFT protocol implementation written in Java, was chosen for evaluation.

3.1 BFT Replicas Generation

BFT Image. OpenShift uses Docker containers [9] that are built from Docker *images* for application deployment and management. A *Dockerfile* containing all necessary commands is needed for assembling an image. For building the BFT replica image, we use an off-the-shelf Java image as the basis and customize it to import the BFT-SMaRt source code. The necessary ports for connecting to other replicas as well as the associated application replica are declared. We eventually push the built image to a Docker Hub [10] repository, so that it can be conveniently imported to the PaaS cloud as an image stream for creating BFT containers.

BFT Pods and Services. In OpenShift, the smallest deployable and manageable unit, the so-called *pod*, is responsible for holding the runtime environment of a set of containers. In BFT-DEP, we specify a JSON file to explicitly describe the features of BFT replica pods. A unique *name* as well as a *label* are assigned to distinguish pods. When creating replicated BFT pods, the BFT image is imported and the ports declared in the image need to be opened by the pod as well. BFT-DEP enforces those pods' allocations by assigning each one to an individual host of the PaaS installation, as replicas should always be distributed to different machines. We achieve this by specifying a *hostPort* item in the BFT pod description file so that according to the default scheduling policy, pods with the same hostPort number cannot be allocated onto the same host.

The unit *service* in OpenShift is defined as an abstraction of one or multiple pods, being responsible for exposing a stable service entry point regardless of underlying pod changes. A *label selector* is used to find all matching pods for the same service. We build BFT services upon individual BFT pods to forward external traffic. A temporary helper pod is used to configure and setup a cluster. It collects IP addresses of all BFT pods to update their host settings and then starts the BFT-SMaRt replica inside each pod. This way, BFT-SMaRt replicas can eventually connect to each other to agree on the order of client requests.

3.2 BFT Application Deployment and Networking

In OpenShift, customers use a *template* (a description file) to package application runtime dependencies for deployment. BFT-DEP offers a specific template for deploying BFT services and replicated applications. When using this template, BFT services are automatically generated and so are the application replicas, while their allocations are enforced by BFT-DEP as explained above. Each BFT service thereby connects to the application replica on the same host via socket connections. BFT services first order the received requests via public IPs, and forward to the corresponding application replicas for execution, and eventually send the replies back to the clients.

3.3 Interim Evaluation

We installed OpenShift v3 on a cluster of AWS EC2 instances (all in US East), composed of one master and four plain nodes. Each EC2 instance is equipped with an elastic IP for public accesses from PaaS customers and clients.

We have conducted an interim evaluation of our preliminary BFT-DEP prototype using a simple key-value store application and the YCSB benchmark [20]. A workload of combined read and update operations is used for testing three deployment scenarios, as shown in Fig. 2: (1) BFT and application deployed on EC2 instances together, (2) BFT and application deployed in OpenShift together, and (3) BFT and application deployed by BFT-DEP separately. Results of average latency indicate that the extra delay of using BFT-DEP introduced by the socket connections between BFT replicas and application services is low.

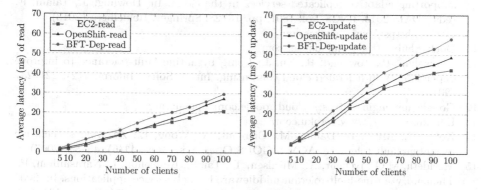

Fig. 2. Evaluation of read and update latencies with YCSB benchmark.

4   Conclusion and Future Works

We presented BFT-DEP, a framework leveraging existing PaaS facilities to address reliability demands of stateful application services. By integrating BFT protocols into the cloud platform as a built-in service layer, BFT-DEP offers customers the capability of automatically deploying and coordinating fault-tolerant applications while the PaaS platform itself can be left unchanged. Our preliminary BFT-DEP prototype has been implemented on top of OpenShift. The interim evaluation shows that the overhead that is added by a containerized BFT protocol implementation is low.

For future works, we plan to make BFT-DEP more generically applicable and enable reconfiguration and distribution changes as supported by BFT-SMaRt.

References

1. Behl, J., Distler, T., Kapitza, R.: Consensus-oriented parallelization: how to earn your first million. In: Proceedings of the 16th Annual Middleware Conference, Middleware 2015, pp. 173–184. ACM (2015)
2. Bessani, A., Correia, M., Quaresma, B., André, F., Sousa, P.: Depsky: dependable and secure storage in a cloud-of-clouds. ACM Trans. Storage (TOS) 9(4), 12 (2013)
3. Bessani, A., Sousa, J., Alchieri, E.E.: State machine replication for the masses with bft-smart. In: 2014 44th Annual IEEE/IFIP International Conference on Dependable Systems and Networks (DSN), pp. 355–362. IEEE (2014)
4. Bft-smart. https://github.com/bft-smart/library
5. Brenner, S., Garbers, B., Kapitza, R.: Adaptive and scalable high availability for infrastructure clouds. In: Magoutis, K., Pietzuch, P. (eds.) DAIS 2014. LNCS, vol. 8460, pp. 16–30. Springer, Heidelberg (2014)
6. Castro, M., Liskov, B.: Practical byzantine fault tolerance. In: Proceedings of the third USENIX Symposium on Operating Systems Design and Implementation (OSDI 1999), pp. 173–186 (1999)
7. Cloud foundry. https://www.cloudfoundry.org/
8. Cogo, V.V., Nogueira, A., Sousa, J., Pasin, M., Reiser, H.P., Bessani, A.: FITCH: supporting adaptive replicated services in the cloud. In: Dowling, J., Taïani, F. (eds.) DAIS 2013. LNCS, vol. 7891, pp. 15–28. Springer, Heidelberg (2013)
9. Docker. https://www.docker.com/
10. Docker hub. https://hub.docker.com/
11. Garraghan, P., Townend, P., Xu, J.: Using byzantine fault-tolerance to improve dependability in federated cloud computing. Int. J. Softw. Inform. 7(2), 221–237 (2013)
12. Google app engine. https://cloud.google.com/appengine/
13. Heroku. https://www.heroku.com/
14. Kotla, R., Alvisi, L., Dahlin, M., Clement, A., Wong, E.: Zyzzyva: speculative byzantine fault tolerance. ACM SIGOPS Oper. Syst. Rev. 41(6), 45–58 (2007)
15. Merideth, M.G., Iyengar, A., Mikalsen, T., Tai, S., Rouvellou, I., Narasimhan, P.: Thema: Byzantine-fault-tolerant middleware for web-service applications. In: 2005 24th IEEE Symposium on Reliable Distributed Systems (SRDS), pp. 131–140. IEEE (2005)
16. Openshift. https://www.openshift.com/
17. Openshift origin v3. https://github.com/openshift/origin
18. Schneider, F.B.: Implementing fault-tolerant services using the state machine approach: a tutorial. ACM Comput. Surv. 22, 299–319 (1990)
19. Verissimo, P., Bessani, A., Pasin, M.: The tclouds architecture: Open and resilient cloud-of-clouds computing. In: 2012 IEEE/IFIP 42nd International Conference on Dependable Systems and Networks Workshops (DSN-W), pp. 1–6. IEEE (2012)
20. https://github.com/brianfrankcooper/YCSB
21. Yin, J., Martin, J.P., Venkataramani, A., Alvisi, L., Dahlin, M.: Separating agreement from execution for byzantine fault tolerant services. In: Proceedings of the Nineteenth ACM SIGOPS Symposium on Operating Systems Principles (SOSP 2003), pp. 253–267. ACM (2003)
22. Zhang, Q., Cheng, L., Boutaba, R.: Cloud computing: state-of-the-art and research challenges. J. Internet serv. appl. 1(1), 7–18 (2010)

BFT-Bench: Towards a Practical Evaluation of Robustness and Effectiveness of BFT Protocols

Divya Gupta[1], Lucas Perronne[1], and Sara Bouchenak[2(✉)]

[1] Univ. Grenoble Alpes, LIG, Grenoble, France
{Divya.Gupta,Lucas.Perronne}@imag.fr
[2] Univ. Lyon, INSA Lyon, LIRIS, Lyon, France
Sara.Bouchenak@insa-lyon.fr

Abstract. Byzantine Fault Tolerance (BFT) is an interesting means to make computing systems resilient in presence of failures and attacks. That being said, designing and implementing BFT protocols is a hard and tedious task. This first comes from the inherent complexity of designing BFT distributed protocols, reasoning about their correctness, and implementing the software prototype of the protocols in a consistent and efficient way. Another reason that makes BFT protocols hard and error prone is the lack of tools for testing and evaluating protocols implementations in various and realistic settings. Furthermore, BFT protocols differ in many aspects, ranging from the faulty behaviors they handle, to the communication patterns and cryptographic mechanisms they apply. Thus, a comprehensive benchmarking environment is still missing to easily analyze and compare the effectiveness and performance of these protocols. In this paper, we present *BFT-Bench*, the first benchmarking framework for evaluating and comparing BFT protocols in practice. *BFT-Bench* includes different BFT protocols implementations, their automatic deployment in a distributed setting, the ability to define and inject different faulty behaviors and workloads, and the online monitoring and reporting of performance and dependability measures. The experimental results of the evaluation of *BFT-Bench* show the effectiveness of the framework, easily allowing an empirical comparison of different BFT protocols, in various workload and fault scenarios.

Keywords: Fault tolerance · Byzantine faults · Fault injection · Performance · Robustness · Benchmarking

1 Introduction

Cloud computing environments are now increasingly common. With their expansion, unpredictable events such malicious attacks, network delays, data corruption, and other types of Byzantine faults require specific fault tolerance

© IFIP International Federation for Information Processing 2016
Published by Springer International Publishing Switzerland 2016. All Rights Reserved
M. Jelasity and E. Kalyvianaki (Eds.): DAIS 2016, LNCS 9687, pp. 115–128, 2016.
DOI: 10.1007/978-3-319-39577-7_10

mechanisms. Byzantine Fault Tolerance (BFT), based on state machine replication, consists in replicating the critical service in several replicas running on different nodes, and thus, ensuring service availability despite failure occurrence [13]. When clients access the service, this is done through a specific BFT communication protocol that ensures that client requests are processed by replicas in the same order.

There has been a large amount of work on Byzantine Fault Tolerance (BFT) protocols. Early efforts have explored the practicality of Byzantine Fault Tolerance, with PBFT protocol [6]. Other efforts have been made to improve the performance of the protocols and reduce the cost they induce due to many message rounds and cryptographic operations. Thus, some BFT protocols focus on improving performance in fault-free cases [2,9,15], while other protocols improve performance in presence of failures, each one proposing and applying techniques to counter specific types of faults such as network contention, system overload, etc. [3,7].

However, there has been very little in the way of empirical evaluation of BFT protocols. Evaluations of the protocols have often been conducted in an ad-hoc way, which makes them difficult to reproduce, and compare with new protocols. Moreover, it is generally admitted that BFT protocols are too complex to implement, thus, re-implementing them each time a new protocol must be compared with existing ones is not realistic.

In this paper, we present *BFT-Bench*, a benchmarking environment for evaluating performance and robustness of Byzantine fault tolerance systems. *BFT-Bench* enables the definition of various execution scenarios and faultloads, their automatic deployment in an online system, and the production of various monitoring statistics. This provides a means to analyze and compare the effectiveness of the protocols in various situations. *BFT-Bench* is an open framework that includes state-of-the-art BFT protocols, and may be extended with new BFT protocols. In addition, the paper presents an evaluation with *BFT-Bench*, empirically comparing different BFT protocols, and exhibiting their level of performance and robustness in different scenarios.

The remainder of the paper is structured as follows. Section 2 discusses the related work. Section 3 presents *BFT-Bench*. Section 4 describes the experimental evaluation, and Sect. 5 concludes the paper.

2   Related Work

A Byzantine fault tolerant system is able to counter arbitrary faults, ranging from hardware crash, to message corruption, network congestion, or any other misbehavior. In the following, we review the related work on Byzantine fault tolerance, and BFT benchmarking.

BFT from Theory to Practice. BFT State Machine Replication (SMR) consists in replicating the underlying service in several replicas, to ensure service availability and correctness despite fault occurrence [13]. Such a service handles requests coming from concurrent clients. Thus, to ensure consistency among service replicas, an agreement protocol is applied to guarantee that client requests are executed in the same order by correct service replicas. Reaching an agreement requires $3f + 1$ replicas to handle upto f arbitrary faults [11].

BFT Performance Improvement in Fault-Free Conditions. One of the main drawbacks of BFT was its cost. Thus, several protocols were proposed to enhance the performance of BFT protocols while maintaining their correctness. A first family of BFT protocols aims at improving the performance of the protocols in the absence of faults. They usually run a lightweight version of the protocol in fault-free cases, and switch to a more robust version of the protocol at fault occurrence. This is interesting in scenarios where faults occur rarely, and where it is more interesting to provide priority to fault-free cases. Examples of such protocols are Zyzzyva [9], Chain [15], and Aliph [2], allowing to improve clients request throughput/latency.

BFT Performance Improvement in Presence of Faults. Another family of BFT protocols intends to improve performance in presence of faults. Roughly speaking, these protocols provide practical and efficient mechanisms to specifically handle some misbehaviors (i.e., fault types). Aardvark [7], Prime [1], Spinning [16], and RBFT [3] are examples of such protocols.

BFT Simulation and Benchmarking. General performance benchmarks have been proposed to evaluate the performance of application servers, web servers, data management systems, etc. Other solutions consider benchmarking dependability to provide a means to characterize system behavior in presence of faults. They consider different underlying systems such as MapReduce [12], or web servers [8]. Less effort has been done for benchmarking BFT systems. BFT-SMaRt is a replication engine that implements a BFT protocol; it interestingly includes a tool for evaluating the BFT protocol [4]. However, it is limited to the assessment of that particular protocol. Simulators of BFT protocols were also proposed [10,14]; in contrast, in this paper we consider the empirical evaluation of BFT. Thus, there is a need for a comprehensive benchmarking environment to help researchers and practitioners to conduct empirical studies and better analyze and evaluate the performance and robustness of BFT protocols.

3   *BFT-Bench* Framework

BFT-Bench framework allows empirical evaluation and comparison of state-of-the-art and new Byzantine fault-tolerance systems. Figure 1 describes the major components of *BFT-Bench*: (i) several BFT protocols implementations, (ii) fault scenarios to be injected in the underlying BFT system, (iii) load to be injected in the running underlying system, and (iv) monitoring statistics to report performance and dependability statistics the system.

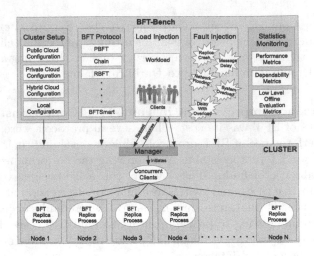

Fig. 1. Overview of *BFT-Bench*

Thus, *BFT-Bench* enables automatic deployment of the experiments in a distributed system that consists of several nodes running the replicas of the BFT protocol, and one or multiple nodes emulating clients sending concurrent requests to the BFT system.

3.1 BFT Protocols

BFT-Bench is intended to be an open framework that can be extended with new BFT protocols to evaluate, new fault models. In this paper, the following state-of-the-art BFT protocols are considered: PBFT for being the first practical BFT protocol [6]; Zyzzyva, Chain, and Aliph for their performance efficiency in fault-free conditions [2,9,15]; Aardvark, and RBFT as instances of robust protocols that improve performance in presence of failures [3,7]. These protocols were chosen for their variety of features, their variety of communication patterns as described in Fig. 2, and their variety in terms of fault types the protocols prototypes actually handle (see Sect. 3.2).

Practical BFT Protocol. PBFT's communication pattern is used as a baseline many other protocols such as Aardvark and RBFT [3,7]. In PBFT, upon a client request the primary sends pre-prepare messages to other replicas with assigned sequence number to the request. Then, prepare messages and commit messages are exchanged to agree on the sequence number. If PBFT suspects the primary to be malicious, it undergoes a *view change* to replace the primary by another replica.

Protocols Enhancing Performance in Fault-Free Conditions. Zyzzyva is a speculative, high throughput BFT protocol [9]. Its design is meant to bypass

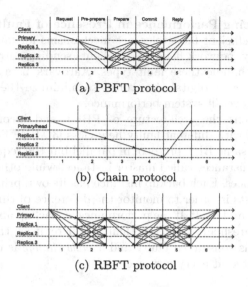

(a) PBFT protocol

(b) Chain protocol

(c) RBFT protocol

Fig. 2. Examples of communication patterns of BFT protocols

the expensive agreement steps of PBFT in fault-free settings. In such scenario, the clients send their requests to the primary in charge of assigning sequence numbers. The primary then forwards the ordered requests to the other replicas, which speculatively execute these requests and send the responses to the clients. If a client receives $3f + 1$ consistent matching responses, it commits. Otherwise, clients apply additional steps such as collecting commit certificates and creating proofs of misbehaviors to trigger view change.

Chain protocol, as its name suggests and as described in Fig. 2(b), follows a chain-like communication pattern where clients send requests to the head replica, which itself sends messages to its successor replica, and so on [15]. Chain greatly benefits from batch optimization where multiple messages are sent in one batch, which improves system throughput, with a peak of performance when the system is completely saturated (i.e., when the network link between any two servers is fully loaded). However, Chain by itself is unable to ensure Byzantine fault tolerance, and must rely on a protocol switching mechanism when subject to failures.

Aliph protocol involves several sub-protocols [2]. Its initial configuration, Quorum, is dedicated to provide high performance if the system does not involve asynchrony, contention, or failures. When facing contention, Quorum is replaced by Chain. Finally, upon occurrence of Byzantine behaviors, Chain is replaced by a backup protocol that handles Byzantine faults, for example PBFT. In Quorum, clients directly send requests to all replicas. These replicas independently execute the requests, updates their local history and reply to the clients. Note that the ordering phase commonly performed by the primary replica is skipped in Quorum, thus providing a better response time. Thus, in Aliph the client side of the protocol is responsible of managing inconsistencies, and relies on a panicking mechanism to trigger sub-protocol switching.

Protocols Enhancing Performance in Presence of Faults. Aardvark prototype implements efficient fault tolerance mechanisms for faults such as intentional message delay, network flooding, or clients sending corrupted requests to the system [7]. To handle these fault types, Aardvark uses mechanisms such as replica blacklisting or digital signatures, to minimize the impact of faulty components on the overall system performance.

RBFT strengthens the architecture of PBFT and incorporates adaptive mechanisms to deal with different faulty behaviors [3]. RBFT runs $f + 1$ multiple instances of the same BFT protocol in parallel but the requests are executed only by one of the instances called master instance, while other f instances are called backup instances. Each backup instance has its own primary which orders the incoming requests in order to monitor the difference of throughput between the master instance and itself. If the performance at backup and master instance differs by a given threshold at not less than $2f + 1$ replicas, the primary replica at master instance is considered faulty and a *view change* is triggered, where a new primary is elected at every instance.

3.2 Fault Injection

In the following, we first describe the fault types that are handed by state-of-the-art BFT protocols presented in Sect. 3.1, and how *BFT-Bench* injects them in a running system. We then present how to describe a *faultload*, i.e. fault scenario to be injected by *BFT-Bench*.

Fault Types Examples

Replica Crash. Upon a replica crash, the replica stops and does not participate in any further communication with the clients or the other replicas of the BFT protocol. In practice, *BFT-Bench* remotely connects to the target replica node and kills the replica process. Note that the implementation of this fault type injection is BFT protocol-independent, thus, it does not require changes to BFT protocols prototypes.

Message Delay. When a replica starts delaying messages, it slows down all future operations of the protocol depending on these messages, thus, leading to degradation in performance. As a result, this Byzantine behavior is especially critical when it occurs at the primary replica. In practice, BFT protocols prototypes are extended to integrate the injection of this type of fault. When *BFT-Bench* triggers this type of fault, instead of sending messages according to the protocol specifications, the replica process sleeps during a given delay, before resuming to send any messages to other replicas.

Network Flooding. Network flooding is a common denial-of-service attack. It is meant to overload the network with malicious messages which can not be said invalid until verified. This verification of messages is computation-intensive and prevents the system from focusing on correct messages. In practice, BFT protocols prototypes are extended to integrate the injection of this type of fault. When *BFT-Bench* triggers this type of fault, the faulty replica transmits corrupted messages of a chosen size to other replicas.

System Overload. Overloading the system with a large number of concurrent client requests can affect system performance to a large extent. Although none of the servers behave maliciously in this attack, but continuous increase in concurrent clients can eventually deteriorate the performance or lead to system thrashing. To inject this behavior, *BFT-Bench* remotely connects to the node in charge of emulating concurrent clients, and starts additional client processes.

Faultload. A *faultload* in *BFT-Bench* is described in a file. Each line of the faultload file consists of the following elements: the time at which a fault occurs (relative to the beginning of the experiment), the type of fault that occurs, where the fault occurs, and optionally, additional parameters that depend on the type of fault. A fault belongs to one of the fault types handled by BFT protocols prototypes, and introduced in Sect. 3.2. A fault occurs in one of the BFT protocol replicas; this replica may be either explicitly specified in the faultload or randomly chosen among the set of replicas.

Thus, a faultload in *BFT-Bench* may contain the following element to describe the injection of fault of type crash:

$< [fault\ trigger\ time],\ replica\ crash,\ replica_x >$

It may contain the following element to describe the injection of fault of type message delay, specifying among others the delay to be injected, and the duration of occurrence of this type of fault:

$< [fault\ trigger\ time],\ message\ delay,\ replica_x,\ ([injected\ message\ delay], [fault\ occurrence\ duration]) >$

A faultload in *BFT-Bench* may also contain the following element to describe the injection of fault of type network flooding, specifying among others the size of the message used for flooding, and the duration of occurrence of this type of fault:

$< [fault\ trigger\ time],\ network\ flooding,\ replica_x,\ ([flooding\ message\ size], [fault\ occurrence\ duration]) >$

The overall architecture of *BFT-Bench* fault injection is presented in Fig. 3. In this example, the cluster has $N + 2$ nodes, where $N = 3f + 1$ nodes are BFT replicas, one node hosts concurrent clients emulator, and one node runs *BFT-Bench*. *BFT-Bench* faultload injector uses faultload to determine which type of fault is to be triggered, at what time this fault will be injected, and other required fault parameters. The fault injector runs a daemon that communicates directly with the replicas to trigger faults. For instance, in case of *replica crash*, the daemon waits until the *fault trigger time* is reached, then calls remotely interacts with the target replica to actually trigger the fault.

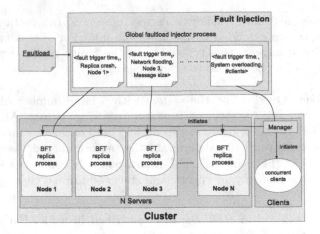

Fig. 3. Architecture of faultload injection

3.3   Load Injection

The workload is first characterized by number of concurrent clients sending requests to the BFT system. Client requests are executed in FIFO order in a closed loop, where a clients submits a request, waits for the request to get processed and receives a response, before sending another request. The workload is also characterized by the size of client request/response messages exchanged with the BFT system. It is an important parameter as large size messages affect BFT system performance, due to time consuming cryptographic operations executed by BFT protocols. *BFT-Bench* includes a client emulator implementing multi-client behavior, where each client process sends requests to the underlying BFT system, and receives the corresponding responses. In *BFT-Bench*, the workload may contain one or several elements as follows to describe the load to be injected:

$<$ *[load injection time]*, *[#concurrent clients]*, *[request message size]*, *[response message size]*, *[request processing time]*, *[load injection duration])$>$

3.4   Monitoring

BFT-Bench produces performance statistics for evaluating and comparing the performance of BFT protocols. *Throughput* and *Latency* are the main performance parameters considered when evaluating Byzantine Fault Tolerance protocols, both experimentally and theoretically. *Latency* is the time elapsed from the moment a client submits a request until the complete response is received by this client. *Throughput* is measured as the number of client requests handled by the system per unit of time. Latency and throughput are measured by *BFT-Bench* at the client-side, and thus include network communication times between the client and the replicas. Furthermore, *BFT-Bench* produces low-level system monitoring information such as cpu, memory and network usage, that can help better explaining the behavior and possible bottlenecks of the system.

3.5   On Extensibility of BFT-Bench

BFT-Bench is an open framework intended to help BFT protocol designers and practitioners to easily evaluate their protocols. *BFT-Bench* includes, among others, existing implementations of BFT protocols. In this paper, we illustrated the use of *BFT-Bench* with several state-of-the-art BFT protocols prototypes. In the following, we describe how to integrate a new BFT protocol prototype to *BFT-Bench*, and benefit from its benchmarking features. Although most of the components of *BFT-Bench* framework are general and can be easily reused for new BFT protocols, there are some exceptions that we describe below. Workload injection is based on the client emulator program that comes with a BFT protocol prototype. Such a program is pretty simple, and its reuse to allow dynamic workload variation as provided by *BFT-Bench* is straightforward. For the implementation of faultload injection for faults like replica crash or system overload, the implementation is independent from the actual BFT protocol prototype. This is not the case of faults of type message delay or network flooding that need an extension of the underlying BFT protocol prototype.

4   Experimental Evaluation

4.1   Experimental Setup

The experiments presented in this paper were conducted on a cluster of Grid'5000 [5]. Each node hosts two Quad-Core Intel Xeon E5420, with 2.50 GHz, 8 GB of RAM, and 160 GB of storage; nodes are connected through 1 GB Ethernet. *BFT-Bench* framework currently includes six BFT protocols, namely PBFT, Chain, RPFT, Aardvark, Aliph, Zyzzyva [2,3,6,7,9,15]. We used the original C++ code of these protocols. When needed by the evaluated BFT protocol, multiple virtual network interfaces are created on a single physical network interface controller to exploit the robustness of protocol, e.g., Aardvark, RBFT.

For each protocol under evaluation, four nodes are used for running the replicas of the service (i.e., application), thus, $f = 1$. Two other nodes are used for the experiments, one for emulating the clients that concurrently send requests to the replicated service, and one node for hosting *BFT-Bench*. Similarly to state-of-the-art evaluations, each replica runs an echo service [6]. Client request size and client response size are 4 KB each. Furthermore, to emulate the computation performed by the service, a delay of 100 ($\pm 10\%$) μs is introduced before sending the response to the client. The results of the experiments are obtained after a warm-up phase of 180 s, to let the system reach a stable stage before actually measuring the behavior of the system. The graphs presented in the following are obtained after the warm-up phase.

4.2   Evaluation in Presence of Replica Crash

In this use case, five concurrent clients access the replicated service, when the crash of the primary replica of the service occurs. Thus, the following faultload is provided to *BFT-Bench*, which triggers a fault at time 300 s:

<300 s, replica crash, {primary}>

Figure 4 presents the measured latency and throughput. Upon crash of the primary, PBFT induces a sudden increase in latency, and throughput drops sharply. This is due to the view change mechanism used by the protocol to replace the faulty primary. Aliph follows the same pattern since it switches to PBFT upon fault occurrence. Upon crash, Chain cannot maintain its pipeline structure as the successor of the crashed server never receives any message. In theory, Chain must switch to PBFT upon crash, but unfortunately this mechanism is not present in the Chain prototype. Zyzzyva prototype implements only the fault free version of the protocol and, thus, does not deal with fault occurrence. In Aardvark and RBFT where clients broadcast requests to all replicas, and because of the absence of a crash handling mechanism at client side, this fault is not handled.

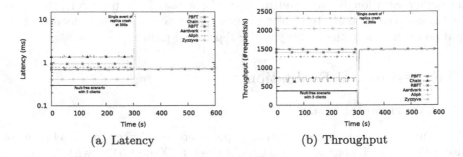

(a) Latency   (b) Throughput

Fig. 4. Performance evaluation in presence of replica crash

4.3   Evaluation in Presence of Message Delay

In this use case, a replicated service is accessed by two concurrent clients, when the service starts misbehaving by inducing intentional and unjustifiable message delay. The following faultload is provided to *BFT-Bench* to inject this misbehavior in the running replicated service:

<300 s, message delay, replica$_x$, (500 ms, 300 s)>

Here, starting from time 300 s there is a message delay of 500 ms, and this misbehavior continues during 300 s (i.e., until the end of the experiment). Since the BFT protocols under evaluation use different architectures and communication patterns, message delays are introduced by *BFT-Bench* in different ways to these protocols, as explained in the following. For instance in case of PBFT, Aardvark, RBFT, and Zyzzyva, a delay is injected at the primary replica-side, when this replica receives a client request and sends the initial message to other replicas for processing that request (i.e., usually known as the *pre-prepare* phase in these protocols). In case of Chain, a message delay is injected before the head replica initiates the communication protocol with the other replicas. For Aliph which does not have a dedicated replica (i.e., no primary, no head), a chosen replica induces message delay.

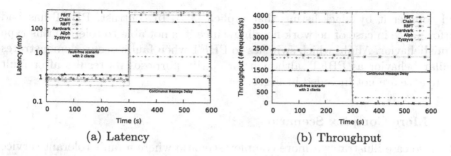

(a) Latency   (b) Throughput

Fig. 5. Performance evaluation in presence of intentional message delay

Figure 5 presents the results of these experiments. We can observe that the impact of this type of fault is different from one protocol to another. For instance, Fig. 5(a) shows that message delay faults induce a latency increase of two orders of magnitude for PBFT, Zyzzyva, Aliph, Chain protocols, and a latency increase of one order of magnitude for Aardvark. Interestingly, due to its robustness to this type of fault, RBFT is able to smoothly tolerate this misbehavior without a perceptible impact on performance.

4.4 Evaluation in Presence of Network Flooding

In this case, ten clients concurrently access a replicated service, when the service starts misbehaving by inducing network flooding. The following faultload is provided to *BFT-Bench* to inject this misbehavior in the running replicated service:

<300 s, network flooding, replica$_x$, (4 KB, 300 s)$>$

Thus, starting from time 300 s, replica$_x$ starts sending corrupted messages of size 4 KB to other replicas, during 300 s. Figure 6 presents the results of these experiments. Interestingly, Aardvark and RBFT are robust in case of such misbehavior. They are able to detect that a replica performs network flooding,

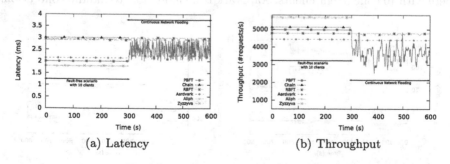

(a) Latency   (b) Throughput

Fig. 6. Performance evaluation in presence of network flooding. Results of Aliph after fault occurrence are not included; Aliph switches to PBFT when fault occurs and demonstrates similar behavior as PBFT.

and counter it by black-listing that replica [3,7]. In contrast, PBFT has bad performance in case of network flooding, since it is not able to tolerate this type of misbehavior. Aliph, which switches to PBFT when faults occur, demonstrates similar behavior as PBFT, although for clarity purposes its results after fault occurrence are not included in Fig. 6.

4.5   More Complex Scenario

This use case illustrates a more complex scenario where a fault tolerant service faces a Byzantine fault, in addition to service contention. Here, the following faultload is used by *BFT-Bench*:

$<200\ s,\ message\ delay,\ (replica_x,\ 500\ ms,\ 600\ s)>$

And in order to increase service contention, the following *workload* is provided to *BFT-Bench*:

$<0\ s,\ 2,\ 4\ KB,\ 4\ KB,\ 100\ \mu s,\ 400\ s>$
$<400\ s,\ 5,\ 4\ KB,\ 4\ KB,\ 100\ \mu s,\ 200\ s>$
$<600\ s,\ 10,\ 4\ KB,\ 4\ KB,\ 100\ \mu s,\ 200\ s>$

Thus, the replicated service is first accessed by two concurrent clients. Then at time 200 s, the service starts misbehaving by inducing abnormal message delay of 500 ms, during 600 s (i.e., until the end of the experiment). In addition, the service load increases from 2 clients at the beginning of the experiment to 5 clients at time 400 s, and then to 10 clients at time 600 s. And as described in Sect. 4.1, client request and response message sizes are 4 KB.

Figure 7 presents the results of the experiment. We can observe that RBFT is able to transparently tolerate the Byzantine fault of type message delay when service contention is not too high. However, when 10 clients concurrently access the service, RBFT is no more able to handle contention and terminates. In case of Aardvark, the Byzantine fault tolerant service is able to face message delay fault, but at the expense of a performance overhead of one order of magnitude. Interestingly, Aardvark smoothly handles service contention increase without a perceptible impact on performance. This holds up to a given service load, where with 10 concurrent clients, Aardvark is no more able to handle contention,

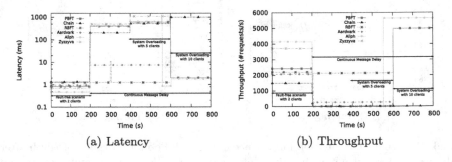

(a) Latency   (b) Throughput

Fig. 7. Performance evaluation - combination of message delay and system overload

and terminates. Zyzzyva and Chain are able to face the Byzatine fault of type message delay. But they induces a high performance overhead of two orders of magnitude when such a fault occurs. In addition, when the service has a high contention (10 concurrent clients), Chain-based replicated service is three orders of magnitude slower, while Zyzzyva crashes. PBFT and Aliph (which switches to PBFT upon fault occurrence) have similar behavior after the occurrence of the fault at time 200 s, with a drop of latency of two orders of magnitude. After a while, PBFT and Aliph undergo a *view change*, i.e. they replace the faulty primary by a new primary. This has a direct impact on service performance which drastically improves.

5   Conclusion

Performance and dependability are important requirements of today's computing systems. Byzantine Fault Tolerance (BFT) is a general approach to make these systems, theoretically, tolerate arbitrary faults. BFT protocols were extensively investigated in the last years, and various prototypes were proposed. However, to the best of our knowledge, there is no practical solution to precisely identify the varying nature of Byzantine behaviors, no general tool for real-time injection of these misbehaviors in a system, and no reusable environment for the empirical evaluation of various BFT protocols. This paper presents *BFT-Bench*, the first framework for evaluating BFT implementations under different faulty behaviors and workloads. *BFT-Bench* framework includes several state-of-the-art BFT protocols, automatically deploys them, injects different types of faults at different rates, and produces performance and dependability measures. The evaluation results show that *BFT-Bench* is able to successfully compare various BFT protocols, in various faulty behaviors. We wish to make BFT benchmarking easy to adopt by developers and end-users of BFT protocols. *BFT-Bench* framework aims to help researchers and practitioners to better analyze and evaluate the effectiveness and robustness of BFT systems. Although this paper concentrates on presenting the current version of *BFT-Bench* with some BFT protocols and their related fault types, we believe that the proposed approach can be easily extended to other BFT protocols, and other faulty behaviors.

Acknowledgement. This work was supported by AMADEOS (Architecture for Multi-criticality Agile Dependable Evolutionary Open System-of-Systems), a collaborative project funded under the European Commission's FP7 (FP7-ICT-2013-610535). The experiments were conducted on the Grid'5000 experimental testbed, developed under the INRIA ALADDIN development action with support from CNRS, RENATER and several Universities, as well as other funding bodies.

References

1. Amir, Y., Coan, B.A., Kirsch, J., Lane, J.: Byzantine replication under attack. In: The 38th Annual IEEE/IFIP International Conference on Dependable Systems and Networks (DSN 2008) (2008)

2. Aublin, P.-L., Guerraoui, R., Knezevic, N., Quéma, V.: The next 700 BFT protocols. ACM Trans. Comput. Syst. **32**(4), 1–45 (2015)
3. Aublin, P.-L., Mokhtar, S.B., Quéma, V.: RBFT: redundant byzantine fault tolerance. In: The IEEE 33rd International Conference on Distributed Computing Systems (ICDCS 2013) (2013)
4. Bessani, A.N., Sousa, J., Alchieri, E.A.P.: State machine replication for the masses with BFT-SMART. In: The 44th IEEE/IFIP International Conference on Dependable Systems and Networks (DSN 2014) (2014)
5. Cappello, F., Caron, E., Dayde, M., Desprez, F., Jégou, Y., Primet, P., Jeannot, E., Lanteri, S., Leduc, J., Melab, N., et al.: Grid'5000: a large scale and highly reconfigurable grid experimental testbed. In: The 6th IEEE/ACM International Workshop on Grid Computing (2005)
6. Castro, M., Liskov, B.: Practical byzantine fault tolerance. In: The 3rd Symposium on Operating Systems Design and Implementation (OSDI 1999) (1999)
7. Clement, A., Wong, E.L., Alvisi, L., Dahlin, M., Marchetti, M.: Making byzantine fault tolerant systems tolerate byzantine faults. In: USENIX Symposium on Networked Systems Design and Implementation (NSDI 2009) (2009)
8. Durães, J., Vieira, M., Madeira, H.: Dependability benchmarking of web-servers. In: The 23rd International Conference on Computer Safety, Reliability and Security (Safecomp'2004) (2004)
9. Kotla, R., Alvisi, L., Dahlin, M., Clement, A., Wong, E.L.: Zyzzyva: speculative byzantine fault tolerance. ACM Trans. Comput. Syst. **27**(4), 1–39 (2009)
10. Lee, H., Seibert, J., Hoque, E., Killian, C., Nita-Rotaru, C.: Turret: a platform for automated attack finding in unmodified distributed system implementations. In: The 34th International Conference on Distributed Computing Systems (ICDCS 2014) (2014)
11. Pease, M., Shostak, R., Lamport, L.: Reaching agreement in the presence of faults. J. ACM **27**(2), 228–234 (1980)
12. Sangroya, A., Serrano, D., Bouchenak, S.: Benchmarking dependability of MapReduce systems. In: The IEEE International Symposium on Reliable Distributed Systems (SRDS) (2012)
13. Schneider, F.B.: Implementing fault-tolerant services using the state machine approach: a tutorial. ACM Comput. Surv. **22**(4), 299–319 (1990)
14. Singh, A., Das, T., Maniatis, P., Druschel, P., Roscoe, T.: BFT protocols under fire. In: The 5th USENIX Symposium on Networked Systems Design and Implementation (2008)
15. van Renesse, R., Schneider, F.B.: Chain replication for supporting high throughput and availability. In: The 6th Symposium on Operating Systems Design and Implementation (OSDI 2004) (2004)
16. Veronese, G.S., Correia, M., Bessani, A.N., Lung, L.C.: Spin one's wheels? byzantine fault tolerance with a spinning primary. In: SRDS (2009)

Self-Balancing Job Parallelism and Throughput in Hadoop

Bo Zhang[1], Filip Křikava[2]([✉]), Romain Rouvoy[1], and Lionel Seinturier[1]

[1] University of Lille/Inria, Villeneuve-d'ascq, France
{bo.zhang,romain.rouvoy,lionel.seinturier}@inria.fr
[2] Czech Technical University, Prague, Czech Republic
krikava@gmail.com

Abstract. In Hadoop cluster, the performance and the resource consumption of MapReduce jobs do not only depend on the characteristics of these applications and workloads, but also on the appropriate setting of Hadoop configuration parameters. However, when the job workloads are not known *a priori* or they evolve over time, a static configuration may quickly lead to a waste of computing resources and consequently to a performance degradation. In this paper, we therefore propose an on-line approach that dynamically reconfigures Hadoop at runtime. Concretely, we focus on balancing the job parallelism and throughput by adjusting Hadoop capacity scheduler memory configuration. Our evaluation shows that the approach outperforms vanilla Hadoop deployments by up to 40 % and the best statically profiled configurations by up to 13 %.

1 Introduction

Along the years, Hadoop has emerged as the *de facto* standard for big data processing and the MapReduce paradigm has been applied to large diversity of applications and workloads. In this context, the performance and the resource consumption of Hadoop jobs do not only depend on the characteristics of applications and workloads, but also on an appropriately configured Hadoop environment. Next to the infrastructure-level configuration (*e.g.* the number of nodes in a cluster), the Hadoop performance is affected by job- and system-level parameter settings. Optimizing the job-level parameters to accelerate the execution of Hadoop jobs has been a subject to a lot of research work [2,9,13–16].

Beyond job-level configuration, Hadoop also includes a large set of system-level parameters. In particular, YARN (*Yet Another Resource Negotiator*), the resource manager introduced in the new generation of Hadoop (version 2.0) defines a number of parameters that control how the applications (*e.g.* MapReduce jobs) are scheduled in a cluster which influence jobs performance. Among YARN parameters, the MARP (*Maximum Application Master Resource in Percent*: yarn.scheduler.capacity.maximum-am-resource-percent) property directly affects the level of MapReduce job parallelism and associated throughput. This property balances the number of concurrently executing MapReduce jobs versus

Published by Springer International Publishing Switzerland 2016. All Rights Reserved
M. Jelasity and E. Kalyvianaki (Eds.): DAIS 2016, LNCS 9687, pp. 129–143, 2016.
DOI: 10.1007/978-3-319-39577-7_11

the number of the corresponding map/reduce tasks. An inappropriate MARP configuration will therefore either reduce the number of jobs running in parallel resulting in idle jobs, or reduce the number of map/reduce tasks and thus delay the completion of jobs. However, finding an appropriate MARP value is far from trivial. On the one hand, the diversity of MapReduce applications and workloads suggests that a simple, *one-size-fits-all* application-oblivious configuration, will not be broadly effective—*i.e.* one MARP value that works well for one MapReduce application/workflow combination might not work for another [22]. On the other hand, YARN configuration is static and as such it cannot reflect any changes in workload dynamics. The only possibility is to do a *best-effort* configuration based on either experience or a static profiling in the case the jobs and workloads are known as *a priori*. However, (1) this might not be always possible, (2) it requires additional work, and (3) any unpredictable workload changes (*e.g.* a load peak due to node failures) will cause performance degradation.

In this paper, we therefore focus on dynamic MARP configuration. The main contributions are the following:

(1) an analysis of the effects of the MARP parameter on the MapReduce job parallelism and throughput, and
(2) a feedback control loop that self-balances MapReduce job parallelism and throughput.

Our evaluation shows that our approach systematically achieves better performance than static configurations. Concretely, we outperform the default Hadoop configuration by up to 40 % and up to 13 % for the *best-effort* statically profiled configurations, yet without any need for prior knowledge of the application or the workload shape, nor any need for any learning phase.

The rest of this paper is organized as follows. In Sect. 2, we introduce the architecture of YARN. The motivation of our research is placed in Sect. 3. Section 4 illustrates the memory and performance issues usually faced by Hadoop clusters. Section 5 describes the methodology we adopt and Sect. 6 evaluates our solution using various Hadoop benchmarks. We discuss related work in Sect. 7 before concluding in Sect. 8.

2   Overview of YARN

YARN is a cluster-level computing resource manager responsible for resource allocations and overall jobs orchestration. It provides a generic framework for developing distributed applications that goes beyond the MapReduce programming model. It consists of two main components (cf. Fig. 1): a per-cluster ResourceManager acting as a global computing resource arbiter and a per-node NodeManager responsible for managing node-level resources and reporting their usage to the ResourceManager.

Figure 1 depicts the architecture of YARN. The ResourceManager contains a scheduler that allocates resources for the running applications, like the Job-Tracker in previous version of Hadoop. However, ResourceManager does not

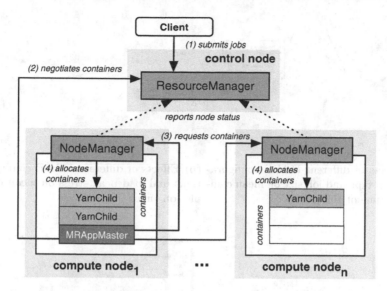

Fig. 1. High-level YARN architecture.

do any application monitoring or status tracking. This responsibility is left for the per-job instance of *Application Master* (AM). AM is an application-specific process that negotiates resources from the ResourceManager and collaborates with the NodeManager(s) to execute and monitor its individual tasks. The scheduling is based on the application resource requirements and it is realized using an abstract notion of *containers*. Essentially, each computing node is partitioned into a number of containers which are fixed-size resource blocks running AMs and their corresponding tasks.

3   Motivation

To understand the limitation of static configuration, we first study how the number of tasks to be processed and the MARP affects the overall completion time of Hadoop jobs. All experiments were performed using an Hadoop cluster made of 11 physical hosts[1] (1 control node and 10 compute nodes) deployed on the GRID5000 infrastructure. We use Hadoop 2.6.0.

Figure 2a reports on the completion time of the three applications provided by the HiBench benchmark suite [11]: Wordcount, Terasort, and Sort. For each of the input workloads—*i.e.* 30MB and 3GB—we observe the impact of the MARP parameter on the mean completion time of 100 jobs. To guarantee the comparisons visible, the values are normalized according to the absolute completion time of the vanilla Hadoop configuration—*i.e.* MARP = 0.1. The absolute completion time can be found at the paper web companion page: https://spirals-team.github.io/had-loop/DAIS2016.html

---

[1] 2 Intel Xeon L5420 CPUs with 4 cores, 15GB RAM, 298GB HDD.

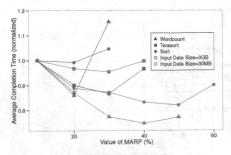

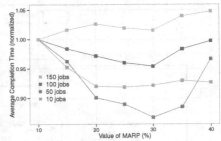

(a) Effects of different MARP configurations, job type and job size on mean completion time of 100 jobs.

(b) Effects of different MARP configurations and load peak stress on mean completion time.

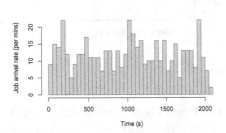

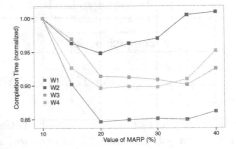

(c) A job distributions generated by SWIM used for W1.

(d) Effects of different MARP configurations and different SWIM generated workloads on overall completion time.

Fig. 2. Effects of MARP and an example of job distributions in SWIM.

As expected, the vanilla configuration does not provide the best configuration for any of the workloads. Furthermore, one can observe that the best performance is not achieved by a single value of MARP, but rather tends to depend on the type and the size of the job. In particular, increasing the value of MARP—thus allowing more jobs running in parallel—tends to benefit the smaller Hadoop jobs, while large jobs complete faster when more resources is dedicated to the YarnChild containers which are responsible for processing requests.

Next, we stress the Hadoop cluster by running a different number of jobs in parallel in order to observe the impact of a load peak on the job mean completion time. Figure 2b shows the performance when running Terasort with 3GB workload under various stress conditions. Compared to Fig. 2a, one can observe that by increasing the number of concurrently running jobs, the optimal value of MARP differs from the previous experiment. Therefore, while a MapReduce job can be profiled for a *best-effort* MARP configuration in a specific Hadoop cluster, any unpredictable changes in the workload dynamics will lead to a performance degradation.

Finally, we consider heterogeneous workloads. Concretely, we use SWIM (*Statistical Workload Injector for Mapreduce*) [3] to generate 4 realistic MapReduce workload. SWIM contains several large workloads (thousands of jobs), with complex data, arrival, and computation patterns that were synthesized from historical traces from Facebook 600-nodes Hadoop cluster. The proportion of job sizes in each input workloads has been scaled down to fit our cluster size using a Zipfian distribution (see http://xlinux.nist.gov/dads/HTML/zipfian.html). (cf. Fig. 2c).

As previously observed for homogeneous workloads, Fig. 2d demonstrates that not a single MARP value fits all the workloads and the best configuration can only be set by having a deep understanding of the Hadoop jobs and their dynamics.

Synthesis. These preliminary experiments demonstrate that the MARP configuration clearly impacts Hadoop performances. They show that the default value is not optimal. While one can profile the different applications to identify the *best-effort* static configuration, we have shown that any unforeseen change in the workload dynamics can degrade the overall performance. We therefore advocate for a self-adaptive approach that continuously adjusts the MARP configuration based on the current state of the Hadoop cluster. In next section, we will analyse How MARP affects the system performance of the Hadoop cluster.

4   Memory Consumption Analysis

In this section, we focus on memory consumption (YARN can manage CPU and memory, but in this paper, we only consider memory) and analyze the causes of the performance bottlenecks.

In an Hadoop cluster, the memory can be divided into four parts: M_{system}, M_{AM}, M_{YC}, and M_{idle}. M_{system} is the memory consumed by the system components—*i.e.* ResourceManager, NodeManager in YARN and NameNode, DataNode in HDFS. M_{system} is constant in a Hadoop cluster.

The other three parts represents the memory held by NodeManager(s) as a result of processing MapReduce jobs:

M_{AM} is the memory allocated to all the MRAppMaster containers across all compute nodes. This is controlled by the MARP configuration—*i.e.* $M_{AM}^* = M_{compute} \times$ MARP. During the processing of jobs, $M_{AM} \leqslant M_{AM}^*$.

M_{YC} is the memory used by all the YarnChilds to process map/reduce tasks across all the concurrently running jobs on all the computing nodes. This part directly impacts the job processing rate. A larger M_{YC} means that the more map/reduce tasks can be launched in parallel and the faster ongoing jobs are completed.

M_{idle} is the unused memory across all the computing nodes. High M_{idle} value together with pending jobs is a symptom of a waste of resources.

Their relationship with the overall computing memory of a Hadoop cluster, $M_{compute}$, can be expressed as follows: $M_{compute} = M_{AM} + M_{YC} + M_{Idle}$. Upon starting an Hadoop cluster, $M_{compute}$ is fixed (unless new computing nodes are enlisted or existing discharged from the cluster).

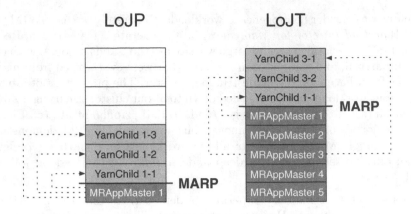

Fig. 3. LoJP and LoJT in Hadoop.

4.1 Loss of Jobs Parallelism

The maximum number of concurrently running jobs, N_{max}, in an Hadoop cluster is $N_{max} = \frac{M^*_{AM}}{M_{container}}$ where $M_{container}$ is the NodeManager container size (by default it is 1GB). The smaller the MARP value is, the smaller N_{max} will be and the less jobs will be able to run in parallel.

In the case the number of running jobs equals to N_{max}, all available application master containers are exhausted and ResourceManager cannot schedule any more jobs. Therefore, $M_{compute} = M^*_{AM} + M_{YC} + M_{idle}$. Where M_{idle} will emerge with a low N_{max}. When the number of running jobs reaches N_{max}, $M_{AM} = M^*_{AM}$ and no more pending jobs can be run even though $M^*_{AM} + M_{YC} < M_{compute}$. Therefore, we can observe that the lower $M^*_{AM} + M_{YC}$ is, the higher M_{idle} is. This indicates a memory / container waste that in turn degrades performances. We call this situation the *Loss of Jobs Parallelism* (LoJP). Figure 3 illustrates such a situation. An Hadoop cluster with 8 containers has the MARP value set too low, allowing only one job to be executed at a time. Any pending job have to wait until the current job has finished, despite the fact that some containers are unused.

4.2 Loss of Job Throughput

As shown in the previous section, small N_{max} limits the jobs parallelism within an Hadoop cluster. However, large N_{max} may also impact the job performance. By increasing N_{max} (or M^*_{AM}) in order to absorb M_{idle}, $M_{compute}$ can be rewritten as follow: $M_{compute} = M_{AM} + M_{YC}$.

In this case, when an Hadoop cluster processes a large number of concurrent jobs, M_{AM} becomes a major part of $M_{compute}$ and thus it limits M_{YC}. MRApp-Master is a job-level controller and it does not participate in any map/reduce task processing. Therefore, a limited M_{YC} decreases significantly the processing throughput of an Hadoop cluster. This symptom is identified as a *Loss of Job*

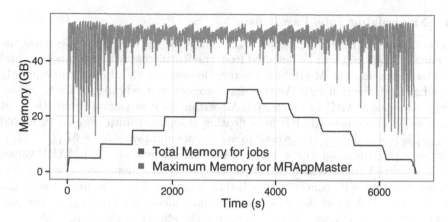

Fig. 4. Amplitude of memory drops depending on the MARP value.

Throughput (LoJT) and is also illustrated in Fig. 3. In this case, we have set the MARP too high, which allows many jobs to run in parallel, yet the actual processing capacity is limited by the low number of available container for running YarnChild.

4.3 Large Drops of Memory Utilization

Depending on the size of the jobs and the memory used in YarnChild containers, the dynamic allocation of resources can result in abruptly large drops of memory utilization (cf. Fig. 4). This is especially true when the tasks are rather fast to complete.

These memory drops usually appear at the end of concurrently running jobs. When a job comes to the end, all its corresponding M_{YC} will be quickly released. But its MRAppMaster is still running to organize data, and to report results to users. Due to the running MRAppMaster, idle jobs cannot get the permission to access memory for processing. Meanwhile, if other concurrently running jobs do not have enough unscheduled map/reduce tasks to consume these M_{idle} (released M_{YC}), the memory utilization will drop. A higher MARP value means more concurrently running jobs, which probably have more unscheduled map/reduce tasks to avoid the memory drops, and vice versa.

The memory drops cause temporarily high M_{idle}, and therefore reduce the average memory utilization—*i.e.* this phenomenon also contributes to performance degradation. Moreover, the frequent and large memory drops can also disturb the users to accurately detect the state of the Hadoop cluster.

5 Memory Consumption Balancing

Based on the previous section, we propose a self-adaptive approach for dynamically adjusting the MARP configuration based on the current state of the cluster.

5.1 Maximizing Jobs Parallelism

The symptom of LoJP—*i.e.* small N_{max}, large M_{idle} leading to decrease the memory utilization— can be detected from the ResourceManager component and fixed by increasing the MARP parameter. However, it should not consequently cause LoJT (cf. Section 4.2). We therefore propose a greedy algorithm to gradually increase the MARP parameter (cf. Algorithm 1). It is a simple heuristics that periodically increments MARP by a floating step (*inc*) until a given threshold (T_{LoJP}) is reached—*i.e.* the overall memory consumption $M_U = M_{AM} + M_{YC}$ falls below the threshold $M_U < T_{LoJP}$. Both, the current M_U and MARP values can be observed from ResourceManager. Once the increment becomes effective, ResourceManager will continue to schedule any pending jobs until the N_{max} limit is reached. A short delay between the increment steps (*delay*) is therefore required to let the cluster settle and observe the effects of the increment.

Algorithm 1. Fixing LoJP by incrementing MARP.

---
procedure LoJP(T_{LoJP}, inc, delay)
   $M_U \leftarrow$ actual memory utilization
  if $M_U < T_{LoJP}$ **then**
     $MARP \leftarrow$ current MARP value
     $MARP \leftarrow MARP +$ inc
     RELOAD($MARP$)
     SLEEP(delay)

5.2 Maximizing the Job Throughput

The LoJT symptom is more difficult to detect since, at the first glance, the Hadoop cluster appears to fully utilize its resource. However, this situation can be also a result of the cluster saturation with too many jobs running in parallel. It therefore requires to better balance the resources allocated to M_{AM} and M_{YC}. Algorithm 2 applies another greedy heuristics to gradually reduce the amount of memory allocated to MRAppMaster by a floating step (*dec*) until we detect that the overall memory utilization (M_U) falls below the maximum memory utilization threshold T_{LoJT}.

To avoid an oscillation between the two strategies, we combine them in a double-threshold (T_{LoJP}, T_{LoJT}, where $T_{LoJP} < T_{LoJT}$) heuristic algorithm that ensures that they work in synergy (cf. Algorithm 3). When memory usage is higher than 0.9, it is enough to prove that LoJP disappears. Meanwhile, an stably over-high memory usage (*e.g.* 0.95) is probably caused by LoJT. The increment and decrement steps are not fixed. Instead, they are computed in each loop iteration based on the difference between the memory utilization and the target threshold. This allows the system to automatically achieve the translation between rapid and fine-gained tuning—*i.e.* if the M_U is near a threshold, the square root will be small, while shall the memory utilization be far from a threshold, the increment or decrement will be large.

Algorithm 2. Fixing LoJT by decrementing MARP.

> **procedure** LoJT(T_{LoJT}, dec, delay)
> $M_U \leftarrow$ actual memory utilization
>   **if** $M_U > T_{LoJT}$ **then**
> $MARP \leftarrow$ current MARP value
> $MARP \leftarrow MARP - \text{dec}$
>   RELOAD($MARP$)
>   SLEEP(delay)

Algorithm 3. Balancing LoJP and LoJT.

> **procedure** BALANCE(delay)
> $M_{compute} \leftarrow$ overall maximum memory
> $T_{LoJP} \leftarrow 0.9 \times M_{compute}$
> $T_{LoJT} \leftarrow 0.95 \times M_{compute}$
>   **loop**
> $M_U \leftarrow$ actual memory utilization
>   **if** $M_U < T_{LoJP}$ **then**
>   LoJP(T_{LoJP}, $\frac{\sqrt{T_{LoJP} - M_U}}{M_{compute}}$, delay)
>   **else if** $M_U > T_{LoJT}$ **then**
>   LoJT(T_{LoJT}, $\frac{\sqrt{M_U - T_{LoJT}}}{M_{compute}}$, delay)

5.3 Handling Drops of Memory Utilization

Drops of memory utilization are caused by the completion of map/reduce tasks that release large blocks of memory. Such memory fluctuation can result in MARP oscillations when the Algorithms 1, 2 and 3 will be constantly scaling up and down the MARP value. To prevent this, we use a Kalman filter to smooth the input—*i.e.* the memory utilization. It helps to stabilize the value and eliminate the noise induced by the memory fluctuation [18]. Concretely, we apply a 1D filter defined as: $M(t + \delta_t) = A \cdot M(t) + N(t)$. where M refers to the state variable—*i.e.* the memory usage—A is a transition matrix and N the noise introduced by the monitoring process.

6   Evaluation

In this section, we evaluate the capability of our self-balancing approach to address the problem of MapReduce job parallelism and throughput. We start with an quick overview of the implementation of the self-balancing algorithm followed by a series of experiments. The evaluation has been done using a cluster of 11 physical hosts deployed on the GRID5000 infrastructure, the same as we used in Sect. 3. We use Hadoop 2.6.0. Additional configuration details and experiment raw values are also available at the paper web companion page.

6.1   Implementation Details

The implemation is based on the feedback control loop that implements the balancing algorithm introduced in the previous section. It follows the classical MAPE (*Monitor-Analyze-Plan-Execute*) decomposition [12].

The control loop is implemented in Java and runs on the control node alongside with YARN. The memory information are collected using the Resource-Manager services. The MARP value is accessed via YARN configuration and is changed by the YARN ResourceManager admin client (`yarn rmadmin` command). For the Kalman filter, we used the jkalman library[2]. It can smooth the memory utilization to avoid unnecessary MARP adjustments. The completion time of one map task is about 10 seconds. It is a reasonable value for *delay* to ensure the capture of memory fluctuation.

6.2   Job Completion Time

We start the evaluation by running the same set of MapReduce benchmark as we did at the beginning in Sect. 3—*i.e.* WORDCOUNT, TERASORT and SORT from the HIBENCH benchmark suite, each with two datasets (30MB and 3GB). Figure 5 shows the mean job completion time of 100 jobs using, the vanilla Hadoop 2.6.0 configuration (MARP = 10%), the *best-effort* statically profiled configuration where the values were obtained from our initial experiments (cf. Fig. 2a), and finally our self-balancing approach (dyn). The values were normalized to the vanilla configuration.

For each of the considered applications and workloads, our self-balancing approach outperforms both other configurations. Often the difference between the statically profiled configuration and our dynamic one is small. This is because the *best-effort* MARP value already provides a highly optimal configuration so the applications cannot execute much faster. The important thing to realize is

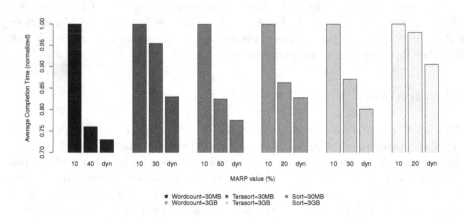

Fig. 5. Performance comparisons of 3 HIBENCH applications and 2 datasets.

---

[2] http://sourceforge.net/projects/jkalman.

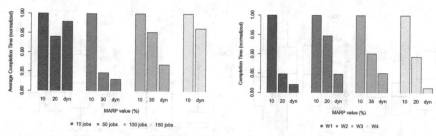

(a) Performance comparisons of Terasort (b) Performance comparisons of 4 SWIM configured with 3GB under 4 workloads. workloads.

Fig. 6. Performance comparisons

that our approach adapts to any application and does not require any profiling effort. It continuously finds a MARP configuration under which the application executes at least as fast as under the *best-effort* configuration.

Next, we evaluate how the approach performs under different workload sizes. Figure 6 shows the completion time of the Terasort with 3 GB input data size benchmark under varying number of concurrently running jobs—*i.e.* 10, 50, 100 and 150. In this case, the self-balancing algorithm outperforms the other configurations in all but the first case of a small number of jobs. The reason is that our solution always starts with the default MARP configuration which is 10 % and converges towards the optimal value (20 % in this case) along the execution. However, the overall completion time of the 10 jobs is too short and the jobs finish before our algorithm converges. Furthermore, the dynamic MARP values are also available at the paper web companion page.

Finally, we evaluate our approach with 4 time-varying workloads generated by SWIM. We use the same workloads as we presented in Sect. 3. The job size distribution varies across the different workloads: each job has only one reduce task and a varying number of map tasks chosen randomly from a given map size set. The actual configuration of the 4 workloads is given in Table 1. Each map task manipulates (reads or writes) one HDFS block; in our case 64MB. The complete input size of the workload is shown in the last column.

Figure 7 compares the per-job completion time distributions for static and dynamic MARP values. For each workloads, one can observe that, compared

Table 1. Configuration of SWIM workloads.

	#Jobs	#Maps	Map size set	Total input size
W1	500	10460	$\{5, 10, 40, 400\}$	335 GB
W2	500	25605	$\{5, 10, 50, 100, 300, 400\}$	819 GB
W3	1000	5331	$\{1, 2, \ldots, 35\}$	342 GB
W4	500	15651	$\{26, 27, \ldots, 50\}$	500 GB

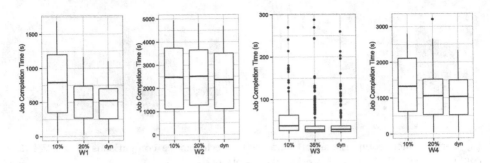

Fig. 7. The comparison of per-job completion time distribution observed for static and dynamic configuration parameters.

to the vanilla configuration, our approach can significantly reduce the job completion times (*e.g.* up to 40 % in W1). It also systematically delivers a better performance than the *best-effort* configurations.

The job-level accelerations can be accumulated and lead to the improvement of workloads-level performance. The overall completion times of the four SWIM workloads is further shown in Fig. 6. Similarly, our approach outperforms all the other configurations.

7   Related Work

Recently, the performance optimization for MapReduce systems has become a main concern in the domain of Big Data. This has resulted in a number of different approaches that aim to improve Hadoop performances.

Auto-Configuration in Hadoop. AROMA [14] is an automatic system that can allocate resources from a heterogeneous cloud and configure Hadoop parameters for the new nodes to achieve the service-quality goals while minimizing incurred cost. But, the VMs in the Cloud require to be provisioned and installed with the required Hadoop system *a priori*. Changlong *et al.* [15] also propose a self-configuration tool named AACT to maintain the performance of an Hadoop cluster. However, the adjustment of configurations for parallel requests are likely to conflict each others. The purpose of Starfish [9] is to enable Hadoop users and applications to get good performance automatically throughout the data life-cycle in analytics. Starfish measures the resource consumption of MapReduce jobs like CPU cycles and I/O throughput of HDFS to estimate average map execution time. However, the prediction may largely differ from the runtime situation. In concurrent case, due to its complex analytic steps, the over-head will also increase significantly. Gunther [16] is a search-based approach for Hadoop MapReduce optimization. It introduces an evolutionary genetic algorithm to identify parameter setting, resulting in near-optimal job performance. But, due to the complexity of the genetic algorithm, identifying an optimal configuration requires Gunther to repeat computing, thus causing performance to degrade.

Many other researches focusing on dynamic configuration like [19,20,23] also exist. Authors design self-adaptive models to optimize system performance, but their compatibility needs to be reconsidered for YARN.

Scalability at Runtime. Ghit *et al.* [5] have investigated a multi-allocation policies design, FAWKES, which can balance the distribution of hosts among several private clusters. In this case, FAWKES is focused on the dynamic redistribution of compute nodes between several clusters while the sum of compute nodes is fixed. However, due to the strict isolation between users, the clusters need to frequently grow or shrink to balance the scales, thereby penalizing each cluster. Chen *et al.* [2] propose a resource-time-cost model, which can display the relationship among execution time, input data, available system resource and the complexity of Reduce function for an ad-hoc MapReduce job. This model is a combination of the white-box [8] and machine-learning approaches. Its main purpose is to identify the relationship between the amount of resources and the job characteristics. Hadoop clusters can benefit from this research to optimize resource provisioning while minimizing the monetary cost. Finally, Berekmeri *et al.* [1] introduce a proportional-integral controller to dynamically enlist and discharge existing compute nodes from live Hadoop cluster in order to meet a given target service-level objectives.

Other Optimization Approaches. Some other studies look beyond Hadoop configuration optimization and scalability to library extensions and runtime improvements. FMEM [24] is a *Fine-grained Memory Estimator for MapReduce jobs* to help both users and the framework to analyze, predict and optimize memory usage. iShuffle [6] decouples shuffle-phase from reduce tasks and converts it into a platform service. It can proactively push map output data to nodes via a novel *shuffle-on-write* operation and flexibly schedule reduce tasks considering workload balance to reduce MapReduce job completion time. Seokyong *et al.* [10] propose an approach to eliminate fruitless data items as early as possible to save I/O throughput and network bandwidth, thus accelerating the MapReduce data processing. Benjamin *et al.* [7] deal with a geo-distributed MapReduce system by a two-pronged approach, which provide high-level insights and corresponding *cross-phase* optimization techniques, to minimize the impact of data geo-localization. Manimal [13] performs static analysis of Hadoop programs and deploys optimizations, including B-tree indexing, to avoid reads of unneeded data. Panacea [17] is a domain-specific compiler which performs source-to-source transformations for jobs to reduce the synchronization overhead of iterative jobs. Twister [4] introduces a new in-memory MapReduce library to improve the performance of iterative jobs. Some researches like [21,25] propose new MapReduce task scheduler to improve resource utilization while observing job completion time goals.

Since our contribution works on the YARN level, we believe that it complements these approaches.

8   Conclusion

Optimizing the performance of Hadoop clusters has become a key concern for big data processing. In YARN, inappropriate memory usage may lead to significant performance degradation. In this paper, we propose a self-adaptation approach based on a closed feedback control loop that automatically balances the memory utilization between YARN MapReduce processes. We have shown that it outperforms the default Hadoop configuration as well as the *best-effort* statically profiled ones. While in this paper we focus on MapReduce, our approach works on YARN level and therefore we plan to look for other applications based on YARN. For the further work, CPU management of YARN will be considered as a new part of this research. Furthermore, we look forward to explore the potential of this research on multi-queues basis, and also focus on HDFS I/O throughput to complement our approach with a support for I/O intensive jobs.

Acknowledgments. This work is partially supported by the Datalyse project www. datalyse.fr. Experiments presented in this paper were carried out using the Grid'5000 testbed, supported by a scientific interest group hosted by Inria and including CNRS, RENATER and several Universities as well as other organizations (see https://www. grid5000.fr).

References

1. Berekmeri, M., Serrano, D., Bouchenak, S., Marchand, N., Robu, B.: A control approach for performance of big data systems. In: IFAC World Congress (2014)
2. Chen, K., Powers, J., Guo, S., Tian, F.: CRESP: towards optimal resource provisioning for MapReduce computing in public clouds. IEEE Trans. Parallel Distrib. Syst. **25**, 1403–1412 (2014)
3. Chen, Y., Ganapathi, A., Griffith, R., Katz, R.H.: The case for evaluating MapReduce performance using workload suites. In: IEEE/ACM MASCOTS (2011)
4. Ekanayake, J., Li, H., Zhang, B., Gunarathne, T., Bae, S.H., Qiu, J., Fox, G.: Twister: a runtime for iterative MapReduce. In: HPDC (2010)
5. Ghit, B., Yigitbasi, N., Iosup, A., Epema, D.H.J.: Balanced resource allocations across multiple dynamic MapReduce clusters. In: ACM SIGMETRICS (2014)
6. Guo, Y., Rao, J., Zhou, X.: iShuffle: Improving hadoop performance with shuffle-on-write. In: Proceedings of the 10th International Conference on Autonomic Computing (ICAC 2013) (2013)
7. Heintz, B., Chandra, A., Sitaraman, R., Weissman, J.: End-to-end optimization for geo-distributed MapReduce. IEEE Trans. Cloud Comput. **PP**(99), 1–14 (2014)
8. Herodotou, H., Babu, S.: Profiling, what-if analysis, and cost-based optimization of MapReduce programs. PVLDB **4**(11), 1111–1122 (2011)
9. Herodotou, H., Lim, H., Luo, G., Borisov, N.: Starfish: a self-tuning system for big data analytics. In: Conference on Innovative Data Systems Research (2011)
10. Hong, S., Ravindra, P., Anyanwu, K.: Adaptive information passing for early state pruning in MapReduce data processing workflows. In: Proceedings of the 10th International Conference on Autonomic Computing (ICAC 2013) (2013)

11. Huang, S., Huang, J., Dai, J., Xie, T., Huang, B.: The HiBench benchmark suite: characterization of the MapReduce-based data analysis. In: Proceedings of the 26th International Conference on Data Engineering (ICDE)
12. IBM: An Architectural Blueprint for Autonomic Computing, 4 edition. Technical report, IBM (2006)
13. Jahani, E., Cafarella, M.J., Ré, C.: Automatic optimization for MapReduce programs. Proc. VLDB Endow. **4**, 385–396 (2011)
14. Lama, P., Zhou, X.: AROMA: automated resource allocation and configuration of mapreduce environment in the cloud. In: ICAC (2012)
15. Li, C., Zhuang, H., Lu, K., Sun, M., Zhou, J., Dai, D., Zhou, X.: An Adaptive auto-configuration tool for hadoop. In: ICECCS (2014)
16. Liao, G., Datta, K., Willke, T.L.: Gunther: search-based auto-tuning of MapReduce. In: Wolf, F., Mohr, B., an Mey, D. (eds.) Euro-Par 2013. LNCS, vol. 8097, pp. 406–419. Springer, Heidelberg (2013)
17. Liu, J., Ravi, N., Chakradhar, S., Kandemir, M.: Panacea: towards holistic optimization of MapReduce applications. In: CGO (2012)
18. Nzekwa, R., Rouvoy, R., Seinturier, L.: A flexible context stabilization approach for self-adaptive application. In: Proceedings of the 8th Annual IEEE International Conference on Pervasive Computing and Communications (PerCom). IEEE (2010)
19. Padala, P., Hou, K., Shin, K.G., Zhu, X., Uysal, M., Wang, Z., Singhal, S., Merchant, A.: Automated control of multiple virtualized resources. In: Proceedings of the 2009 EuroSys (2009)
20. Padala, P., Shin, K.G., Zhu, X., Uysal, M., Wang, Z., Singhal, S., Merchant, A., Salem, K.: Adaptive control of virtualized resources in utility computing environments. In: Proceedings of the 2007 EuroSys (2007)
21. Polo, J., Becerra, Y., Carrera, D., Torres, J., Ayguade, E., Steinder, M.: Adaptive MapReduce scheduling in shared environments. In:14th IEEE/ACM International Symposium on Cluster, Cloud and Grid Computing, pp. 61–70 (2014)
22. Ren, K., Gibson, G., Kwon, Y., Balazinska, M., Howe, B.: Hadoop's adolescence: a comparative workloads analysis from three research clusters. In: SC Companion on High Performance Computing, Networking Storage and Analysis (2012)
23. Wang, Y., Wang, X., Chen, M., Zhu, X.: Power-efficient response time guarantees for virtualized enterprise servers. In: Real-Time Systems Symposium (2008)
24. Xu, L., Liu, J., Wei, J.: FMEM: a fine-grained memory estimator for MapReduce jobs. In: Proceedings of the 10th International Conference on Autonomic Computing (2013)
25. Zhang, W., Rajasekaran, S., Wood, T., Zhu, M.: MIMP: deadline and interference aware scheduling of hadoop virtual machines. In: IEEE/ACM International Symposium on Cluster, Cloud and Grid Computing, May 2014

Resource Usage Prediction in Distributed Key-Value Datastores

Francisco Cruz(✉), Francisco Maia, Miguel Matos, Rui Oliveira, João Paulo,
José Pereira, and Ricardo Vilaça

INESCTEC and Minho University, Braga, Portugal
{fmcruz,fmaia,miguelmatos,rco,jtpaulo,jop,rmvilaca}@di.uminho.pt

Abstract. In order to attain the promises of the Cloud Computing paradigm, systems need to be able to transparently adapt to environment changes. Such behavior benefits from the ability to predict those changes in order to handle them seamlessly. In this paper, we present a mechanism to accurately predict the resource usage of distributed key-value datastores. Our mechanism requires offline training but, in contrast with other approaches, it is sufficient to run it only once per hardware configuration and subsequently use it for online prediction of database performance under any circumstance. The mechanism accurately estimates the database resource usage for any request distribution with an average accuracy of 94 %, only by knowing two parameters: (i) cache hit ratio; and (ii) incoming throughput. Both input values can be observed in real time or synthesized for request allocation decisions. This novel approach is sufficiently simple and generic, while simultaneously being suitable for other practical applications.

1 Introduction

The ability to predict how a system will behave is critical in Cloud Computing systems. Accurate prediction would allow administrators to make better informed decisions on resource allocation, systems configuration or even the technology to use. Currently, this typically requires extensive testing while still lacking the desirable accuracy levels. This is particularly true for massive scale distributed key-value datastores (often named NoSQL databases), Notably, their highly desirable performance, scalability and availability properties cannot be achieved without careful resource allocation and judicious data placement, which requires extensive testing.

In this paper we demonstrate that, for distributed key-value datastores, it is possible to achieve accurate performance prediction, in real-world scenarios, resorting to only a small fraction of the systems resources. NoSQL datastores make heavy use of buffer caching, specially to improve the performance of read requests. In this work we show that the success of such caching layer is directly related to the datastore's resource consumption and we leverage such relation for resource prediction purposes. In fact, it is known that, for a given throughput, the

© IFIP International Federation for Information Processing 2016
Published by Springer International Publishing Switzerland 2016. All Rights Reserved
M. Jelasity and E. Kalyvianaki (Eds.): DAIS 2016, LNCS 9687, pp. 144–159, 2016.
DOI: 10.1007/978-3-319-39577-7_12

higher the cache hit ratio, the lower the resource usage of the NoSQL datastore. This is true since each cache hit avoids resource consumption stemming from lower layer access. Moreover, contrary to relational databases, which due to their inherent complexity require more elaborate models, in this work we show that for distributed key-value datastores this correlation is actually enough to accurately predict resource usage of any workload. Such accurate prediction of resource usage then allows system optimization, preparation, and simulation under different conditions. This is particularly important if we aim to effectively deploy NoSQL data stores in the pay-as-you-go model, which is common in the Cloud Computing paradigm.

Contributions. (a) We provide a mechanism to build a read operation resource usage model and a write operation resource usage model. Both models are hardware dependent, meaning they need to be rebuilt when the hardware changes, but they are generated only once per hardware configuration and can then be used to predict the resource usage for any workload. (b) Leveraging these models, we are able to predict a NoSQL datastore resource usage, only by knowing two parameters: (i) the cache hit ratio and (ii) the incoming throughput. From our experiments using HBase, we accurately predict resource usage for any request distribution and any throughput of read-only and a mix of read and update operations. We achieve an average prediction accuracy of 94 %.

Roadmap. The rest of this paper is organized as follows. We begin by providing some background about caching mechanisms and NoSQL datatores in Sect. 2. Section 3 presents evidence on the correlation between the cache hit ratio of NoSQL datastores and resource usage. Section 4 focuses on the prediction of resource usage for read-only operations while Sect. 5 focuses on write operations. We validate our mechanism using HBase and mixed (read/write) workloads in Sect. 6, present related work in Sect. 7 and conclude with Sect. 8.

2   Background

Caching mechanisms. Databases make use of buffer caching to improve their read performance. By keeping most frequently accessed data in fast access structures (either implemented by software or hardware) performance can be significantly improved. As a result, the flow of a read request usually takes the following path: (i) the client issues a request to read some tuple; (ii) the database verifies if the requested tuple is in cache; (iiia) if it does the tuple is returned to the client, (iiib) otherwise the database tries to fetch the tuple from secondary memory. When using caching one of the main goals is to try to maximize the percentage of requests that are served from cache, also known as the cache hit ratio. A high hit cache rate means that a good number of requests are being served exclusively by the cache, thus avoiding higher CPU and I/O costs from using less efficient storage mediums. When the data size exceeds the cache size, eventually, some data in the cache needs to be removed to give room to more frequently accessed data. This is handled by cache replacement algorithms [23].

There are several cache replacement algorithms, however one of the most widely used algorithms is the Least Recently Used (LRU) algorithm [25]. Under this replacement algorithm when the cache is full, the algorithm discards data that was least recently used. This algorithm is the one typically used by distributed key-value datastores [12,18].

Distributed key-value datastores. Distributed key-value datastores run in a distributed setting with tenths to hundreds of nodes, usually composed of commodity hardware. The application data is partitioned and these partitions are assigned to the available nodes according to a data placement strategy. Contrasting with relational database management systems (RDBMS), these datastores only provide a simple key-value interface to manipulate data by means of put, get, delete, and scan operations and they do not offer strong consistency criteria. Complex operations like joining and aggregation are not present and data is denormalized. Considering these characteristics, the success of caching mechanisms is key for performance. In this paper, we focus on HBase which is one of the most successful and widely used key-value datastores [12]. Inspired by BigTable [4], HBase's data model implements a variant of the entity-attribute-value (EAV) model and can be thought of as a multi-dimensional sorted map. This map is called *HTable* and is indexed by the row key, the column name and a timestamp. HBase follows a hierarchical architecture where there is a Master node and there is one or more slave nodes called *Regionservers*. The row range of a *HTable* is horizontally partitioned into *Regions* and distributed over different nodes. Each *Region* is stored as an append-only file in the Hadoop Distributed File System (HDFS) [3], whose instances are called *DataNodes*. Usually, *RegionServers* are co-located with *DataNodes* to promote the locality of the data being served by the *RegionServer*. HBase has a *block cache* implementing the LRU replacement algorithm. Several key-values are grouped into blocks of configurable size and these blocks are the ones used in the cache mechanism. The block size within the *block cache* is a parameter but defaults to 64 KB.

3   Interdependence of Resource Usage and Cache Hit Ratio

Let us consider a server usage metric related to the CPU waiting time on I/O operations (I/O_{wait}), the time spent on user space (CPU_{user}) and the time spent on kernel space (CPU_{system}) in the form: $Server_{usage} = I/O_{wait} + CPU_{user} + CPU_{system}$. In the following we show the cache hit ratio is effectively related to server usage. To this end, we set up three experiments using a HBase deployment and YCSB [6] as the workload generator. These experiments cover a wide spectrum of possible behaviors. With these we are able to show a clear and direct relationship between the cache hit ratio and server usage in NoSQL systems, which lays the foundation for the rest of the paper.

Experimental setting: In all experiments, one node acts as master for both HBase and HDFS, and it also holds a Zookeeper [14] instance running in standalone mode, which is required by HBase. Our HBase cluster was composed of 1

RegionServer, configured with a heap of 4 GB, and 1 *DataNode*. HBase's LRU *block cache* was configured to use 55 % of the heap size, which HBase translates into roughly 2.15 GB. The *RegionServer* was co-located with the *DataNode*. The YCSB workload generator ran in a separate node and was configured with a *readProportion* of 100 % (read-only), and with a fixed throughput of 2000 operations per second with 75 client threads. All experiments were set to run for 30 min with 150 s of ramp up time and the results are the computed average of 5 individual runs. The server usage was logged every second in the *RegionServer/-DataNode* machine using the UNIX *top* command. The *top* command gives us the CPU_{idle} metric that is converted to our $Server_{usage}$ metric in the form: $Server_{usage} = 100\% - CPU_{idle}$. By the end of each experiment, we gathered the *RegionServer*'s achieved cache hit ratio. All nodes used for these experiments have an Intel i3 CPU at 3.1 GHz, 8 GB of main memory, a 7200 RPM SATA disk, and are interconnected by a switched Gigabit network.

First Experiment: In this first experiment, a single *region* was populated using the YCSB generator with 4,000,000 records (4.3 GB). This means that the *region* cannot be fitted entirely into the *block cache*: about 1.1 millions records (1.21 GB) remain on secondary memory and must be brought into main memory when requested. There were four different scenarios each with a differently configured request popularity:

1. A *uniform* popularity distribution, that is all records have equal probability of being requested (the case where the cache hit ratio is minimum);
2. A *hotspot* popularity distribution, where 50 % of the requests access a subset of keys that account for 30 % of the key space;
3. A *zipf scrambled* popularity distribution, highly skewed, but because it is scrambled it means the most popular keys are spread across the key space;
4. A *zipf clustered* popularity distribution, highly skewed, and clustered, meaning the most popular keys are contiguous, which makes them fall in the same cache block.

The results for this experiment are depicted in Table 1. As expected, the *uniform* request popularity is the one that achieves the lower cache hit ratio ($p_{hit} = 49\%$), and thus consumes more server resources (58.35 %) while the *zipf clustered* request popularity has the higher cache hit ratio (93 %). This is true because popular keys are found in the same block, which is maintained in memory avoiding cache misses.

Second experiment: We set up a second experiment, to demonstrate that the behavior observed in the first experiment is independent of request popularities. This experiment is identical to the first one except for the *region* size, which has now 2,000,000 records (2.14 GB). As a result the *region* fits entirely into the *block cache*, thus the expected cache hit ratio is 100 %. Table 2 depicts the results. As all data is served only by the *block cache*, the different request popularities are, as expected, irrelevant to server resource consumption and all distributions use roughly the same resources.

Table 1. Average $Server_{usage}$ and cache hit ratio (p_{hit}) with a *region* larger than the *block cache.*

Distribution	p_{hit}	Average $Server_{usage}$	#Records
Uniform	49 %	58.35 %	4,000,000
Hotspot	56 %	46.19 %	4,000,000
Zipf Scrambled	68 %	35.91 %	4,000,000
Zipf Clustered	93 %	19.28 %	4,000,000

Table 2. Average $Server_{usage}$ and cache hit ratio (p_{hit}) with a *region* that fits in *block cache.*

Distribution	p_{hit}	Average $Server_{usage}$	#Records
Uniform	100 %	12.29 %	2,000,000
Hotspot	100 %	12.14 %	2,000,000
Zipf Scrambled	100 %	12.92 %	2,000,000
Zipf Clustered	100 %	12.89 %	2,000,000

Third experiment: In this experiment we show that two different distributions, with different data sizes but with the same cache hit ratio, will have the same server resources consumption if subject to the same fixed throughput. We used a similar setting to the first experiment's but changed the number of records of the *uniform* distribution to 2,141,881(2.3 GB) so its cache hit ratio could also be 93 %. The throughput is again fixed at 2000 operations per second. Table 3 depicts the results that support our claim that, for a given throughput, an identical cache hit ratio, regardless of the data size and the distribution results in the same resource consumption.

Correlation between server usage and cache hit ratio: A correlation test using the *Fisher's z transformation* [11] with the data from the previous experiments, shows that in fact there is a negative correlation for *p-value* < 0.001, making it statistically significant. Based on these results, we argue that it is possible to estimate the server usage given the incoming throughput and the cache hit ratio and, in the following sections, we show how this can be done.

Table 3. Average $Server_{usage}$ and cache hit ratio (p_{hit}) results for 2 distributions with different sizes, but with same cache hit ratio.

Distribution	p_{hit}	Average $Server_{usage}$	#Records
Zipf Clustered	93 %	19.28 %	4,000,000
Uniform	93 %	19.76 %	2,141,881

4   Estimating Resource Usage of Read Operations

Previous section demonstrated that there is an intrinsic relation between resource usage and cache hit ratio. The cache hit ratio reflects not only the data size, but also the underlying distribution of requests which, in combination with an incoming throughput, corresponds to a given server usage. Furthermore, for a fixed throughput this relation is univocal: for some throughput if two distinct workloads consume the same amount of resources, then they must have the same cache hit ratio. In this section, we show how the server usage of any workload can be estimated simply by knowing its cache hit ratio and incoming throughput. We build on the aforementioned properties to build a tridimensional model, that models the server usage for a NoSQL datastore, when the cache hit ratio and the throughput vary. The objective is to build a model that, for a given hardware configuration, a given hit cache ratio and certain request throughput of an HBase node, allows to predict the resource consumption of such node. To achieve this we require an initial training step, which is hardware dependent. Consequently, each generated model is only valid for a single hardware configuration but is required to be generated only once. Once we have the model we are able to predict HBase node resource usage for any given workload. As shown previously, request distribution is irrelevant in terms of the relationship between hit cache ratio and resource consumption. Taking advantage of this observation we always consider the uniform distribution in the generation of the prediction models. In fact, such model will still be valid if, on runtime, a different request distribution is observed.

In order to generate the model, our approach is to judiciously choose a number of representative combinations of cache hit ratio and throughput, test them against the desired hardware configuration and then, by using linear interpolation between the different server usage levels measured, we are able to build a tridimensional model that correlates data size, with throughput and expected server usage. Notably, with this approach we are able to achieve very high levels of accuracy. At this point, it is important to note that, for a generic workload generator, it is not possible to define the desired cache hit ratio. Instead we can only set the data size and desired throughput. However, we can take advantage of a simple approach proposed by *Che et al.* [5] that provides an estimation without error of the cache hit ratio for the uniform distribution. This way, we can represent the cache hit ratio by its correspondent data size when building the model. Therefore, in the remainder of this section we will mention data sizes implicitly mentioning their correspondent cache hit ratios. Another reason for choosing the uniform distribution is because it allows to reduce the overall training time since it represents the worst case for LRU caches (lowest possible hit ratio for a given data size), thereby the time it takes to populate the data in the NoSQL database is smaller.

Regarding the process of choosing the representative measures to take, let's begin by looking at an illustrative example. Figure 1 shows the behavior of incoming throughput when data sizes increase for a fixed server usage percentage. Note that, if the data size is smaller than the cache size then only the throughput

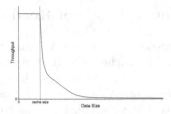

Fig. 1. Typical relation between cache size and throughput for a fixed $Server_{usage}$.

impacts server usage. In this case, the cache hit ratio is always 100 % and the throughput constant for all possible data sizes between 0 and *cache size*. For larger data sizes, the cache hit ratio drops and cache swapping begins, which in turn means that in order for the server usage to stay the same the throughput must decrease. As a result, this is a boundary point (where *data size* equals to the *cache size*). This observation allows us to reduce the number of points to calculate for that section as we just need to build the model from that point onwards. Then, other observations help us choosing the points to measure. For data sizes slightly larger than the boundary point, there is a big drop on throughput in order to resource usage to remain the same. This drop can be more or less abrupt depending on the speed of the secondary memory. In order to capture this behavior in the model we need to increase the number of tested combinations of pairs data size and throughput immediately after the boundary point. Conversely, when the data size is largely increased we can be confident of a long and flat tail, thus not requiring many training points to achieve high accuracy.

The uniform distribution server usage model is automatically generated resorting to a developed Python script and using YCSB as the workload generator[1]. Generally, this script has 2 main parameters: (i) a list of cache hit ratios and (ii) a list of targeted server usage levels. Hit cache ratios are, as explained earlier, converted to data sizes using the Che's approximation. Then, resorting to a binary search, the script tries to find the necessary throughput of read operations to achieve each specific percentage of server usage for each data size defined as input. Fixing the server usage level and allowing the throughput to be experimentally calculated via the script, allows us to have a representative number of server usage levels without having to test multiple cache hit ratio and throughput combinations in order to have a usable model. When a sufficient number of points for a specific server usage level are found and we resort to interpolation between those points. Namely, using the monotonic spline interpolation of the R project[2] embedded into the Python script. This process is repeated for each of the targeted server usage levels. This list does not comprehend all of the possible values between 0 and 100 %. Instead, from our experience we noted that a few of them is sufficient (usually 5 equally spaced). Furthermore, by again using linear interpolation between the different server usage levels we achieve very accurate

---

[1] All the scripts used in this work are openly available at github.com/fmcruz/suhcr/.
[2] http://www.r-project.org.

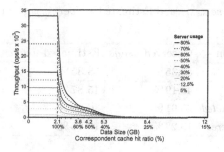

Fig. 2. Instantiation of the server model for read operations based on a uniform distribution.

results, and ultimately build a tridimensional model that correlates data size, with throughput and expected server usage.

Model Instantiation in Our Cluster. We ran the automatic server model generator in our cluster using the same setting as the experiments of Sect. 3. The generated server model is as depicted in Fig. 2. There were defined 10 different cache hit ratios: 100 %, 95 %, 90 %, 80 %, 70 %, 60 %, 50 %, 40 %, 25 %, and 15 %. These cache hit ratios were then transformed in their data size equivalents to be used as input in the model generator. The first point is the boundary point corresponding to 2,000,000 of YCSB records. As previously stated, for data sizes slightly larger than the *cache size* we need to increase the density of points tested to ensure the model is more accurate. Thus, the next point is only a 5 % decrease, and the subsequent 6 points are decreases of 10 % in the cache hit ratio. On the other hand, predicting a flat long tail from that point on, we just defined 2 points much more apart from each other, 25 % and 15 % of cache hit ratio, corresponding to 8,000,000 and 12,000,000 records.

In Fig. 2 the solid lines correspond to the 5 targeted levels of server usage, namely 80 %, 60 %, 40 %, 20 % and 5 %. It is general practice in frameworks for automated elasticity of NoSQL datastores [17] that the rule governing the addition of new nodes indicate 80 % as the maximum usable CPU before a new node is needed in the cluster. This is an empirical higher bound on usable CPU to accommodate operating systems processes, account for possible load spikes and compactions. Therefore, the highest defined level was 80 %. When eventually the generator has finished searching for the throughput needed to reach the targeted levels of server usage for the various data sizes, it then interpolates the data that resulted in the represented continuous curves. Finally, we just need to do a final and linear interpolation between these curves. The curves that correspond to the linear interpolation are represented by dotted lines for the server usage levels of 70 %, 50 %, 30 % and 12.5 %, which are example levels.

Model Accuracy. Revisiting the first experiment of Sect. 3, we can now use the generated model to estimate the server usage for the different distributions.

Table 4. Observed $server_{usage}$ and Estimated $server_{usage}$ results under four different distributions.

Distribution	Observed *usage*	Estimated *usage*	Accuracy
Uniform	58.35 %	58.35 %	100 %
Hotspot	46.19 %	45.87 %	99.31 %
Zipf Scrambled	35.91 %	36.29 %	98.94 %
Zipf Clustered	19.28 %	19.15 %	99.33 %

The results are depicted in Table 4. As can be seen, the estimated server usage is almost the same as the observed average server usage, despite all four different distributions with very different cache hit rates. It should be noted that, as expected, the approach predicts the server usage of the uniform distribution with accuracy of 100 % due to the similarity between the input usage levels of the model and the ones used in the test. We can also use the generated model to accurately estimate the server usage when the incoming throughput varies. In that regard, we set up two different experiments using the exact same setting as in the experiments of Sect. 3. For every data point there were 3 independent runs, and the results presented are the computed average. In the first experiment, we populated the HBase instance with 4,000,000 records (4.3 GB). The YCSB's client was configured to use the *zipf clustered* distribution with 100 % read operations, and for a fixed throughput ranging from 250 ops/s to 10,000 ops/s. We also wanted to validate what happens when using a data size not used in the model generator. As a result, we populated the HBase cluster with 3,000,000 records (3.15 GB), and this time using the *zipf scrambled* distribution, which yields a much lower cache hit ratio (78.8 %). As a result, the configured read throughput ranged from 250 ops/s to 7,000 ops/s. The results for each experiment are depicted in Fig. 3(a) and in Fig. 3(b). They show the estimated server usage compared to the observed one. The estimated results are drawn from our approach using the generated model for read operations, and observing the cache hit ratio as provided by HBase exported metrics. As expected, the estimated server usage in both experiments is very similar to the observed counterpart.

Discussion. The approach described in this section allows to accurately estimate the server usage resorting to an offline trained model based on the uniform distribution. Using the cache hit ratio and the incoming throughput as the only parameters that affect resource utilization may appear oversimplifying. Specially, when taking account related approaches to usage prediction in RDBMS. However, key-value datastores are fundamentally different from relational databases. In order to attain high scalability, high throughput and high availability, these datastores offer a simple key-value interface based on put and get operations without providing multi record atomic operations nor complex operations like joins and aggregations. On the other hand, RDBMS must cope with a large

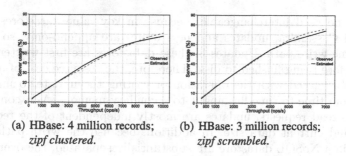

(a) HBase: 4 million records;   (b) HBase: 3 million records;
    zipf clustered.   *zipf scrambled.*

Fig. 3. Experiments for read-only operations.

number of concurrent and lock-prone ACID transactions and need different more complex models for resources, such as CPU, RAM, disk I/O and database locks. These differences allow our simple but effective technique to work. The empirical intuition of why other parameters, such as the I/O costs, do not need to be considered separately is because they are already concealed in the training model. Taking a closer look into the behavior of each distribution in the first experiment, and decomposing the overall throughput into operations hitting and missing the cache, we have:

- *Uniform* - 49 % of cache hit ratio; thus 980 ops/s are cache hits, the remaining 1020 ops/s miss the *block cache*;
- *Hotspot* - 56 % of cache hit ratio; thus 1120 ops/s are cache hits, the remaining 880 ops/s miss the *block cache*;
- *Zipf Scrambled* - 68 % of cache hit ratio; thus 1360 ops/s are cache hits, the remaining 640 ops/s miss the *block cache*;
- *Zipf Clustered* - 93 % of cache hit ratio; thus 1860 ops/s are cache hits, the remaining 140 ops/s miss the *block cache*.

By looking at the average resource usage for each distribution, it is obvious that the cost of a cache miss is greater than the cost of accessing the *block cache*. This implies that the server usage for read operations can be decomposed as the sum of two costs: $Usage_{read} = Usage_{hit} + Usage_{miss}$. The $Usage_{hit}$ is the cost of only accessing the cache, while the $Usage_{miss}$ represents the cost of a miss in the cache. It covers not only the cost of bringing a block into the cache (either from main memory or disk), but also the cost of discarding the least recently used data to make room for the new data block. Thus, when two workloads have identical cache hit ratios and identical incoming throughputs, it means that both workloads have the same number of operations hitting the cache and the same number of operations missing the cache. As a result, once two workloads exhibit the same $Usage_{hit}$ and $Usage_{miss}$, ultimately exhibit the same server usage.

5   Estimating the Resource Usage of Update Operations

Although workloads are generally dominated by reads, most applications also have updates. We apply a similar approach to update operations. Updates and writes can be used interchangeable, because in key-value datastores, such as HBase and Cassandra, updates and new writes are append-only, so they follow the same write path. Updates in these datastores are first written to main memory before being flushed to disk. Therefore, the resource cost of an update is essentially related with the operation of writing the update to main memory and, from time to time flushing it to secondary memory. As a consequence, contrary to read requests, updates are mostly independent of the request distribution and current data size. In addition, because the write path and the read path in a NoSQL datastore are substantially separated, the overall server usage can be defined as the sum of the usage related with read operations and the usage related with update operations: $ServerUsage_{overall} = ServerUsage_{read} + ServerUsage_{update}$. As updates are independent of the request distribution and the data size, creating a model to predict the server usage of update operations is simpler than the read model counterpart. The only variable affecting the server utilization is, thus the write throughput.

Analogous to the model generator for read operations, we used a Python developed script to generate the server usage model for update operations. It also uses YCSB as the workload generator, but this time configured for updates. As the update model only depends on the throughput, the script has only one main parameter: a list of targeted update throughput points to test. For every element of targeted update throughput there are 3 independent runs, and the server utilization is logged every second in the remote machine where the datastore node is running. When all the defined points are finished, we also resort to interpolation between those points. Like the server model of read operations, the automatic server model generator was used on our own cluster, using the exact same setting. The generated server model for updates is depicted in Fig. 4. There were defined 28 different targeted update throughputs from 5 updates per second to 10,000 updates per second. For increased accuracy, the first 10 targeted throughputs fall within the interval of 5 to 1000 updates per second. From that point on, there were 500 increments until 10,000 updates per second, which is the point where the server usage reaches 80 %. As can be seen the server utilization for update operations grows linearly with the increased throughput.

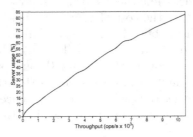

Fig. 4. Instantiation of the model for update operations.

6   Resource Estimation for Read-Write Workloads

Along this section we validate our approach using HBase showing that we can accurately predict resource consumption for any given workload even if there is a mix between read and update operations. In the experiments we used the exact same setting as in the experiments of Sect. 3. For every data point there were 3 independent runs, and the results presented are the computed average. By using both the read and the update model, we are able to estimate the server usage for read operations and update operations independently. However, as described in Sect. 5 the write path and the read path are mostly separated, thus we are able to estimate the overall server usage just by adding both estimations. In order to validate this assumption, we set up an experiment configured with different read and update mixes, namely: 90 % read and 10 % update; 80 % read and 20 % update; 50 % read and 50 % update; 20 % read and 80 % update; 10 % read and 90 % update. The *region* was populated with 4,000,000 records (4.3 GB) and the requests followed the uniform distribution with a fixed throughput of 118 ops/s, 562 ops/s, 1250 ops/s, 1958 ops/s and 2921 ops/s. These tested throughputs correspond to 5 %, 20 %, 40 %, 60 % and 80 % server usage levels, as generated by the server model for the uniform distribution. In Fig. 5 is depicted the results for this experiment. It shows that our approach is valid and it accurately predicts the server usage even when there are read and update operations simultaneously. However, as seen in Fig. 5(c) and (d) for the higher values of throughput the observed server usage is higher than the estimated one. These differences can be explained by compactions occurring during the test period that disrupt the readers of records stored on disk. Figure 6 shows the server usage along the entire 30 min run for the 20 % read and 80 % update mix (Fig. 5(d)) for the 2912 ops/s throughput. Until the compaction process starts (at 1277 s) the observed server

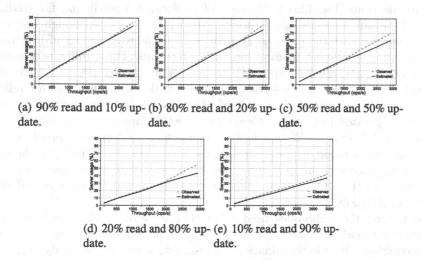

(a) 90% read and 10% up-   (b) 80% read and 20% up-   (c) 50% read and 50% update.   date.   date.

(d) 20% read and 80% up-   (e) 10% read and 90% update.   date.

Fig. 5. Read and update operations mix experiments in HBase.

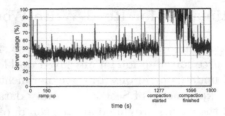

Fig. 6. Observed server usage along a 30 min run for the 20 % read and 80 % update mix for 2912 ops/s throughput.

usage average is the same as the estimated one (44 %). Then, the compaction process greatly increases server usage to levels near 100 %. When compaction ends regular behavior is resumed. This process greatly impacts the overall server usage average, but even at this point our estimated server usage is only off by 12 %, which is the greatest difference observed. It is worth noting, however, that while more powerful hardware and particularly SSDs would attenuate the problem and help improve the estimation, in [2] it is proposed to offload compactions to a dedicated compaction server to prevent the significantly degraded read performance during compactions.

7   Related Work

A significative group of approaches aims at predicting the resource usage of generic systems such as, virtual machines, thus requiring complex models that must take into account many parameters [26,27]. As mentioned in the literature, in order to obtain accurate models with fewer variables, it is key to focus on specific applications [15]. This is the case of performance prediction for RDBMS focused on online transaction processing (OLTP) [21,22]. Although our work has similarities with the previous approaches, such as resorting to off-line model training, it has different assumptions from RDBMS. These differences significantly change the required approach to accurately predict the performance of key-value datastores. A single resource model is also not achievable for related work that predicts the performance of SQL queries by using models for each database operator (e.g., Sort, Merge Join), which are not present in NoSQL datastores [19]. It is worth mentioning the work on performance prediction for database consolidation, where several database instances are running in the same server and processing different types of workloads and, in many cases, even distinct schemas [1,8]. Once again, this work needs to deal with the added complexity of RDBMS.

Regarding the techniques used to predict systems' performance, machine learning and analytical modeling are the most commonly used [20]. These can be used exclusively or in combination, by resorting to time-series analysis [13,16], regression models [9,28], and clustering [24]. These approaches require lengthy training phases to estimate accurately different workload distributions. It is however possible to reduce the duration of this initial phase by using a less accurate model and then refine it, in runtime, with other machine learning algorithms [10]. Because we target a specific type of system, we are able to reduce our model to only two parameters, the cache hit ratio and incoming throughput. Our approach achieves high accuracy without needing runtime improvements for the model. To the best of our knowledge our approach is the only work that can accurately predict the performance of a NoSQL datastore with a single model. Even if our solution needs offline training, it does not require system traces or runtime mechanisms to improve the precision of the estimation.

8 Conclusion

Along this paper we focused on a mechanism for distributed key-value datastores resource usage prediction. Our mechanism is able to accurately predict the resource utilization for every data size, request distribution and throughput combination. In contrast with previous approaches on prediction systems for cloud environments, we take advantage of focusing on a specific cloud component to improve prediction accuracy and its applicability. In particular, we observed that the majority of the NoSQL systems make use of buffer caching mechanisms to improve performance. Moreover, the effectiveness of such mechanisms is directly related with the performance and, as a consequence, to the resource utilization of the database. This effectiveness can be measured in terms of the hit ratio that the caching mechanism exhibits. The higher the cache hit ratio the more effective the cache mechanism is, and thus more efficient is the database. In this work, we show that a NoSQL workload can be characterized by the incoming throughput and by its cache hit ratio, as the latter is a reflection of the data size and of the distribution of requests. From such observation, we can use the cache hit ratio and the throughput to build a server usage model, that can then be used to predict the resource utilization of any workload only by knowing those two parameters. In our experiments the average prediction accuracy achieved is 94 % with a standard deviation of 5.6. Notably, our approach can be effectively used for several practical applications. Examples are automated online load balancing systems, automated resource allocation and even cost-benefit assessment of hardware upgrades to mention a few. In effect, we are currently implementing this mechanism in an automated elasticity tool (MET [7]) aiming at improving its load balancing capabilities.

Acknowledgment. This work is part-funded by: ERDF - European Regional Development Fund through the Operational Programme for Competitiveness and Internationalization - COMPETE 2020 Programme, and by National Funds through the FCT - Fundação para a Ciência e a Tecnologia (Portuguese Foundation for Science and Technology) within project POCI-01-0145-FEDER-006961; and project LeanBigData (FP7-619606).

References

1. Ahmad, M., Bowman, I.T.: Predicting system performance for multi-tenant database workloads. In: Proceedings of the Fourth International Workshop on Testing Database Systems, DBTest 2011, pp. 6:1–6:6 (2011)
2. Ahmad, M.Y., Kemme, B.: Compaction management in distributed key-value datastores. Proc. VLDB Endow. 8(8), 850–861 (2015)
3. Apache. Hadoop (2015). http://hadoop.apache.org/
4. Chang, F., Dean, J., Ghemawat, S., Hsieh, W.C., Wallach, D.A., Burrows, M., Chandra, T., Fikes, A., Gruber, R.E.: Bigtable: a distributed storage system for structured data. In: OSDI (2006)
5. Che, H., Tung, Y., Wang, Z.: Hierarchical web caching systems: modeling, design and experimental results. IEEE J. Sel. Areas Commun. 20, 1305–1314 (2002)
6. Cooper, B.F., Silberstein, A., Tam, E., Ramakrishnan, R., Sears, R.: Benchmarking cloud serving systems with YCSB. In: SoCC (2010)
7. Cruz, F., Maia, F., Matos, M., Oliveira, R., Paulo, J.A., Pereira, J., Vilaça, R.: Met: workload aware elasticity for NOSQL. In: Proceedings of the 8th ACM European Conference on Computer Systems, EuroSys, pp. 183–196 (2013)
8. Curino, C., Jones, E.P., Madden, S., Balakrishnan, H.: Workload-aware database monitoring and consolidation. In: Proceedings of ACM SIGMOD International Conference on Management of Data, SIGMOD 2011, pp. 313–324 (2011)
9. Desnoyers, P., Wood, T., Shenoy, P., Singh, R., Patil, S., Vin, H.: Modellus: automated modeling of complex internet data center applications. ACM Trans. Web 6, 1–29 (2012)
10. Didona, D., Quaglia, F., Romano, P., Torre, E.: Enhancing performance prediction robustness by combining analytical modeling and machine learning. In: Proceedings of the 6th ACM/SPEC International Conference on Performance Engineering, pp. 145–156 (2015)
11. Fisher, R.A.: On the probable error of a coefficient of correlation deduced from a small sample. Metron 1, 3–32 (1921)
12. George, L.: HBase: The Definitive Guide. O'Reilly, Sebastopol (2011)
13. Gong, Z., Gu, X., Wilkes, J.: Press: predictive elastic resource scaling for cloud systems. In: International Conference on Network and Service Management, pp. 9–16 (2010)
14. Hunt, P., Konar, M., Junqueira, F.P., Reed, B.: Zookeeper: wait-free coordination for internet-scale systems. In: Proceedings of USENIX Conference on USENIX Annual Technical Conference, USENIXATC 2010, p. 11 (2010)
15. Jennings, B., Stadler, R.: Resource management in clouds: survey and research challenges. J. Netw. Syst. Manage. 23(3), 567–619 (2014)
16. Khan, A., Yan, X., Tao, S., Anerousis, N.: Workload characterization and prediction in the cloud: a multiple time series approach. In: Network Operations and Management Symposium (NOMS), pp. 1287–1294 (2012)
17. Konstantinou, I., Angelou, E., Tsoumakos, D., Boumpouka, C., Koziris, N., Sioutas, S.: Tiramola: elastic nosql provisioning through a cloud management platform. In: International Conference on Management of Data (SIGMOD Demo Track) (2012)
18. Lakshman, A., Malik, P.: Cassandra - a decentralized structured storage system. In: LADIS (2009)
19. Li, J., König, A.C., Narasayya, V., Chaudhuri, S.: Robust estimation of resource consumption for SQL queries using statistical techniques. Proc. VLDB 5, 1555–1566 (2012)

20. Matsunaga, A., Fortes, J.A.B.: On the use of machine learning to predict the time and resources consumed by applications. In: Proceedings of IEEE/ACM International Conference on Cluster, Cloud and Grid Computing, CCGRID, pp. 495–504 (2010)
21. Mozafari, B., Curino, C., Jindal, A., Madden, S.: Performance and resource modeling in highly-concurrent OLTP workloads. In: Proceedings of the ACM SIGMOD International Conference on Management of Data, pp. 301–312 (2013)
22. Mozafari, B., Curino, C., Madden, S.: Dbseer: resource and performance prediction for building a next generation database cloud. In: Conference on Innovative Data Systems Research (CIDR) (2013)
23. Puzak, T.R.: Analysis of Cache Replacement-algorithms. Ph.D. thesis (1985). AAI8509594
24. Singh, R., Sharma, U., Cecchet, E., Shenoy, P.: Autonomic mix-aware provisioning for non-stationary data center workloads. In: Proceedings of the 7th International Conference on Autonomic Computing, pp. 21–30 (2010)
25. Sleator, D.D., Tarjan, R.E.: Amortized efficiency of list update and paging rules. Commun. ACM **28**, 202–208 (1985)
26. Sudevalayam, S., Kulkarni, P.: Affinity-aware modeling of cpu usage for provisioning virtualized applications. In: 2011 IEEE International Conference on Cloud Computing (CLOUD), pp. 139–146 (2011)
27. Wood, T., Cherkasova, L., Ozonat, K., Shenoy, P.D.: Profiling and modeling resource usage of virtualized applications. In: Issarny, V., Schantz, R. (eds.) Middleware 2008. LNCS, vol. 5346, pp. 366–387. Springer, Heidelberg (2008)
28. Zhang, Q., Cherkasova, L., Smirni, E.: A regression-based analytic model for dynamic resource provisioning of multi-tier applications. In: Proceedings of the 4th International Conference on Autonomic Computing, p. 27 (2007)

A Performance Evaluation of Erasure Coding Libraries for Cloud-Based Data Stores

(Practical Experience Report)

Dorian Burihabwa, Pascal Felber, Hugues Mercier, and Valerio Schiavoni[(✉)]

Université de Neuchâtel, Neuchâtel, Switzerland
{dorian.burihabwa,pascal.felber,hugues.mercier,
valerio.schiavoni}@unine.ch

Abstract. Erasure codes have been widely used over the last decade to implement reliable data stores. They offer interesting trade-offs between efficiency, reliability, and storage overhead. Indeed, a distributed data store holding encoded data blocks can tolerate the failure of multiple nodes while requiring only a fraction of the space necessary for plain replication, albeit at an increased encoding and decoding cost. There exists nowadays a number of libraries implementing several variations of erasure codes, which notably differ in terms of complexity and implementation-specific optimizations.

Seven years ago, Plank *et al.* [14] have conducted a comprehensive performance evaluation of open-source erasure coding libraries available at the time to compare their raw performance and measure the impact of different parameter configurations. In the present experimental study, we take a fresh perspective at the state of the art of erasure coding libraries. Not only do we cover a wider set of libraries running on modern hardware, but we also consider their efficiency when used in realistic settings for cloud-based storage, namely when deployed across several nodes in a data centre. Our measurements therefore account for the end-to-end costs of data accesses over several distributed nodes, including the encoding and decoding costs, and shed light on the performance one can expect from the various libraries when deployed in a real system. Our results reveal important differences in the efficiency of the different libraries, notably due to the type of coding algorithm and the use of hardware-specific optimizations.

1 Introduction

Cloud-based storage has seen an impressive growth over the last few years, notably thanks to the availability of affordable solutions from large companies like Dropbox, Google, Amazon, Microsoft, or Apple. While these services mainly target the general public, several companies have also specialized in the development of dedicated solutions offering specific properties in terms of security or dependability, support for deployment on premises, or customized application

© IFIP International Federation for Information Processing 2016
Published by Springer International Publishing Switzerland 2016. All Rights Reserved
M. Jelasity and E. Kalyvianaki (Eds.): DAIS 2016, LNCS 9687, pp. 160–173, 2016.
DOI: 10.1007/978-3-319-39577-7_13

support. There is also a great interest from the scientific community to develop their own solution to finely control and tune a complete Cloud-based stack, be it in terms of communication, processing, or storage.

In the era of "Big Data", the amount of information to manage can quickly become a bottleneck. Storage space is plenty but not infinite, and data must be stored redundantly for reliability purposes. It must therefore be replicated but at the same time remain relatively compact in size. There is therefore a tension between space efficiency and performance, as any form of compression comes with associated processing overhead.

A common approach to address this challenge is to use erasure coding. This technique, already used since the eighties for redundant array of independent disks, allows infrastructure providers to add some redundancy to stored data without the space overhead of full replication, and with relatively low computation costs and sufficient flexibility in how failed disks or missing data can be recovered.

The theory of erasure codes has been developed over decades, and techniques are mature. Yet, practical libraries for performing the associated computations efficiently in software have truly emerged over the last few years, largely driven by the needs from backup services, data centers, and Cloud-based infrastructures in general ("Anything" as a Service).

Seven years ago, Plank *et al.* [14] have conducted a comprehensive performance evaluation of open-source erasure coding libraries available at the time. The focus of the study was on the raw performance of the libraries and the impact of different parameter configurations. Since then, the landscape has significantly evolved, with improved encoders and new libraries, as well as a shift toward integration within software stacks for data centers.

In this experimental study, we want to take a fresh perspective at the state of practice in erasure coding for data storage. Rather than focusing just on the libraries, we are interesting in evaluating them in realistic settings, i.e., within a complete software stack involving multiple clients and server nodes deployed across a data center. This study does also account for the costs related to data serialization and transmission, the overhead associated with the different APIs, the reads and writes to the back-end databases, etc. Therefore, it allows us to quantify the costs of using the libraries to build a complete storage solution, and to observe how the various configuration parameters affect end-to-end performance.

Our findings notably reveal several interesting lessons. First, modern encoding libraries efficiently exploit specific hardware instructions for better performances, and in a cloud-environment it is important to obtain direct access to the CPU's full instruction set. Second, the usage of high-level languages such as Python, which allow for portable and dependable client-side front-ends, to interact with efficient C-based libraries does not cause noticeable overhead. Third, the deployment of encoded data blocks over storage back-ends require practitioners to accommodate much less data than a solution based on replication. Fourth, the reconstruction of missing blocks is a sensibly more costly operation than the pure decoding when all blocks are available: this is an important factor to take into account in case of disaster-recovery actions to estimate the time to recover missing data.

The remainder of this paper is organized as follows. We first give an overview of erasure coding and related with in Sect. 2. We then describe the different libraries and the storage architecture used as part of this study in Sects. 3 and 4, respectively. We present and discuss experimental results in Sect. 5, and we finally conclude in Sect. 6.

2   Background and Related Work

The objective of error-correcting codes for data storage is to carefully add redundancy to data in order to protect it against corruption when stored on media like DVDs, magnetic tapes or solid-state drives. In these systems, the errors are usually modeled as erasures, meaning that their locations are known. Consider the example shown in Fig. 1, where a coding disk is used to store the XOR ("exclusive or") of k data blocks. If the system realizes that one of the disks has failed, as shown in Fig. 2, it can XOR the healthy disks and recover the failure. This is the maximum decoding capability of this code, and there will be data loss if more than one disk fails.

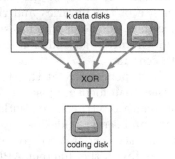

Fig. 1. Redundancy using XOR.

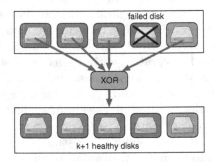

Fig. 2. Failed disk recovered using XOR.

In general, k data blocks are coded to generate $n - k$ coding blocks, as illustrated in Fig. 3. After disk failures, the system will try to decode the original codewords from the healthy disks, like in Fig. 4. The number of recoverable disk failures depends on the code itself.

The most famous class of erasure codes are Reed-Solomon codes (RS), first introduced in 1960 [17]. An (n, k) Reed-Solomon code is a linear block code with dimension k and length n defined over the finite field of n elements. Reed-Solomon codes have many interesting properties. First, they achieve the singleton bound with equality, and thus are maximum distance separable (MDS) [8]. In other words, they can correct up to $n - k$ symbol erasures, i.e., any k of the

n code symbols are necessary and sufficient for decoding. Second, using a large field, they can correct bursts of errors, thus their widespread adoption in storage media where such bursts are common.

Encoding and decoding Reed-Solomon codes is challenging, and optimizing both operations has kept many coding theorists and engineers busy for more than 50 years. There is a large amount of literature on these topics, covering theory (e.g., [5]) and implementation (e.g., [18]), but in a nutshell the best encoding and decoding implementations are quadratic in the size of the data.

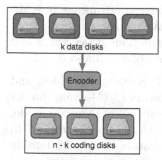

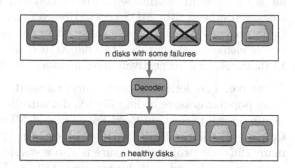

Fig. 3. Generic erasure code encoder.

Fig. 4. Generic erasure code decoder.

Reed-Solomon, while storage-efficient, were not originally designed for distributed storage and are somewhat ill-suited for this purpose. Besides their complexity, their main drawback is that they require at least k geographically distributed healthy disks to recover a single failure, followed by decoding of all the codewords with a block on the failed disk. This incurs significant bandwidth and latency costs. This handicap has led to the development of codes that can recreate destroyed redundancy without decoding the original codewords. The tradeoffs between storage overhead and failure repairability is an active area of research [3,11], and there are many interesting theoretical and practical questions to solve. Among other work of interest, NCCloud [2] reduces the cost of repair in multi-cloud storage if one cloud storage provider fails permanently. We also mention the coding work done for Microsoft Azure [1,6], and XOR-based erasure codes [7] in the context of efficient cloud-based file-systems exploiting *rotated* Reed-Solomon codes. RAID-like erasure-coding techniques have been studied in the context of cloud-based storage solutions [7]. Plank *et al.* [14] studied chosen erasure-coding libraries, which has in great part motivated and inspired the present study.

3   Coding Libraries

We tested four different coding libraries in our experimental evaluation. These libraries are considered state-of-the-art and are widely adopted in storage and networking applications. We describe below the main features of each of them. Table 1 summarizes their principal characteristics.

Liberasurecode. Liberasurecode[1] is an erasure code API library in C that supports pluggable erasure code backends. It supports backends such as jerasure and Intel ISA-L but also provides three erasure codes of its own: a Reed Solomon implementation and two flat XOR implementations. Flat XOR erasure codes [4] are small low-density parity-check (LDPC) codes [10]. With flat XOR codes, each parity element is the XOR of a distinct subset of data elements. Such codes are not maximum distance separable (MDS) and, hence, incur in some additional storage overhead over MDS codes. However, they offer the advantage of additional recovery possibilities, i.e., an element can be recovered using many distinct sets of elements. We evaluate two flat XOR codes constructions, `flat_xor_3` and `flat_xor_4`, that respectively have a Hamming distance of $d = 3$ and $d = 4$.

Jerasure. The Jerasure library,[2] first released in 2007, is one of the oldest and most popular erasure coding library. Jerasure is written in C/C++ and implements several variants of Reed-Solomon and MDS erasure codes (Vandermonde, Cauchy [9], Blaum-Roth, RAID-6 Liberation [12],...). As it has been used in many different projects, Jerasure is also a stable and mature library. It notably provides a rich and well documented API, and has been optimized for speed on modern processors (e.g., by leveraging SIMD instructions since version 2.0). More details about the internals of this library can be found at [15].

Intel ISA-L. Intel Intelligent Storage Acceleration Library (ISA-L)[3] is an implementation of erasure codes optimized for speed on Intel processors [13]. It is written primarily in hand-coded assembler and aggressively optimizes the matrix multiplication operation, the most expensive step of encoding. During the decoding operations, Intel ISA uses a cubic cost Gaussian elimination solver. For our evaluation we the latest version (v2.14).

LongHair. The LongHair library[4] is an implementation of fast Cauchy Reed-Solomon erasure codes in C [16]. It was designed to be portable and extremely fast, and it provides an API flexible enough for file transfer where the blocks arrive out of order.

4   Experimental Cloud-Based Data Store

In order to easily and efficiently evaluate the wide spectrum of coding libraries described previously, and to accelerate the comparison between current and future solutions, we designed and implement a lightweight, yet modular experimental testbed. We describe its components, the internal mechanisms, the deployment infrastructure, and other contextual assumptions in the remainder of this section.

---

[1] https://bitbucket.org/tsg-/liberasurecode.
[2] http://jerasure.org/jerasure/jerasure.
[3] https://software.intel.com/en-us/storage/ISA-L.
[4] https://github.com/catid/longhair.

Table 1. Summary of encoder names and libraries, support for hardware acceleration (HW), and the description of the algorithms (RS stands for Reed-Solomon).

Encoder	Library	HW	Description
`liberasure_rs_vand`	LibErasure	×	Vandermonde RS
`liberasure_flat_xor_3`	LibErasure	×	Flat-XOR ($d = 3$)
`liberasure_flat_xor_4`	LibErasure	×	Flat-XOR ($d = 4$)
`jerasure_rs_vand`	Jerasure	SIMD (SSSE3), CLMUL	Vandermonde RS
`jerasure_rs_cauchy`	Jerasure	SIMD (SSSE3), CLMUL	Cauchy RS
`isa_l_rs_vand`	Intel ISA-L	SIMD (SSE4), AVX(1/2)	Vandermonde RS
`longhair_cauchy_256`	LongHair	SIMD (SSSE3)	Cauchy RS

4.1 Architecture

In its simplest instantiation, a cloud-based data store that leverages erasure coding comprises the following core components, as depicted in Fig. 5: a storage server ("proxy") that mediates interactions between clients and the data store, an encoder, and a set of storage nodes.

The **proxy** component is the main front-end to the system. While there can be an arbitrary number of proxies for a given data store, we only consider one in our evaluation. The proxy exposes a simple *stateless* REST interface to put and get data blocks. The interface mimics the operating principles of well-established services like Amazon S3. More sophisticated operations, such as operating on subsets of the data blocks for a given file, can be easily integrated. The interactions between the proxy and the clients happen via synchronous HTTP messages over pre-established TCP channels. The proxy dispatches/collects data blocks to/from the encoder service.

The **encoder** component performs the actual processing and transformation of data blocks before they are stored, as well as the reverse decoding operation. The encoder is co-localized within the same host as the proxy to maximize

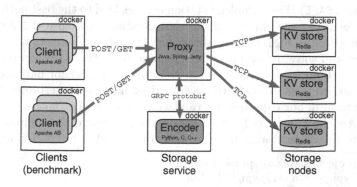

Fig. 5. Architecture of the experimental testbed.

throughput and avoid bottlenecks induced by high pressure on the network stack. To increase the flexibility of our testbed, our encoder provides a plugin mechanism to dynamically load and swap different coding libraries. This mechanism relies on a platform-independent transport mechanism (using `protobuf`) and a stable interface between the proxy and the encoder. The encoder interface currently exposes three main operations: `encode`, `decode`, and `reconstruct`.

Once the blocks have been encoded, they are sent by the proxy to the **storage nodes**. Each storage node is independent from the others and all the interactions are mediated by the proxy. Blocks are dispatched to storage nodes using an explicit placement strategy: the proxy ensures that encoded block parts are spread to distinct nodes so that the failure of one node results in the loss of one part. Upon read, the proxy contacts a random subset of storage nodes of minimal size to reconstruct the requested block.

The **clients** are separate processes running on different nodes in the same data center. They read and write data by contacting the proxy following access patterns defined as part of the workloads.

4.2   Implementation

We used different languages and technologies to implement our testbed and integrate with the open-source erasure coding libraries. Our implementation choices have been largely driven by performance and simplicity considerations, as well as by constraints from the evaluated libraries.

The proxy component is implemented in Java and exploits the exporting facilities of the *Spring Boot* framework[5] (v1.3.1) to leverage industrial-grade application servers. The proxy handles `POST` and `GET` requests via the embedded Jetty web-server.

The encoder component is implemented in Python to facilitate the integration with the PyEClib[6] library (v1.2), the reference Python binding for `liberasure`. This library implements wrappers to uniformly access several encoding libraries.

The open-source libraries under evaluation are implemented in C/C++ (e.g., `liberasure`, `JErasure`, `LongHair`) or a mix of C and hand-written Assembly (e.g., `Intel ISA-L`). These implementation choices lead to the best performances and can take advantage of hardware acceleration, as in the case of `Intel ISA-L` that exploits built-in SIMD CPU instructions. We call the libraries via a common access layer and software wrappers implemented in Python. Python provides an easy mean to bind to such libraries via its built-in support for native code. For completeness, we also evaluate the overhead of using an interpreted language such as Python in our experimental validation. The suite of macro-benchmarks leverages Apache Bench[7] (v2.3) to measure the maximum throughput and per-request latencies. The storage nodes run on top of Redis[8] (v3.0.7), a lightweight

---

[5] https://projects.spring.io/spring-boot/.
[6] https://pypi.python.org/pypi/PyECLib.
[7] https://httpd.apache.org/docs/2.4/programs/ab.html.
[8] http://redis.io.

yet efficient in-memory key-value store. Redis tools provide easy-to-use probing mechanisms (e.g., the `redis-cli` command-line tool) to retrieve the current memory occupied by the stored key-value pairs. We exploit these tools to calculate the storage overhead of the encoded blocks. Our deployment machinery allows us to scale at will all the mentioned components. To do so, we rely on the tools offered by the *Docker*[9] ecosystem (v1.6) and its *Compose*[10] orchestration tool (v1.5.3).

5 Experimental Results

This section presents our extensive evaluation of the previously described coding libraries. We first describe the settings of our evaluation, then we test in isolation the coding libraries via a set of micro-benchmarks, and we finally evaluate the libraries in realistic settings.

5.1 Evaluation Settings

We deploy and conduct our experiments over a cluster of machines interconnected by a 1 Gb/s switched network. Each physical host features 8-Core Xeon CPUs and 8 GB of RAM. We deploy virtual machines (VM) on top of the hosts.

The KVM hypervisor, which controls the execution of the VM, is configured to expose the physical CPU to the guest VM and Docker container by mean of the `host-passthrough`[11] option. This VM configuration allows certain coding libraries (e.g., Intel ISA-L) to exploit ad-hoc CPU instruction sets. In this evaluation, we do not account for any GPU acceleration. The VMs leverage the `virtio` module for better I/O performances.

We deploy one Docker container on each VM without any memory restriction to minimize interferences due to co-locations and maximize performances.

5.2 Micro-benchmark

Our first set of experiments evaluate the throughput of the coding libraries for increasing block sizes of 4 MB, 16 MB and 64 MB. In this scenario, the libraries are tested in isolation via specialized clients that send a continuous stream of data blocks to encode or decode.

For each library we execute 10,000 times the `encode` function and show the average and standard deviation results. All the Reed-Solomon libraries are configured with $k = 10$ and $m = 4$, a typical configuration used in modern data centers (e.g., at Facebook [19]). To approach a similar configuration, the Flat XOR libraries are set to $k = 10$ and $m = 5$. For reference purposes, we compare against a baseline `striping` encoder/decoder that simply splits the data in the

---

[9] https://www.docker.com.
[10] https://docs.docker.com/compose/.
[11] http://www.linux-kvm.org/page/Tuning_KVM.

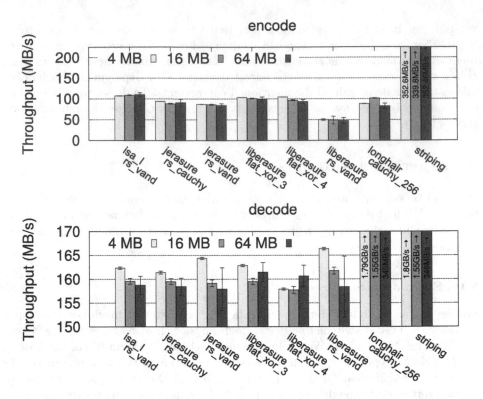

Fig. 6. Micro-benchmark: `encode` (top) and `decode` (bottom) throughput for several coding libraries and block sizes.

requested number of blocks (typically one block per stripe) and immediately returns them to the client without any further processing.

Figure 6 presents our results for encoding (top) and decoding (bottom). We notice that `liberasure_rs_vand` is the slowest in the encoding phase, achieving at most 52.35 MB/s for a 4 Mb block size. The Jerasure implementation of the same coding technique (`jerasure_rs_vand`) and Intel's `isa_l_rs_vand` perform *twice* as fast for the same block size, respectively up to 87 MB/s and 107 MB/s.

We can explain the performance gap between different implementations of the same coding techniques by two main reasons: (1) the longer foray of such libraries in the open-source community (the original design of Jerasure dates back to 2007) thus benefiting from several contributions and code scrutiny, and (2) native support for hardware acceleration for the Intel ISA and Jerasure libraries.

Finally, `longhair_cauchy_256` outperforms the other implementations for any block size. Indeed, not only is its implementation based on the Jerasure source code, but it embeds carefully hand-crafted low-level optimizations (e.g., selection of the minimal Cauchy matrix, faster matrix bootstrap, etc.).

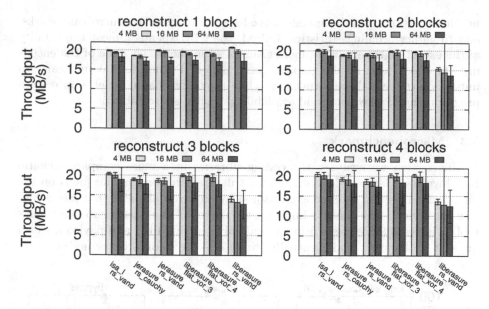

Fig. 7. Micro-benchmarks: throughput of `reconstruct` for increasing number of missing blocks and block sizes.

In the decoding scenario, the `decode` function is fed with all the available blocks. As expected, when all the blocks are available, the libraries can decode very efficiently, achieving throughputs that are never below 157 MB/s for any block size. For example, `liberasure_flat_xor_4` achieves a 158.13 MB/s throughput with 4 MB blocks, and `jerasure_rs_cauchy` reaches 164.87 MB/s. The highly optimized `longhair_cauchy_256` achieves results that are orders-of-magnitude better also in decoding (up to 1.79 GB/s for 4 MB blocks).

Finally, Fig. 7 shows the cost of reconstructing missing blocks. We present the achieved throughput of the coding libraries in reconstructing from 1 to 4 missing blocks (from top-left to bottom-right). Figure 7 presents the average throughput for 100 executions. Notice how `liberasure_rs_vand` achieves the best result (20.77 MB/s) in reconstructing 1 missing block with 4 MB block sizes but steadily decreases with bigger block sizes and more to reconstruct. This result confirms the measures of the same library in pure decoding shown previously in Fig. 6. The other libraries perform consistently across the spectrum of parameters, and all operate between 17.15 MB/s and 19.19 MB/s. These results need to be taken carefully into account to decide which is the best fitting library to adopt in a cloud setting.

We performed a breakdown analysis of the computing times for each of the microbenchmarks. The goal of this analysis is to verify that the cost of using a high-level language such as Python did not hinder our results and thus negatively impacted on the observed performances. We exploit the `cProfile` module[12] to

---

[12] https://docs.python.org/2/library/profile.html.

profile the execution of the `encode`, `decode`, and `reconstruct` microbenchmarks, and to gather profiling statistics. Indeed, the CPU spends almost the totality of the execution time (always more than 99 %) in the native code of the encoding libraries. These results confirm the choice of Python as having near-zero impact on the overall performances, while providing major benefits in ease of programming, deployment, and availability of open-source libraries.

5.3   Macrobenchmark

In this section we evaluate the coding libraries in a more complex scenario that involves a large-scale storage infrastructure service. First we focus on the observed per-request latency as measured by an external client that stores files into the system. The client is implemented on top of the Apache **ab** benchmark tool. It issues `POST` requests using a randomly generated key and payload, which are sent to the proxy and eventually stored into the Redis storage nodes.

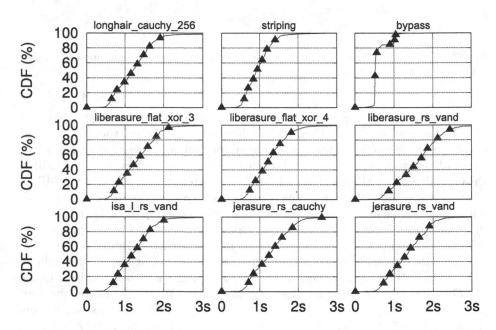

Fig. 8. Latency distribution of 500 requests measured by Apache **ab** client.

Figure 8 shows the cumulative distribution function (CDF) of the latencies as observed by the client. These results include two additional variants that concretely avoid any encoding actions: **striping** and **bypass**. The **striping** variant simply splits the file into the desired number of blocks and immediately returns them to the client. We implemented this solution as an additional back-end to the PyECLib library. The **bypass** technique allows to circumvent any communication overhead between the proxy and the encoder components (see

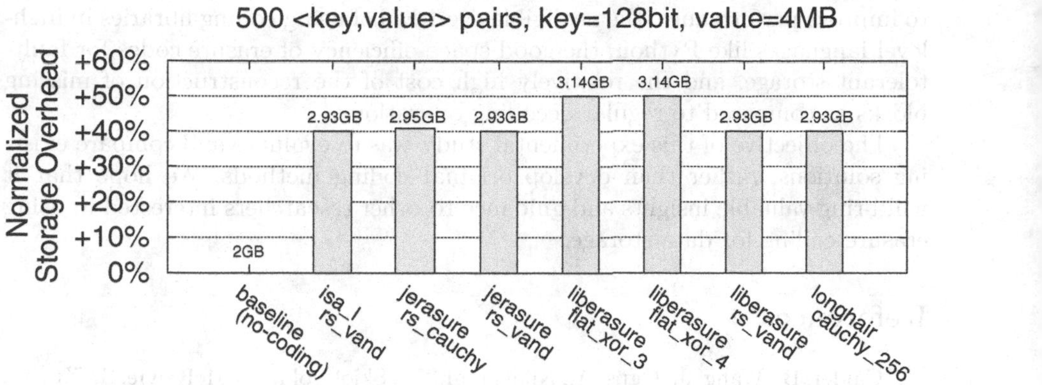

500 <key,value> pairs, key=128bit, value=4MB

Fig. 9. Storage overhead.

Fig. 5). The difference between the `bypass` and `striping` indicate the price one pays to send the files back and forth between the proxy and the encoder. We observe that `isa_l_rs_vand` and `longhair_cauchy_256` achieve the best overall performances, with the 99th percentile of the latencies below 2.645 s and 2.482 s respectively, and the median latencies as low as 1.192 s and 1.133 s.

We conclude our experimental evaluation by comparing the storage overhead induced by the choice of a given coding library. Figure 9 presents our results. The client sequentially stores 500 files of 4 MB each, for a total of 2 GB of data. The baseline results indicate the cost of storing the files without any form of coding. On the y-axis we show the storage overhead normalized against the baseline cost, while for each library we indicate the total space requirements. In our experiments, the Flat XOR erasure codes are on average 8 % more demanding than the other codes: they require a total of 3.14 GB of storage space (corresponding to a +63 % of the original data).

6 Conclusion

We have studied and compared, in this practical experience report, the performance of several open-source erasure coding libraries that are widely used to implement error correction in distributed systems. These libraries notably differ in terms of coding algorithms, implementation quality, and hardware-specific optimizations. Unlike the seminal study of Plank *et al.* [14] published seven years ago, we focus here on the latest generation of coding libraries when used in realistic settings for cloud-based storage, and deployed on modern hardware inside a data centre.

We conducted a wide range of experiments with these libraries to not only measure their raw speed at encoding and decoding data, but also evaluate their performance when used to store and retrieve actual content. Our observations notably highlight the importance of specific hardware instructions such as SIMD to improve performance, the negligible overhead of using coding libraries in high-level languages like Python, the good space efficiency of erasure codes for fault-tolerant storage, and the relatively high cost of the reconstruction of missing blocks as compared to regular decoding operations.

The objective of this experimental study was to evaluate and compare existing solutions, rather than develop original coding methods. We hope that it will bring valuable insights and guidance to other researchers interested in using erasure coding for data storage.

References

1. Calder, B., Wang, J., Ogus, A., Nilakantan, N., Skjolsvold, A., McKelvie, S., Xu, Y., Srivastav, S., Wu, J., Simitci, H., Haridas, J., Uddaraju, C., Khatri, H., Edwards, A., Bedekar, V., Mainali, S., Abbasi, R., Agarwal, A., Fahim ul Haq, M., Ikram ul Haq, M., Bhardwaj, D., Dayanand, S., Adusumilli, A., McNett, M., Sankaran, S., Manivannan, K., Rigas, L.: Windows Azure Storage: a highly available cloud storage service with strong consistency. In: Proceedings of the Twenty-Third ACM Symposium on Operating Systems Principles, SOSP 2011, pp. 143–157. ACM, New York (2011)
2. Chen, H.C., Hu, Y., Lee, P.P., Tang, Y.: NCCloud: a network-coding-based storage system in a cloud-of-clouds. Trans. Comput. **63**(1), 31–44 (2014)
3. Dimakis, A., Godfrey, P., Wu, Y., Wainwright, M., Ramchandran, K.: Network coding for distributed storage systems. IEEE Trans. Inf. Theory **56**(9), 4539–4551 (2010)
4. Greenan, K.M., Li, X., Wylie, J.J.: Flat XOR-based erasure codes in storage systems: constructions, efficient recovery, and tradeoffs. In: 2010 IEEE 26th Symposium on Mass Storage Systems and Technologies (MSST), pp. 1–14. IEEE (2010)
5. Guruswami, V., Sudan, M.: Improved decoding of Reed-Solomon and algebraic-geometry codes. IEEE Trans. Inf. Theory **45**(6), 1757–1767 (1999)
6. Huang, C., Simitci, H., Xu, Y., Ogus, A., Calder, B., Gopalan, P., Li, J., Yekhanin, S.: Erasure coding in Windows Azure Storage. In: Proceedings of the USENIX Annual Technical Conference, USENIX ATC, pp. 15–26 (2012)
7. Khan, O., Burns, R.C., Plank, J.S., Pierce, W., Huang, C.: Rethinking erasure codes for cloud file systems: minimizing I/O for recovery and degraded reads. In: Proceedings of the 7th Conference on File and Storage Technologies, FAST 2012, p. 20. USENIX Association (2012)
8. Lin, S., Costello, D.J.: Error Control Coding, 2nd edn. Pearson Prentice Hall, Englewood Cliffs (2004)
9. Luby, M., Zuckermank, D.: An XOR-based erasure-resilient coding scheme. Technical report (1995)
10. Luby, M.G., Mitzenmacher, M., Shokrollahi, M.A., Spielman, D.A., Stemann, V.: Practical loss-resilient codes. In: Proceedings of the Twenty-Ninth Annual ACM Symposium on Theory of Computing, pp. 150–159. ACM (1997)
11. Oggier, F.E., Datta, A.: Self-repairing codes - local repairability for cheap and fast maintenance of erasure coded data. Computing **97**(2), 171–201 (2015)
12. Plank, J.S.: The raid-6 Liber8Tion code. Int. J. High Perform. Comput. Appl. **23**, 242–251 (2009)
13. Plank, J.S., Greenan, K.M., Miller, E.L.: Screaming fast Galois field arithmetic using Intel SIMD instructions. In: FAST, pp. 299–306 (2013)

14. Plank, J.S., Luo, J., Schuman, C.D., Xu, L., Wilcox-O'Hearn, Z.: A performance evaluation and examination of open-source erasure coding libraries for storage. In: Proceedings of the 7th Conference on File and Storage Technologies, FAST 2009, pp. 253–265. USENIX Association, Berkeley (2009)
15. Plank, J.S., Simmerman, S., Schuman, C.D.: Jerasure: A library in C/C++ facilitating erasure coding for storage applications-version 1.2. Technical report, Technical Report CS-08-627, University of Tennessee (2008)
16. Plank, J.S., Xu, L.: Optimizing Cauchy Reed-Solomon codes for fault-tolerant network storage applications. In: 2006 Fifth IEEE International Symposium on Network Computing and Applications, NAC 2006, pp. 173–180. IEEE (2006)
17. Reed, I.S., Solomon, G.: Polynomial codes over certain finite fields. J. Soc. Ind. Appl. Math. 8(2), 300–304 (1960)
18. Sankaran, J.: Reed Solomon decoder: TMS320C64x implementation. Application Report SPRA686, Texas Instruments (2000)
19. Sathiamoorthy, M., Asteris, M., Papailiopoulos, D., Dimakis, A.G., Vadali, R., Chen, S., Borthakur, D.: XORing elephants: novel erasure codes for big data. Proc. VLDB Endow. 6(5), 325–336 (2013)

Dynamic Load Balancing Techniques for Distributed Complex Event Processing Systems

Nikos Zacheilas[1]([✉]), Nikolas Zygouras[2], Nikolaos Panagiotou[2],
Vana Kalogeraki[1], and Dimitrios Gunopulos[2]

[1] Athens University of Economics and Business, Athens, Greece
{zacheilas,vana}@aueb.gr
[2] University of Athens, Athens, Greece
{nzygouras,n.panagiotou,dg}@di.uoa.gr

Abstract. Applying real-time, cost-effective Complex Event processing (CEP) in the cloud has been an important goal in recent years. Distributed Stream Processing Systems (DSPS) have been widely adopted by major computing companies such as Facebook and Twitter for performing scalable event processing in streaming data. However, dynamically balancing the load of the DSPS' components can be particularly challenging due to the high volume of data, the components' state management needs, and the low latency processing requirements. Systems should be able to cope with these challenges and adapt to dynamic and unpredictable load changes in real-time. Our approach makes the following contributions: (i) we formulate the load balancing problem in distributed CEP systems as an instance of the job-shop scheduling problem, and (ii) we present a novel framework that dynamically balances the load of CEP engines in real-time and adapts to sudden changes in the volume of streaming data by exploiting two balancing policies. Our detailed experimental evaluation using data from the Twitter social network indicates the benefits of our approach in the system's throughput.

1 Introduction

In recent years we observe a significant increase in the need for processing and analyzing voluminous data streams in a variety of application domains, ranging from traffic monitoring [19] to financial processing [4]. In order to analyze this huge amount of data and detect events of interest, Complex Event Processing (CEP) systems have emerged as an appropriate solution. In CEP systems, like Esper[1], users define queries (i.e. rules) that process incoming *primitive* events and detect complex events when some conditions are satisfied. CEP systems are easy to use as most of them offer a query language for expressing the rules.

One significant shortcoming of CEP systems is that they lack in scalability due to their centralized architecture, making them inadequate for applications

---

[1] www.esper.codehaus.org.

© IFIP International Federation for Information Processing 2016
Published by Springer International Publishing Switzerland 2016. All Rights Reserved
M. Jelasity and E. Kalyvianaki (Eds.): DAIS 2016, LNCS 9687, pp. 174–188, 2016.
DOI: 10.1007/978-3-319-39577-7_14

that require processing large volumes of data streams. On the other hand, Distributed Stream Processing Systems (DSPS) like Infosphere Streams[2], Spark Streaming[3] and Storm[4] are commonly used for performing scalable and low latency complex event detection. However, current DSPSs lack the expressiveness and ease of use of CEP systems. So combining the two approaches provides a scalable and easy to use framework.

A common approach to increase the system's throughput is to distribute different CEP engines across the cluster nodes, using DSPS [19]. In this work we follow this approach and focus on applications that apply the *key-grouping* partitioning schema for distributing the input data to the CEP engines. *Key-grouping* partitioning assigns the tuples to the appropriate CEP engines based on a specific key attribute of the tuples, which ensures that tuples sharing the same *key* will end up in the same engine. However, when applying a static partitioning schema, which remains the same during the topology's lifetime, it is highly possible to create imbalanced cluster nodes. This usually happens in scenarios where the data load that share the same *key* varies significantly over time. For example, in applications that monitor stock prices (i.e. where the grouping *key* is the stock's name), the number of particular stock transactions may vary significantly during the day. Thus, sudden changes in the system's load and performance are quite common [8]. So it is important to implement techniques that are able to dynamically adapt to such changes in the data load and ensure that the system remains balanced [12,14]. These techniques should consider the size of the data that will be transferred across the engines. Many data re-transmissions result to increased recovery time (i.e. *rebalancing cost*).

Another technique that is widely used in order to cope with the data deluge is elasticity [5]. Elastic systems are able to decide the appropriate number of engines (i.e. scale-out, scale-in) and adapt to changes in the observed load (e.g. unexpected load bursts). In our previous work [18], we have described a novel technique that enables the automatic adjustment of the number of running engines. In order to keep the system's performance stable the load balancing problem and the elasticity problem are *orthogonal*. When the system is unable to process the incoming data, actions that balance the load should be taken firstly and if this fails then scale-out actions should be applied. Furthermore, load balancing techniques can be beneficial when applications run in cloud infrastructures like Amazon's EC2[5]. In such environments users are charged on an hourly-basis, so having overloaded engines can lead to increased monetary cost as they would require more time to process their assigned data.

In this paper we focus on the problem of automatically balancing the load between concurrently running CEP engines. Our work aims at dynamically adapting to unexpected changes in the input load and minimizing the amount of

---

[2] www.ibm.com/software/products/us/en/infosphere-streams.

[3] https://spark.apache.org.

[4] http://storm.apache.org/.

[5] http://aws.amazon.com/ec2/.

data that needs to be exchanged between the engines so that the state migration overhead is reduced. Our contributions are the following:

- We formulate our problem as an instance of the *job shop scheduling* problem.
- We propose a novel Dynamic Load Balancing (*DLB*) algorithm that balances the engines' load and at the same time minimizes the required state migrations. We examine two different policies for deciding which *keys* should be moved.
- We add an extra component in Storm, named *Splitter*, in order to support these load balancing algorithms and handle the necessary state migrations that guarantee the system's consistency.
- Finally, we evaluate our proposals in our local Storm cluster with a Twitter application that performs First Story Detection [11] on incoming tweets. Our experimental results demonstrate that our framework effectively balances the load between the CEP engines and improves the system's throughput compared to other state-of-the-art techniques [12,14].

2   System Architecture and Model

2.1   System Architecture

We have built our system using Apache's Storm as the DSPS and Esper as the CEP system.

Esper. Esper is one of the most commonly used Complex Event Processing (CEP) systems, applied to streaming data for detecting events of interest. Users can define queries (i.e. Esper rules) via the Event Processing Language (EPL), which bears a lot of similarities with SQL thus it is easy to use and learn. Incoming data are examined and when they satisfy the rules' conditions an event is triggered. The windows of the data streams, based on their expiration policy, could be either *length-based* (for a fixed number of data points) or *time-based* (contain the tuples received during a sliding time window). Esper keeps incoming data in in-memory buffers for the time period needed and then discards them.

Storm. We chose to use Apache's Storm mainly due to its scalability features that allow us to process voluminous data streams [11]. Applications in Storm are expressed as a graph, called topology. The graph consists of nodes that encapsulate the processing logic (implemented by the users) and edges that represent the data flows among components. There can be two types of *components*: *spouts* and *bolts*. Spouts are the input sources in the system which feed the framework with raw data (e.g. simple events). Bolts process these incoming tuples with user-defined Java functions. From an architectural perspective Storm consists of a Master node, called Nimbus, and multiple worker nodes. The user can easily tune the parallelism of the components (spouts/bolts) by adjusting the number of threads (i.e. *executors* in Storm's terminology) that will be used for the components' execution. These threads run on the workers' processors, enabling the topology's distributed execution in the cluster's nodes.

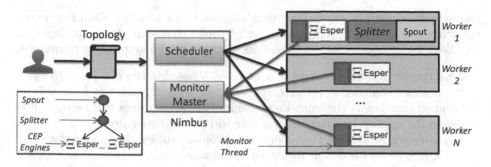

Fig. 1. System architecture

Combining DSPS and CEP. In Fig. 1 we present our system architecture. Users decide the components to be used (e.g. spouts and bolts) and the Esper rules to run. We added a special type of bolt called EsperBolt that contains an Esper engine that processes incoming tuples and invokes the user-defined rules. This way we exploit the ease of use of Esper as users need to define only the rules that would execute and the actual evaluation of the rules is applied by the Esper engines. Furthermore, users can set the parallelism (i.e. number of threads) of the EsperBolt. In the topology presented in Fig. 1, the component that contains the EsperBolt has its parallelism set to N so we have N CEP engines running in our topology, and each one of them executes in a separate processor. Also we added an extra monitor thread per worker's processor to report periodically the performance (e.g. latency, input rate) of its assigned components.

Our system is able to receive and distributively process voluminous sequential data from a wide range of input sources (e.g. Twitter data, bus mobility data and stock prices). In this work we focus on rules that group together tuples based on some common characteristic, named as *key*; tuples that refer to a specific *key* should be transmitted always to the same Esper engine. So we need a partitioning schema that maps the possible *keys* to the available engines. Another challenge arises from the fact that the amount of tuples that correspond to each *key* may vary significantly overtime and this can affect the system's performance.

In many real-world applications, content-aware partitioning is required in order to preserve system's functionality. It is extremely possible to miss events or to identify wrong ones, if tuples with the same *key* are assigned to different CEP engines. For example, in an application that monitors the evolution of different stock prices, the tuples that refer to the same stock should be sent to the same CEP engine. Following this approach, each CEP engine is responsible to process a subset of the input *keys*.

2.2 System Metrics

Each Storm topology is associated with a set of Esper *Engines* that will be responsible for the distributed event processing and a set of *Keys* that distinctly characterize a group of tuples (i.e. tweet's topics, stock's name). Each Esper rule monitors and identifies events on the set of tuples that share the same *key*.

We define the following set of metrics to measure the system's performance:

- *keys_map[k]*: a data structure that maps each possible *key* $k \in \{1, ..., |Keys|\}$ to an Esper engine $e \in \{1, ..., |Engines|\}$. As a result, different *keys* will be grouped together in the same Esper engine. Streaming data will be transmitted to the appropriate engine according to this data structure.
- *keys_load[k]*: represents the amount of incoming tuples that share the same *key* k in a pre-defined time or length based window.
- *eng_load[e]*: represents the amount of incoming tuples emitted to the engine e in the examined window defined as:

$$eng\_load[e] = \sum_{(k \in Keys | e = keys\_map[k])} keys\_load[k], \forall e \in Engines \qquad (1)$$

- *imbScore(eng_load)*: is a function, defined in Sect. 3.1, that depicts the system's *imbalance* score given as input the engines' load. The goal of this work is to minimize this metric.

3   Methodology

In this work we focus on the problem of balancing the load among concurrently running CEP engines by determining the appropriate assignment of *keys* to engines that will keep the system's performance steady even in the case of varying *keys* load. Initially, we formulate our problem and describe a metric that measures the system's imbalance. Then, we propose an algorithm, Dynamic Load Balancing (*DLB*), which solves efficiently the problem. Furthermore, we consider two policies, *DLB-L* and *DLB-H*, for determining the *keys* that should be moved in order to balance the load. Finally, we present how we extended our system to support these techniques and appropriately migrate the engines' state to guarantee that our CEP engines report correct events. For the latter, we use a distributed database for storing and retrieving the in-memory tuples of the Esper engines when the algorithm changes the partitioning schema.

3.1   Problem Definition

Our problem can be represented as a variation of a well-known *NP-hard* optimization problem, the *job shop scheduling* problem [3]. More formally our optimization problem can be formulated as follows:

> Given a set of Keys where each key $k \in Keys$ receives keys_load[k] tuples/sec, a set of Engines where each engine $e \in Engines$ receives eng_load[e] tuples/sec and a current allocation of keys to engines keys_map[ ], our goal is to find a new assignment of keys to engines keys_map'[ ] that minimizes imbScore metric and also minimizes the data that will be transferred across the different engines.

Algorithm 1. Dynamic Load Balancing

1: **Input:** $keys\_map$, $keys\_load$, eng_load, θ, $policy$
2: **Output:** $keys\_map$
3: $imbScore \leftarrow measure\_imbalance(eng\_load)$
4: **while** $imbScore > \theta$ **do**
5:     $sort_{DESC}(eng\_load)$
6:     $e_{min} \leftarrow arg\,min_e(eng\_load)$
7:     $eng\_load_{temp} \leftarrow eng\_load$
8:     **while** $eng\_load.hasNext()$ **do**
9:         $e_{loaded} \leftarrow eng\_load.getNext()$
10:        **if** $e_{loaded} == e_{min}$ **then**
11:            **return** $keys\_map$
12:        $k^* \leftarrow selectKey(policy, keys\_load[\,])$
13:        $eng\_load_{temp}(e_{loaded}) \leftarrow eng\_load_{temp}(e_{loaded}) - keys\_load(k^*)$
14:        $eng\_load_{temp}(e_{min}) \leftarrow eng\_load_{temp}(e_{min}) + keys\_load(k^*)$
15:        $imbScore\_new \leftarrow measure\_imbalance(eng\_load_{temp})$
16:        **if** $imbScore\_new < imbScore$ **then**
17:            $keys\_map[k^*] \leftarrow e_{min}$
18:            $eng\_load \leftarrow eng\_load_{temp}$
19:            $imbScore \leftarrow imbScore\_new$
20:            $break$
21: **return** $keys\_map$

In the *job shop scheduling* problem we have a set of identical machines and we want to schedule a set of jobs in these machines in order to minimize some performance metric (e.g. the total makespan which is the total length of the schedule). In our setting, *Engines* can be seen as the identical machines of the *job shop scheduling* problem, while *Keys* correspond to the jobs that must be assigned into these machines and *imbScore* is the performance metric we want to minimize. Note that in our problem we also consider state migrations when a *key* must move to a different engine, ensuring that the CEP will remain consistent.

As imbalance function we decided to use the relative standard deviation ($RSTD$) among the engines' load which is a commonly used metric for expressing imbalances in a system [6]. We compute the *imbScore* as follows:

$$imbScore(eng\_load[\,])) = 100 * \frac{std(eng\_load[\,])}{mean(eng\_load[\,])} \tag{2}$$

where $mean()$ and $std()$ are functions that compute the mean and the standard deviation respectively. The higher the relative standard deviation is, the more imbalanced are the CEP engines. When this quantity exceeds a pre-defined threshold we assume that the load is unequally distributed across the engines so a balancing algorithm must be applied in order to rebalance the load across the engines and minimize this metric.

3.2 Dynamic Load Balancing

Our proposed algorithm can be thought as an extension of the LPT algorithm (Longest Processing Time) [3], which is a greedy approximation for the *job shop scheduling* problem. The main difference with the *LPT* algorithm is that in our case *Keys* are already assigned into a finite number of *Engines*, but their load changes over time, resulting to significant load imbalances. This will be the result of an increase or decrease of the aggregated volume in some specific engines. When a balancing algorithm applies a new partitioning schema to react to this, then a set of tuples is transferred to the new engine. This ensures the consistency of the system's state after the rebalancing. A key feature of our approach is its low complexity as it does not need to monitor system resources (*e.g.,* CPU) but focuses on the data instead. We describe below the two policies of our approach.

Dynamic Load Balancing (DLB), presented on Algorithm 1, addresses the previously described issues by dynamically changing the partitioning of different *keys* to the available Esper engines. Initially it checks whether the imbalance score (*imbScore*) exceeds a predefined threshold θ. If the set up criterion is not satisfied then iteratively starts the rebalancing procedure. The rebalancing procedure, presented in Algorithm's 1 lines 5–20, initially sorts in descending order the loads of the different engines, so the engines that receive more data will be examined firstly in order to reduce their incoming load. Also the least loaded engine, e_{min}, is identified in order to transfer load to this engine. Then our algorithm examines the most loaded engine e_{loaded} and checks whether transferring one *key* k^* from e_{loaded} to e_{min} improves the *imbScore*. If the *imbScore* is improved then k^* is transferred from e_{loaded} to e_{min} and this procedure is repeated till the imbalance criterion is satisfied. In case that *imbScore* is not improved e_{loaded} examines the next most loaded engine. Finally if all engines are examined and the balancing criterion is still not met the rebalancing procedure terminates and the best possible found allocation is returned.

Our algorithm supports different policies in order to select the appropriate *key*, k^* that will be transferred from a loaded engine to the least loaded engine, in Algorithm's 1 line 12. Below we describe the two main policies that we considered in this work:

- *Pick heavy loaded (*DLB-H*):* This policy selects the most loaded *key* from the engine e_{loaded} that reduces the imbalancing score when it is transferred to the least loaded engine e_{min}.
- *Pick lightly loaded (*DLB-L*):* This policy selects the least loaded *key* from the engine e_{loaded} and transfers it to e_{min}.

The first policy, *DLB-H*, minimizes the number of *keys* that are transferred along the engines. This is achieved as it tries to balance the system, moving few heavy loaded *keys*. On the other hand *DLB-L* policy may favour the movement of many poorly loaded *keys* to ensure balance. The first policy outperforms the second in the *length-based* streams, where each *key* contains the same amount of data. Thus, the system will recur in a shorter time period, as the number of transferred *keys* is minimized and consequently the size of transferred data to the new engine is minimized. The second policy is able to fine tune the system better as moving small *keys* across the different engines achieves a more balanced system. Since the rebalancing procedure is terminated when the *imbScore* does not exceed a threshold θ, we expect from the two methods to have a similar performance in the *time-based* streams, where the volume of data in the system for each *key* is proportional to the *key*'s load.

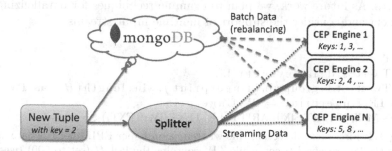

Fig. 2. *Splitter* component, when a new tuple with $key = 2$ is inserted it routes it to the appropriate CEP engine, also coordinates the rebalancing procedure

3.3   Managing the Engines' States Ensuring CEP's Consistency

Our goal is to be able to support load balance and at the same time guarantee that the detected events will be the same as those detected using the default *key-grouping*(KG) approach. In order to achieve our goals, we added *Splitter*, a new component in our Storm topologies. *Splitter* adjusts the engines' load using the Dynamic Load Balancing algorithm described in the previous and also manages the engines' state in order to ensure that event evidence is preserved by performing content-aware load retransmission. This way we avoid both missing events and false positives that could be caused from the balancing mechanism. *Splitter*, illustrated in Fig. 2, is responsible to forward tuples to the appropriate CEP engine based on their *key*. The *Splitter* keeps the *keys_map*[], *keys_load*[] and *eng_load*[] data structures (defined in Sect. 2.2) and is responsible to update them when new data are inserted into the system. Initially, it determines the engine that will process the incoming tuple using a simple modulo hash function on the tuple's *key*. However, when the imbalance threshold is not satisfied (see Sect. 3.2) it invokes Algorithm 1 to balance the load between the engines and update the *keys_map*[] data structure.

We store all incoming tuples into a distributed database (e.g. MongoDB[6]) so that the engines can retrieve them when the rebalancing procedure is applied and avoid information loss. Furthermore, *Splitter* is responsible to coordinate the rebalancing procedure, when a *key* k^* is selected to move from an old engine e_{old}

---

[6] http://www.mongodb.org/.

to a new one e_{new}. The following steps are followed: (i) e_{old} is informed to remove all the tuples related with k^* that are kept in-memory, (ii) e_{new} is informed that from now on it will be responsible for the processing of k^*'s tuples, (iii) e_{new} retrieves the required data regarding k^* from the distributed database, (iv) e_{new} stores incoming tuples regarding k^* in a local buffer until the necessary data are retrieved and then forwards them to the engine, (v) *Splitter* forwards tuples regarding k^* to e_{new}. In our current implementation, the Splitter component can be the bottleneck as it is possible to be overloaded by the amount of data it receives. As future work, we plan to examine techniques for parallelizing this component and consider the support of multiple input streams.

```
SELECT *
FROM Tweet.std:lastevent() LE,
     Tweet.std:groupwin(fingerprint).win:length(H) as TW
WHERE LE.fingerprint = TW.fingerprint
HAVING MAX(TWEET_SIMILARITY(LE.TEXT,TW.TEXT))<= τ
```

Listing 1.1. First story detection rule written as an Esper EPL rule: *LE* data stream contains the last received tweet while *TW* contains the last *H* (set to 500) tweets for each different key. An alarm is fired when the similarity between last received tweet and its closest neighbor sharing the same key is less than a threshold τ (set to 0.2).

4   Evaluation

We have performed an extensive experimental evaluation of our framework in our local cluster consisting of 8 VMs running in two physical nodes. Each VM had attached two CPU processors and $3{,}072$ MB RAM. All VMs were connected to the same LAN and their clocks were synchronized with the NTP protocol. We used Storm 0.8.2, Esper 5.1 and MongoDB 2.6.5. We used a separate physical node where Nimbus runs to avoid overloading the VMs. We evaluated our proposals with a First Story Detection (FSD) [11] application applied on the Twitter data stream. We tested the methods using the default Twitter data order as well as with a modified version that varies the *keys'* load distribution over time using Zipf distribution. In all the experiments described below, 5 Esper engines were used unless stated otherwise. We compared our proposed *DLB* algorithm against two commonly applied techniques, *PKG* [12] and *LPTF* [14]. Furthermore, we also demonstrate how our approach outperforms the *key-grouping* approach (*KG* in Figs. 3 and 4) which is the default grouping applied in Storm that assigns *keys* to engines using a simple hash function (i.e. *key* % |*Engines*|). The threshold of *imbScore* was set to 15 %. MongoDB required 1 ms on average for retrieving a single tweet.

We report results for the following metrics: (1) the system's *throughput* that depicts the amount of tuples per second that have been processed overtime, (2) the *relative standard deviation* of the engines' load which provides insights on how the algorithms balance the engines' load, (3) the *number of complex events* detected by the different techniques, ideally this metric should be equal to the one reported by the *KG* approach as this technique guarantees that tuples with the same *key* will be processed by the same engine and (4) the amount of tuples that are retransmitted by the different techniques in order to balance the system's load. This metric captures the overhead of the rebalancing procedure. It should be *noted* that, in order to test the performance of the proposed methods on extreme conditions, we transmitted the Twitter data to the system with the maximum possible speed, without simulating the original Twitter rate. Also it should be *mentioned* that in order to measure metrics (1), (2) and (4) we run each experiment for 40 min, while in order to measure metric (3) the whole dataset was examined.

Application Description. The FSD algorithm detects the most similar tweet with the current, from a set of the last *H* received tweets. If the similarity with the most similar tweet is lower than a threshold then this tweet is assumed a novel First Story tweet describing a new event. In order to make the problem tractable and scalable, for each newly received tweet Locality Sensitive Hashing (LSH) is used for identifying the *key* of the tweet [13]. This approach ensures that similar tweets will share the same *key*. The algorithm was translated to an Esper query presented on Listing 1.1. We fed our system with approximately 2.95 million tweets (8 GB) and set the number of *keys* to 4,096.

Table 1. Performance of the Different Techniques with FSD

	DLB-L	*DLB-H*	*LPTF*	*PKG*	*KG*
Total Processed Tweets	2,941,246	2,899,076	2,042,201	2,926,853	2,726,628
First Story Events	6,546	6,546	6,546	7,563	6,546
Avg Relative Std (%)	18.34	23.43	14.53	8.6	44.53

As it was mentioned above we selected to transmit the Twitter data to our system with two approaches. The first reads the tweets and transmits them with the default order. The second approach samples the *key* from a Zipf distribution and a tweet with that *key* is transmitted to the system. We selected to vary the Zipf-exponent, ϵ, periodically in order to simulate a use case where the *keys* distribution changes over time. More specifically, initially we started with a low Zipf-exponent, $\epsilon = 0.2$, depicting a rather balanced system, and after five minutes we set ϵ equal to 1.5 creating a highly skewed *key* distribution (approximately 80 % *RSTD* if *KG* is applied). We kept this highly skewed exponent for 10 min and then we repeated the procedure by resetting ϵ to 0.2.

Comparison with Other Load Balancing Techniques. Initially we compared our approaches against *LPTF* and *PKG* in terms of throughput and number of detected events. Figure 3(a) illustrates the system's throughput when the tuples are read in the default order, while Fig. 3(b) depicts the same metric when the periodic Zipf-distribution is applied. It is observed that the two proposed policies (*DLB-L* and *DLB-H*) are able to keep high throughput (approximately

1200 (tuples/sec)) throughout the experiment's execution. On the other hand the *LPTF* approach suffers from an unstable behavior explained by the large amount of data that are retransmitted along the engines.

More specifically, our policies performed seven retransmissions during the application's execution while *LPTF* performed nine. However, *LPTF* in each retransmission moved on average 76 % of the *keys* which corresponded approximately to 677, 886 tweets. So a lot of its execution time was spent to move data between the engines. In contrast, *DLB-L* moved at maximum 30 % of the *keys* which resulted to 380, 000 tweets. Similar results were exhibited by the *DLB-H* approach that moved at maximum 10 % of stored *keys* (70, 400 tweets). When the *keys* are picked using the periodic Zipf-distribution, Fig. 3(b), our approach keeps the throughput steady despite the changes in *keys*' load. When *KG* was applied with $\epsilon = 0.2$ we observed that *RSTD* was around 3 %, while when $\epsilon = 1.5$ the *RSTD* was approximately equal to 77 %. *LPTF* is still penalized by the fact that it moves larger amount of data when a rebalancing occurs and thus has worst performance overtime. More specifically, 12 rebalances occur in the *LPTF* algorithm moving in each rebalance more than 600, 000 tweets. In this case, *DLB-L* performs ten retransmissions moving 47.5 % of the *keys* with 294, 881 moved tweets on average. In contrast, *DLB-L* performs the same number of retransmission as *DLB-H* but moving significantly less data (5 % of the *keys* which corresponded to 57, 750 tweets).

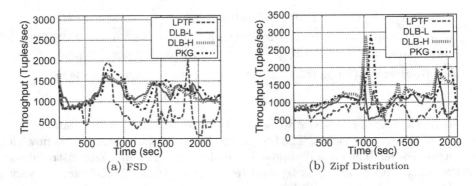

(a) FSD   (b) Zipf Distribution

Fig. 3. Throughput comparison with LPTF and PKG

In Fig. 3(a),(b) we also report the performance of the *PKG* partitioning in terms of throughput. As you can see, its throughput is very stable and similar to the performance of our proposed policies. However, when the system experiences high load (e.g. between 1200–1800 s in Fig. 3(b)) our proposals are able to maintain higher throughput than *PKG* as they migrate the loaded engines' *keys*. The *PKG* approach processed approximately 2, 831, 477 tweets in 40 min while *DLB-H* processed 2, 795, 336 tweets in the same time period. The main limitation of the *PKG* approach is the fact that it can lead to false positive events. *PKG* may assign tuples that correspond to the same *key* to different engines and thus incorrect events may be detected as the engines' state will not be consistent. More specifically, *PKG* detects in total 7,563 first story events while our content-aware approach detects 6,546 events which is the same number of events detected by KG as you can see in Table 1. So *PKG* leads to approximately 13.4 % false positive events.

Comparison with Scale-Out. Finally, in the last set of experiments we examined the performance of our proposals against the *KG* applied by Storm. We report results when *KG* uses 5 and 6 engines as we wanted to point out that scaling-out the system is not always beneficial unless load balancing is also applied. In Fig. 4(a),(b) we illustrate the system's throughput overtime. As you can observe, our approach in the unmodified app outperforms *KG* when it uses 5 engines and has comparable throughput with *KG* using 6 engines. Between 800–1700 s there is a large increase in the relative standard deviation of the engines' load reaching up to 70 % when *KG* is used. *DLB-L* balances the load between the engines keeping it around 20 % in this time period and achieves higher throughput. Also as we report in Table 1, in the end of the experiment, *DLB-L* has processed 2, 941, 246 tweets while *KG* with 6 engines processed 2, 790, 362 tweets and KG with 5 engines 2, 726, 628.

Similar results were observed in the Zipf-distribution scenario. As you see in Fig. 4(b), when the system is not loaded ($\epsilon = 0.2$) using *KG* with six engines outperforms our approach; however, when the exponent is increased (i.e. 300–900, 1200–1800), the relative standard of the engines' load reaches up to 80 % and thus the throughput deteriorates. In contrast, *DLB-H* keeps the load small, at around 40 %, and thus outperforms the other approaches in these time periods. Finally, when the experiment has finished, *DLB-H* has processed 2, 795, 336 tweets, *KG* with 6 engines processed 2, 653, 789 tweets while *KG* with 5 engines processed 2, 586, 169 tweets.

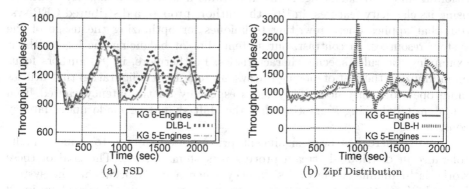

(a) FSD   (b) Zipf Distribution

Fig. 4. Throughput comparison against KG using more engines

5   Related Work

Recent works that examine the load balancing problem in stream processing systems have been described in [12,14]. The dynamic load balancing technique proposed in [12], named Partial Key Grouping (*PKG*), considers the usage of two hash functions for determining two streaming operators and assigns the tuple to the least loaded operator. *PKG* could not be applicable for CEP as it is possible to identify false positive events, as it can send tuples with the same *key* to different engines. More specifically, in CEP systems that use *key-grouping*, each *key* should be emitted to the same engine which contains in memory the previously received tuples with this *key*. In [14] the authors propose the usage of the Longest Processing Time First (*LPTF*) algorithm in offline data and then apply the detected partitioning when the system runs in real-time. *LPTF* is a commonly used greedy approximation of *job shop scheduling* problem that assigns the most loaded *key* to the least loaded engine and repeats this procedure for all the *keys*. The main limitations of this approach are the fact that it requires an offline training phase.

A recent work presented on [10] focused on balancing the load in distributed cache systems. The authors follow an iterative greedy approach which ensures that no node is overloaded by redistributing the node's *keys* to the least loaded one aiming to balance RAM and CPU usage. Another commonly applied technique for balancing the load in DSPS is load shedding [17] which discards some of the incoming data in order to keep the load steady. However, it can lead to significant information loss. In our previous work [19] we examined the feasibility of developing a large-scale event processing system for a traffic monitoring application. Our approach used historical data and applied a static partitioning schema such that all engines receive approximately the same amount of input. The StreamCloud system described in [7] also supports content-aware load partitioning and load balancing. If the latter fails it moves to a new configuration using its elasticity features. In [16], the authors propose a distributed CEP system that applies query rewriting techniques for optimizing the usage of the system resources. In contrast, our system aims at balancing the load without examining the rules specific characteristics. Furthermore, in [8], authors focus on minimizing the cost of moving the system to a new configuration that utilizes more operators' instances. They focus especially on the latency caused from a system rebalancing suggesting that the shift should be made under latency constraints.

Finally, there has been significant prior work in order to achieve fault-tolerance in distributed stream processing systems [1,2,9]. The goal of these works is to minimize the tuples' latency when a crash occurs in the system by exploiting either active replication or upstream backups. The authors in [2] proposed a checkpointing approach to expose the internal operator state. A recent work [9] proposes a hybrid approach by adaptively switching between the two fault-tolerance mechanisms based on the current workload characteristics. Finally, much work has been done in regards to automatically determine the appropriate number of stream processing components like [5,15] and our previous work [18]. These proposals are *orthogonal* to ours, as our aim is to balance the load among the engines and only if this is not possible, increase the system's resources.

6 Conclusions

In this paper we presented a novel framework that automatically balances the system's load, preserving the system's throughput at high rates. We proposed a balancing algorithm for automatically partitioning incoming tuples to the available CEP engines. Our goal was to keep the CEP engines balanced overtime in regards to the tuples they process and at the same time keep the rebalancing cost, due to data movements, low. Our detailed experimental evaluation in our local cluster indicated a clear improvement in the system's throughput when the proposed techniques were applied. For future work, we plan to extend our framework by enhancing its fault-tolerance and remove possible limitations of the MongoDB in the rebalancing procedure.

Acknowledgments. This research has been financed by the European Union through the FP7 ERC IDEAS 308019 NGHCS project and the Horizon2020 688380 VaVeL project.

References

1. Brito, A., Fetzer, C., Felber, P.: Multithreading-enabled active replication for event stream processing operators. In: SRDS, Niagara Falls, New York, USA (2009)
2. Fernandez, R.C., Migliavacca, M., Kalyvianaki, E., Pietzuch, P.: Integrating scale out and fault tolerance in stream processing using operator state management. In: SIGMOD, New York, NY, USA (2013)
3. Coffman, E.G., Bruno, J.L.: Computer and Job-Shop Scheduling Theory. Wiley, New York (1976)
4. Demers, A., Gehrke, J., Hong, M., Riedewald, M., White, W.: Towards expressive publish/subscribe systems. In: Ioannidis, Y., Scholl, M.H., Schmidt, J.W., Matthes, F., Hatzopoulos, M., Böhm, K., Kemper, A., Grust, T., Böhm, C. (eds.) EDBT 2006. LNCS, vol. 3896, pp. 627–644. Springer, Heidelberg (2006)
5. Gedik, B., Schneider, S., Hirzel, M., Wu, K.L.: Elastic scaling for data stream processing. IEEE Trans. Parallel Distrib. Syst. **25**(6), 1447–1463 (2014)
6. Gufler, B., Augsten, N., Reiser, A., Kemper, A.: Handling data skew in MapReduce. In: CLOSER, Noordwijkerhout, The Netherlands (2011)
7. Gulisano, V., Jimenez-Peris, R., Patino-Martinez, M., Soriente, C., Valduriez, P.: Streamcloud: an elastic and scalable data streaming system. IEEE Trans. Parallel Distrib. Syst. **23**(12), 2351–2365 (2012)
8. Heinze, T., Jerzak, Z., Hackenbroich, G., Fetzer, C.: Latency-aware elastic scaling for distributed data stream processing systems. In: DEBS, Mumbai, India (2014)
9. Heinze, T., Zia, M., Krahn, R., Jerzak, Z., Fetzer, C.: An adaptive replication scheme for elastic data stream processing systems. In: DEBS, Oslo, Norway (2015)

10. Jia, Y., Brondino, I., Peris, R.J., Martínez, M.P., Ma, D.: A multi-resource load balancing algorithm for cloud cache systems. In: Proceedings of the 28th Annual ACM Symposium on Applied Computing (2013)
11. McCreadie, R., Macdonald, C., Ounis, I., Osborne, M., Petrovic, S.: Scalable distributed event detection for twitter. In: BigData, Santa Clara, CA, USA (2013)
12. Nasir, M.A.U., Morales, G.D.F., García-Soriano, D., Kourtellis, N., Serafini, M.: The power of both choices: practical load balancing for distributed stream processing engines. In: ICDE, Seoul, Korea (2015)
13. Petrović, S., Osborne, M., Lavrenko, V.: Streaming first story detection with application to twitter. In: Human Language Technologies: The 2010 Annual Conference of the North American Chapter of the Association for Computational Linguistics, pp. 181–189 (2010)
14. Rivetti, N., Querzoni, L., Anceaume, E., Busnel, Y., Sericola, B.: Efficient key grouping for near-optimal load balancing in stream processing systems. In: DEBS, Oslo, Norway (2015)
15. Schneider, S., Hirzel, M., Gedik, B., Wu, K.L.: Auto-parallelizing stateful distributed streaming applications. In: PACT, Minneapolis, MN, USA (2012)
16. Schultz-Møller, N.P., Migliavacca, M., Pietzuch, P.: Distributed complex event processing with query rewriting. In: DEBS, Nashville, Tennessee, USA (2009)
17. Tatbul, N., Çetintemel, U., Zdonik, S.: Staying fit: efficient load shedding techniques for distributed stream processing. In: VLDB, Vienna, Austria (2007)
18. Zacheilas, N., Kalogeraki, V., Zygouras, N., Panagiotou, N., Gunopulos, D.: Elastic complex event processing exploiting prediction. In: BigData, Santa Clara, CA, USA (2015)
19. Zygouras, N., Zacheilas, N., Kalogeraki, V., Kinane, D., Gunopulos, D.: Insights on a scalable and dynamic traffic management system. In: EDBT, Brussels, Belgium (2015)

PAN – Distributed Real-Time Complex Event Detection in Multiple Data Streams

Lukas Probst[✉], Ivan Giangreco, and Heiko Schuldt

Databases and Information Systems Group, University of Basel, Basel, Switzerland
{lukas.probst,ivan.giangreco,heiko.schuldt}@unibas.ch

Abstract. In this paper, we present PAN, a generic middleware for distributed real-time complex event detection (CED) which is able to analyze multiple distributed data streams. In PAN, CED applications are defined as workflows and are executed by dedicated workers in a distributed way in a P2P network. In consequence, PAN is scalable in terms of the number of data streams and the complexity of the analyses. Evaluations based on an extended version of the ACM DEBS 2013 Grand Challenge scenario show the effectiveness and efficiency of PAN.

1 Introduction

The last decade has seen a vast proliferation of devices that sense their environment. As according to the IoT vision most of them are connected to the Internet, they are able to disseminate the data they measure in form of continuous data streams. Hence, the number of data streams and the volume of streamed data has increased enormously. Nevertheless, the analysis of a single or multiple of these Big Data streams in real-time is essential. In particular, the detection of complex events out of the raw streaming data in real-time is a major challenge and at the same time an important aspect in a variety of applications. As an example, consider a soccer team in which each player is equipped with several sensors which produce continuous data streams. These streams need to be analyzed to produce added value on a match for different stakeholders (clients). Hence, different events need to be detected out of all the incoming streams. This requires an infrastructure that (i) allows to implement, in a modular way, basic components for detecting simple events, that (ii) supports the combination of these components for complex event detection into workflows and that (iii) scales with the number of streams and with the complexity of the analyses.

The first generation of complex event detection (CED) systems, also called complex event processing (CEP) systems, has been built with a centralized architecture (e.g., [1,8,10]). This significantly limits their scalability, especially if complex events have to be detected in real-time. More recent approaches (e.g., [2,4,6]) use a distributed architecture and forward streams in a publish/subscribe style between workers that perform parts of the complex event detection.

© IFIP International Federation for Information Processing 2016
Published by Springer International Publishing Switzerland 2016. All Rights Reserved
M. Jelasity and E. Kalyvianaki (Eds.): DAIS 2016, LNCS 9687, pp. 189–195, 2016.
DOI: 10.1007/978-3-319-39577-7_15

In this paper, we introduce PAN (*P2P Analysis Network*), a generic distributed real-time CED middleware which jointly addresses the challenges we have listed above. PAN is able to analyze multiple distributed input data streams and to concurrently handle several analysis requests of different clients. In PAN, CED applications are defined as workflows on top of components implementing basic event detectors or other analysis operators such as aggregators. These workflows are executed in a distributed way in a P2P network based on publish/subscribe communication between workers. As a result, PAN has a high degree of scalability.

The contribution of this paper is twofold. First, we present PAN, a novel middleware architecture for distributed and scalable CED that seamlessly combines ideas from workflow management (definition of CED workflows) and P2P systems (distributed, scalable CED). Second, we provide the results of an evaluation of PAN's performance and scalability characteristics on the basis of a sports use case using an extended version of the ACM DEBS 2013 Grand Challenge scenario [7, 11]. The results show the effectiveness and efficiency of the PAN approach.

The remainder of this paper is organized as follows: We introduce PAN in Sect. 2 and report on the evaluation of PAN in Sect. 3. Section 4 presents related work and Sect. 5 concludes.

2 PAN

In this section, we present and discuss the concepts of PAN. The main idea behind PAN is to obtain a high degree of scalability for real-time CED applications by distributing the workload across several peers in an unstructured P2P network and communicating via publish/subscribe.

2.1 CED Workflows in PAN

In PAN, CED applications are defined by means of *workflows*. They consist of so-called *workers* which provide basic functionality for CED and which are combined using a partial order that allows both sequential and parallel execution of workers, depending on the semantics of a concrete CED application. Figure 1 illustrates a sample workflow which generates the player as well as the team ball possession statistic streams for the soccer use case. This workflow includes several intermediate streams (e.g., *BALLHITS*), i.e., streams that are generated as output streams by some workers and consumed as input streams at other, subsequent workers. The *sensor devices* producing the initial input streams are sources of a workflow. Moreover, there are devices outside PAN called *clients* that consume the output streams of the workers. The clients are the sinks of a workflow and might join it only for a short time.

Each worker is hosted on a *peer*. Each peer, in turn, can host a single or multiple workers. With this design, PAN obtains a high degree of flexibility in terms of workflow distribution since the workflow can be either executed on a

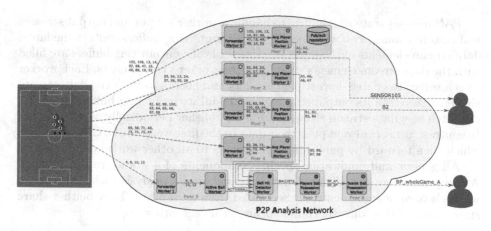

Fig. 1. Sample CED workflow in PAN for soccer game analysis. The initial input streams are taken from the ACM DEBS 2013 Grand Challenge [7,11]. (Soccer field graphic: https://de.wikipedia.org/wiki/Datei:Offsidelarge.svg, Client icon: http://www.flaticon.com/packs/humans-3)

single machine or fully distributed onto a large number of peers hosting workers which compute only small subtasks.

To standardize the interaction between workers in PAN, they only share data via network communication, independent from their deployment.

2.2 Publish/Subscribe

Hard-wiring the communication between the workers would lead to a highly inflexible system, earmarked for a specific workflow. In contrast, the publish/subscribe style of interaction allows to decouple the sender of a data stream and its receiver. PAN uses a central publish/subscribe repository which stores a mapping from the stream identifier to a list of publishers. When a new worker is deployed, it has to publish all its output streams. Subsequently, all potential subscribers (clients or other workers) can use this information to identify the publisher and fetch data stream elements from there. Note that the repository has to be contacted only once, when the link between subscriber and publisher is established. Hence, the central repository does not become a bottleneck.

2.3 PAN Workers

A PAN worker is a building block for the CED workflows. At the interface, each worker generates one or several output stream(s) on the basis of one or several input stream(s) it consumes – either directly from a sensor or from other workers. The input streams are processed by one or several components inside the worker. The output streams contain the analysis results of these components.

PAN uses separate ring buffers to handle a worker's input and output streams and thus to connect two workers. A worker's input ring buffers contain the latest data stream elements of the input streams while the output ring buffers are filled with the data stream elements created by the worker's components. Each worker runs a server to enable downstream workers and clients to fetch the data stream elements stored in its output ring buffers. To fill its input ring buffers, a worker can fetch new data stream elements from a publisher periodically or on demand. In contrast, sensors always push their data to the first workers of a CED workflow which then forward by publishing the streams to all other workers and clients.

All generic and application-specific components of a worker run in parallel. A component can use all input data streams for its analysis task. However, a worker's components are strictly separated from each other. They neither share state, nor can they directly communicate with each other.

2.4   Scalability

Increasing the number of sensor data streams to be analyzed, the number of different analyses that have to be performed, or the complexity of these analyses results in an increased computational effort. PAN can handle this by distributing the overall workload across more workers which can then be deployed on peers with free capacities. In consequence, PAN scales w.r.t. the number of data streams and w.r.t. the complexity and the number of analyses.

3   Evaluation and Implementation

In our evaluation each peer is deployed in the Azure Cloud platform[1]. The ping between two peers is around 0.9 ms. Both clients and (simulated) sensors are deployed on a separate physical server[2] with a ping around 21 ms to the Cloud.

In order to create a CED application that runs on top of PAN one only has to implement the workers in Java and to specify the workflow in a JSON config file, similar to TechniBall's XML approach [9]. The config file is used to automatically deploy the CED system. The actual connection between the workers is done at start-up time using the publish/subscribe repository. Due to space limitations, we refer to [12] for further information on the implementation of PAN.

For evaluation purposes, we have implemented a soccer analysis application that generates ball possession streams using the dataset from the ACM DEBS 2013 Grand Challenge [7,11] in multiple steps (see Fig. 1). The input data streams are created by sensors attached to the shin guards of the players and inside the ball and include position, timestamp, velocity and acceleration info. We have used the first 25 min of the soccer match for our evaluation.

PAN's performance is measured using the *query delay* that indicates how long the system needs to calculate and generate a certain output data stream. It is

---

[1] Small VM instances (standard A1), 1 core 1.6 GHz CPU, 1.75 GB RAM.
[2] Lenovo ThinkPad W530, Intel Core i7-3820QM CPU @ 2.70 GHz, 12 GB RAM.

Table 1. Average query delay with increasing number of peers

Stream	3 peers	6 peers	8 peers	14 peers
SENSOR105	69.76 ms	66.61 ms	73.79 ms	88.96 ms
B2	2923.73 ms	123.99 ms	165.68 ms	114.72 ms
BP_wholeGame_A	1141.07 ms	1078.43 ms	948.44 ms	961.06 ms

defined as the difference between the machine time when receiving an output data stream element at the client $MT(c)$ and the machine time $MT(s)$ at which the corresponding sensor data stream element has been emitted. Note that the query delay comprises also the time for sending the input stream to the first worker and for fetching the stream from the last worker of the CED workflow.

We analyze PAN's performance by varying the number of peers hosting the workers of the ball possession workflow. More precisely, we use four different deployments with 3, 6, 8, and 14 peers. The client periodically (every 20 ms) fetches the latest data element of three streams, produced at different positions in the workflow: a forwarded sensor data stream (*SENSOR105*), an intermediate output data stream (*B2*) and a final output data stream (*BP_wholeGame_A*).

Table 1 lists the results of this evaluation. While the average query delays of the *SENSOR105* and the *BP_wholeGame_A* streams are rather constant, the query delay of the *B2* stream is approximately 20 times higher in the three peers setting than in the other settings. With only three peers, the two peers that are supposed to be responsible for generating the average player position streams are not capable of doing so. However, the evaluation shows that PAN can solve such computational bottlenecks by distributing the workflow onto more peers.

4 Related Work

Similar to PAN, also RACED [4] distributes the detection components in a P2P network and links these components using publish/subscribe. However, since in RACED the data stream requested by a client has to be generated along its shortest path tree (SPT), clients cannot share a workflow if they do not have the same SPT while in PAN no duplication is needed. In [6] the authors of RACED propose a single-tree deployment strategy for their T-REX middleware [5] that allows workflows to be shared by clients such that the same output stream does not have to be generated multiple times. However, while PAN is a worker-based CED middleware, RACED and T-REX are language-based CED middleware approaches that suffer from some limitations as the client can neither define complex calculations nor small programs that have to be performed in order to detect a complex event or to generate the corresponding output data stream element. The same is true for all other language-based CED middleware systems such as, for instance, Amit [1] or Cayuga [8]. Worker-based CED middleware systems like PAN or OSIRIS-SE [2], in contrast, facilitate the implementation of arbitrary workers in a modular way and thus do not suffer from such limitations.

In reply to the ACM DEBS 2013 Grand Challenge [7,11], six systems have been proposed [3]. While the workers and CED workflows of PAN are based on the requirements of the challenge and thus have some similarity with all these systems, PAN's architecture is mainly influenced by the approach of Jergler et al. [10] that proposes a workflow-based architecture for CED in which different workers are connected with non-blocking ring buffers. While [10] states that the concept can in general be implemented in a distributed way using publish/subscribe, only a centralized implementation is presented. Hence, PAN fills a void as it promotes these concepts to a distributed and thus scalable system.

5   Conclusion

In this paper, we have introduced the distributed real-time CED middleware PAN. It uses workflows to define CED applications and distributes the workload onto multiple workers hosted by peers in a P2P network. The worker-based approach allows to implement parts of CED workflows in a modular way, ranging from simple stream forwarding to highly sophisticated analyses. Evaluations have shown that PAN is able to eliminate computational bottlenecks by distributing the workflow on more peers. In our future work, we plan to organize the workers in a structured P2P network to store the mapping of streams to publishers in a distributed and reliable way. Moreover, we plan to further analyze, evaluate and compare different approaches to publish/subscribe-based communication, in particular a pull-based vs. a push-based communication approach.

References

1. Adi, A., Etzion, O.: Amit - the situation manager. VLDB J. 13(2), 177–203 (2004)
2. Brettlecker, G., Schuldt, H.: Reliable distributed data stream management in mobile environments. Inf. Syst. 36(3), 618–643 (2011)
3. Chakravarthy, S., et al. (eds.): The 7th ACM International Conference on Distributed Event-Based Systems, DEBS 2013. ACM, Arlington (2013)
4. Cugola, G., Margara, A.: RACED: an adaptive middleware for complex event detection. In: Proceedings of ARM 2009, Urbana Champaign, IL, USA (2009)
5. Cugola, G., Margara, A.: Complex event processing with T-REX. J. Syst. Softw. 85(8), 1709–1728 (2012)
6. Cugola, G., Margara, A.: Deployment strategies for distributed complex event processing. Computing 95(2), 129–156 (2013)
7. ACM DEBS 2013 Grand Challenge Description. http://www.orgs.ttu.edu/debs2013/index.php?goto=cfchallengedetails
8. Demers, A.J., et al.: Cayuga: a general purpose event monitoring system. In: Proceedings of CIDR 2007, Asilomar, CA, USA (2007)
9. Gal, A., et al.: Grand challenge: the TechniBall system. In: Proceedings of DEBS 2013, Arlington, TX, USA. ACM (2013)
10. Jergler, M., et al.: Grand challenge: real-time soccer analytics leveraging low-latency complex event processing. In: Proceedings of DEBS 2013, Arlington, TX, USA (2013)

11. Mutschler, C., Ziekow, H., Jerzak, Z.: The DEBS 2013 grand challenge. In: Proceedings of DEBS 2013, Arlington, USA (2013)
12. Probst, L.: PAN - a P2P approach for scalable complex event detection in distributed data streams. Master's thesis, University of Basel (2014). http://dbis.cs.unibas.ch/downloads/theses/MSc_Thesis_Lukas_Probst.pdf/at_download/file

Bringing Complex Event Processing
into Multitree Modelling of Sensors

Alexandre Garnier[1][✉], Jean-Marc Menaud[1], and Nicolas Montavont[2]

[1] ASCOLA Research Group, Mines Nantes / Inria / LINA UMR 6241,
Nantes, France
{alexandre.garnier,jean-marc.menaud}@mines-nantes.fr
[2] Institut Mines-Télécom / Télécom Bretagne, Irisa, Rennes, France
nicolas.montavont@telecom-bretagne.eu

Abstract. The recent advances in the Internet of Things allow deploying a large variety of applications for smart cities, home automation or the industry of the future. These applications generate a large amount of data that can be challenging to manage; identifying and parsing this data become a prominent problem. In order to address this issue, we propose a multitree model for the sensor representation which matches the need for heterogeneous applications and user support. From there, we define a complex event processor based on a new language and grammar, in order to filter and identify user specific events. We show that we considerably reduce the size of queries by focusing on end-users knowledges as semantics for data streams.

Keywords: Sensor networks · Domain-specific languages · Complex event processing

1 Introduction

From home automation to smart cities, from amateur weather stations to large deployments of smart power meters in datacenters, Internet of Things (IoT) applications target more and more end-users every day. The link between these users and the IoT is usually provided by applications deployed over a sensor network. A recurring problem concerning sensor networks is the heterogeneity, not only of sensors, but also of the protocols used to access them, often characterized by their low bandwidth and poor reliability. To address this issue, the notion of data streams has emerged, leading to a change of paradigm around data parsing, from traditional DataBase Management Systems (DBMS) to Complex Event Processing (CEP). Instead of processing stored persistent data through volatile queries, CEP parses volatile data stream as it comes through persistent queries. However, parsing the raw data issued from sensors remains a complex

© IFIP International Federation for Information Processing 2016
Published by Springer International Publishing Switzerland 2016. All Rights Reserved
M. Jelasity and E. Kalyvianaki (Eds.): DAIS 2016, LNCS 9687, pp. 196–210, 2016.
DOI: 10.1007/978-3-319-39577-7_16

task. This is due to the endless nature of the data stream and its growing heterogeneity, which reflects the variety of networked things. In order to address this issue, ideally the data has to be adapted to the user's knowledge.

Given that the number of users to consider grows with the IoT coverage, the ability to provide a meaningful access to the data to each user is a prominent problem. If CEP alone is able to notify specific users with data they are interested in, it does not allow to pre-identify these data. To leverage this gap, some kind of semantics, or context, can be attached to the data, in order to assist users when identifying the information they need. To this end, various tracks have been followed, from ontology-based enrichment to context-aware solutions. While ontology-based solutions tend to be harsh to manage for non-expert end-users and do not directly address their needs, context-aware solutions usually lack interoperability between different user contexts. A good compromise could be to provide a cross-context modelling of the data. Such a model would provide a defining frame to the semantical enrichment, while avoiding context partitioning. In order to fully provide to users a simple yet effective access to the data, CEP should be merged with such a modelling of the data.

Our previous work, SensorScript [7], aimed at providing a cross-context modelling of the data. In this paper, we propose to enhance it with a complex event processor, addressable through a new Domain-Specific Language (DSL). The DSL focuses on pre-identified uses and their combinations, relying on end-users oriented knowledge. This allows to reduce lengths of queries an end-user can express as they are able to manipulate nothing more than what he considers to be relevant information. Moreover, decision making can be automated in order to address actuators specific features in addition to sensors data gathering.

The remainder of the paper is organized as follows. Section 2 studies existing work about data semantics and CEP. In Sect. 3 we draw up the motivation for integrating CEP with SensorScript. Sections 4 and 5 introduce the model and the language which ensure complex event processing. Section 6 evaluates the language concision and the underlying query management through a demonstration scenario. Finally, Sect. 7 concludes by presenting future work.

2   Related Work

Data identification has been a prominent track of research over the years. We can divide the existing work into two categories: data semantical enrichment on one hand; context aware data stream mining on the other hand. Several publications about context awareness for the IoT are discussed in [13]. In this paper we will focus on solutions which provide real-time processing of the data stream, as it is a strong requirement for complex event processors.

In [18] data semantics are provided by a separated knowledge base, which is a Resource Description Framework [9] (RDF) store. Thus event queries mix raw events extracted from the data stream and background knowledge retrieved from the knowledge base. That allows to establish relationships between the raw events. RDF knowledge base access is done through SPARQL [20] queries.

This inevitably leads to hybrid queries, which mix SPARQL syntax with complex event paradigm. Use of such semantically enriched complex events is addressed in [17]. It relies on the notion of event stream from which raw data is pulled then pushed back after semantical enrichment and event composition. Furthermore, a partitioning of enriched data stream mining operators is proposed for both CEP (*e.g.* filters or aggregators) and knowledge operators.

SCONSTREAM [10] aims at providing spatial enrichment over the data for the specific case of users tracking in home automation. Queries continually parse the raw data to generate spatialized events when triggered. UbiQuSE [16] proposes a more generic contextual framework for data mining queries. It relies on XML formalism for context-enriched data. Thus it uses XQuery [2] to express queries that address both real-time and historical data querying. This broadens the use of the DBMS, as it stores both contextual and historical data. These two solutions however rely on pre-existing solutions to bundle both data mining (being real-time or periodic) and context-awareness, which leads to hybrid querying over the data. COPAL [11] aims at providing a DSL to broaden the notion of context from sole location to handle processing environments in the case of distributed processing. This DSL provides a complex event processor in order to compose events through a declarative, and quite verbose, developer-centric syntax, in the sense that a user has to learn the underlying model before composing events. A common issue of these solutions remains in the context storage, generally based on a decoupled DBMS, which impacts the simplicity of queries. The runtime additional cost of addressing the DBMS and couple its information with the raw data is addressed by none of these publications.

Concerning CEP languages, other contributions mainly aimed at adapting Structured Query Languages (SQL) to manage data streams and event composition. CQL.[1] is one of the first to do so. The change of paradigm from relational databases to complex event processing focuses on the notion of a relation. A relation is addressed in the *from* clause, like tables in SQL, and mapped over time windows to a finite set of data from. Other than time windows, partitioned windows can also be expressed, providing a partition over the data stream similar to the SQL *group by* clause. TinyDB [12] provides time windows with a dedicated additional clause rather than a mapping over data stream. It also allows to specify a recovery rate for queries execution, jeopardizing efficiency as there is no guarantee that the data will be updated at least the same rate of the accesses defined in queries. Aiming at providing more flexibility over windows specification, Esper [6] provides the notion of pattern which orchestrates both time windows and data filtering with boolean operators. WildCAT [5] aims at coupling Esper Processing Language (EPL) with data context awareness through hierarchical contexts definition. However, this semantic enrichment of data operates as on overlay to Esper rather than being fully integrated within EPL.

Another track focused on declarative event specification. AmbientTalk [19] uses this concept for the actors within mobile ad-hoc networks, as a mean to leverage the problematics specific to these infrastructures. TESLA [4] formalizes an event specification language. Following AmbientTalk, REScala [15] and

EventCJ [8] integrate such a formalism within object-oriented and functional programming. If these languages depart from traditional SQL, they however concentrate on addressing a larger scope rather than simplifying their syntax.

3 Motivation

SensorScript was based on a previous work: btrScript [14]. btrScript is a datacenter monitoring DSL inspired by XPath [3], in particular its queries which allow implicit pathfinding within a tree. Indeed the DSL is backed to two static trees to address both virtualized and physical aspects of a modern datacenter. In [7], we altered the underlying model to manage any number of configurable intricated trees, which allows SensorScript to address the diversity of sensor networks. The trees intrication of the model will be detailed in Sect. 4.

The benefits of such a modelling are two-fold. On one hand it offers a good semanticization over the data by integrating it within tree contexts. On the other hand, queries remain concise as the model still relies on trees. Hence, we consider these features make SensorScript a strong candidate to be integrated within a complex event processor, as existing CEP languages suffer from verbose queries. This led us to deeply alter SensorScript data and query management, and to rethink key components of the DSL grammar.

4 Model

The model consists of two parts, which are the data modelling and the complex event processor. The data modelling consists on a multitree modelling of the data in which each tree corresponds to an end-user field of expertise, or a *context*. Figure 1 illustrates a multitree model with five different contexts. These contexts revolve around a conference site, with lighting monitoring and automation on one hand, and presentations' affluence tracking system on the other hand. These use cases are described in more detail through some examples in Sect. 6.

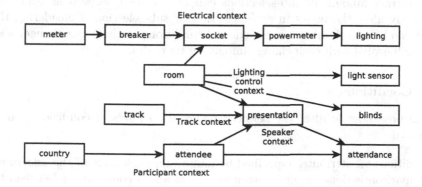

Fig. 1. Example of a multitree model

To set up complex event processing, we propose to change the paradigm on which is based traditional data management. Instead of considering the data as persistent, we assume data streams on which queries are considered persistent. These queries must be constantly aware of any data update. To achieve that, a naive solution would be to rely on a periodic queries-executing process. This is however unsatisfactory because of higher costs in terms of both efficiency and responsiveness, according to the data stream rate. More realistically, both problems will happen at different times, due to the various underlying networks which are not all reliable, and the various number of queries impacting their execution time. Hence, the query model must react dynamically to data changes.

We lean on the multitree model to leverage data accessibility. The hierarchy of nodes within the multitree can and will be accessed through the queries, as it provides meaningful information about contexts, therefore users specific knowledges. As a matter of fact, queries results are updated on real time with the data stream, but also with changes of the multitree structure. Thus the multitree sets a semantical structure down. Queries rely on these semantics in order to access nodes based on the constitutive contexts information of the multitree model. To achieve that, we propose the query object model as illustrated in the UML class diagram of Fig. 2.

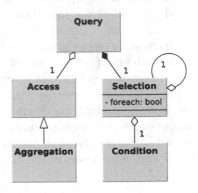

Fig. 2. Query object model

In our query object model, a query consists of three main concepts, which are the node *selection*, on which can be expressed a *condition*, and the optional *access* to selected node attributes or methods.

4.1   Selections

An arbitrary amount of sub-selections can be specified, as well as conditions optionally filter the nodes in each selection or sub-selection. Considering that nodes can be added, moved, removed, and conditions on them can change, selections will evolve with each change impacting its nodes.

4.2   Conditions

Conditions allow to filter the selected nodes. Two kinds of conditions can be expressed:

- conditions on attributes (specified by name): for each node of the selection, a comparison is done either between an access and a constant, or between two accesses over the node;

– conditions on connected nodes (specified by type): for each node of the selection, a boolean set operation is done on all the nodes of the given type that are accessible, upwards or downwards, from this node; for instance, we can restrict the selection of all sockets to the set of sockets with no powermeter.

4.3 Accesses

Accesses are made on each node of the selection, and can be delivered as is or aggregated (thus the *Aggregation* access inheritance).

5 Language

The main objective of the SensorScript language is to allow users to express CEP queries about their own field of expertise, regardless of the complexity of the whole underlying multitree model. As we saw in Sect. 2, existing CEP DSL derive from SQL, thus require users to know more of the underlying model than what should be needed. In contrast, SensorScript comes with a language which leans on the multitree model and takes advantage of the relations between its nodes to provide implicit connections among them, regardless of the distance separating them in the model. As we want to keep the language as concise as possible, we choose to use character operators rather than english words based syntax, which we hope significantly reduces the verbosity of queries. Naturally, the language reflects the selection, access and condition concepts constituting a query as presented in Sect. 4. It is essential however to keep the expression of these three concepts as simple as possible.

Listing 1. SensorScript simplified grammar

```
1:            Query  →  Selection(.Access)? |
                        Selection:Selection.AggregationMethod
2:        Selection  →  AtomicSelection({Condition})?(/Selection)?
3:           Access  →  SimpleAccess | AggregationMethod
4:        Condition  →  SimpleAccess Comparator SimpleAccess |
                        Condition BooleanOperator Condition |
                        (Condition, Duration)
5:    SimpleAccess  →  Attribute | SimpleMethod | Constant
6:       Comparator  →  = | != | < | > | <= | >=
7: BooleanOperator  →  & | | | ;
8: AtomicSelection  →  NodeName | NodeType
```

Non-terminal symbols
Grammar description operators
Terminal symbols

Considering these points, we propose a simplified grammar of the language in Listing 1. We will go through the grammar rule by rule, following the non-terminals as they occur within rules. Rule 1 reflects that a query is either a *selection* or an *access* (simple or aggregated) over a selection.

5.1 Selection

The second rule shows that sub-selections over a selection are expressed by the slash operator between super and sub-selections. Selections are expressed either on node types or node names. For this reason, not only both names and types are unique, but also a name cannot be equal to a type. Considering a sensor network modelled with Fig. 1, the query listing the breakers of room 42, for instance, would be: `room42/breaker`.

5.2 Condition

Rule 2 in Listing 1 also introduces the expression of conditions, within braces operators, over selections. As shown in rule 4, conditions are either simple, consisting of comparisons on *accesses*, or composed of sub-conditions by boolean operators.

Besides traditional *and* and *or* operators, we introduce here the *sequence* operator ";", so that the condition `<selection>{A;B}` ensures that conditions A *then* B are met on nodes of the selection. That does not mean that B has to match after A is satisfied, but that, whether or not B was already satisfied when A matches, B must be checked *chronogically after* A matches for the condition to be met.

Another aspect of time management appears with time conditions, which are simply conditions checked over a duration of time, both of them expressed between parentheses and separated by a comma.

As an example, we consider that one wants to detect the room 42 powermeters that go through an electrical overload. This can be described as the powermeters that have a power consumption that outnumbers their capacity just before it drops to zero, which can be expressed with this query:

```
room42/powermeter{power > capacity; power = 0}
```

As preventing an electrical overload seems to be a better solution, one could create an alert of when a powermeter is soon to be overloaded, for instance when its power consumption remains close to its capacity (with a minimum charge of 90 %) for at least one hour:

```
room42/powermeter{(power > capacity * 0.9, '1 h')}
```

5.3 Access

Accesses are done on each node of a selection, through the dot operator. The access of a query occurs on two occasions on runtime:

– when a node is added to the selection, access on it occurs systematically;
– for a node already in the selection, each node update that affects the access will trigger it.

Rules 3 and 5 in Listing 1 show that they exist several possible accesses on nodes:

Attribute access for each node of a selection, the query will wait for the given attribute to be updated. For instance, to be notified of each power update from powermeters of room 42: `room42/powermeter.power`.

Constant access this access allows to express constants, which is mostly useful for conditional expressions. As shown in rule 4, accesses within conditions are expressed without the dot operator. Considering our previous example, this corresponds to the zero in this query:

`room42/powermeter{power > capacity; power = 0}`

Method access for each node of a selection, the query will recall the method for each node update that might affect the method result. This will exclusively happen for method with parameters that correspond to attribute accesses. For methods with no parameter or only constant parameters, accesses are only provided when nodes are added to the selection and for these nodes only. Two types of methods exist:

- simple methods: similar to attributes accesses, they are called separately for each node of the selection. For instance, this is the get method, which is equivalent to an attribute access: `/room42/powermeter.get(power)`
- aggregation methods: on the contrary, aggregation methods provide a computation which occur on all nodes from the selection to produce one result only; an update on one node of the selection, as well as changes of the selection itself, will trigger the method to be called. As an example, let's consider that one wants to access the total consumption from room 42 powermeters: `room42/powermeter.sum(power)`.

5.4 Foreach

A particular aggregation use case allows to partition the selection to provide a behavior similar to the *group by* clause in MySQL. This is what we call the *foreach* aggregation method access, expressed by the colon operator in rule 1. To explain how it is expressed, we will consider this example and its equivalent in SQL:

SensorScript	SQL
`room42/breaker:powermeter.sum(power)`	`SELECT sum(powermeter.power)`
	`FROM breaker, powermeter`
	`WHERE breaker.room = 42`
	`AND powermeter.brId = breaker.id`
	`GROUP BY breaker.id`

We see here two selections around the colon operator, which are breakers from room 42 for the first one, powermeters for the second one. Besides, the sum method is called on the *power* attribute from powermeters. *De facto*, this query will follow power updates for each room 42 powermeter. But rather than summing the whole power consumption of the room, it will sum the power consumption *for each* breaker accessible from the room 42, considering sockets within a same room are attached to different breakers.

So, if we consider a query of the form A:B.method(access), considering that A and B are selections, this means that *for each* node N from the selection A, the specified aggregation method will be called on nodes from selection B *accessible from* N (or the nodes corresponding to the N/B).

The difference in the concept's name with SQL is to reflect the way it is expressed and avoid confusion: the *group by* clause precedes an attribute, the *foreach* operator follows a node selection.

6   Evaluation

This section proposes to evaluate the language concision through some examples over the model from Fig. 1 and compare them with similar examples from the literature. Then we propose a scenario which reflects a more complex yet realistic use of the language. Both approaches focus only on syntactic concision of the language, performance evaluation will be subject to future work. Futhermore, we will specifically look at timed conditions management as they bring an additional constraint over the model dynamicity. Finally, we will highlight the limitations of SensorScript in terms of features, compared to other CEP languages.

6.1   Comparison with CQL

In the model from Fig. 1, more specifically around the *track*, *speaker* and *participant* contexts, we consider a conference for which name tags distributed to every attendee embed an RFID chip. For each presentation, they are invited to check in by swiping their name tag in an RFID reader. Speakers (which is a role that an attendee assumes for a presentation) also check in when beginning their presentation. Each room of the conference has its own RFID reader. Technically, the data stream is flowing with the presence of attendees in any of the conference rooms.

To keep things as simple as possible, we concentrate here on the three aforementioned contexts:

- the *participant* context, for attendees who attend a presentation;
- the *speaker* contexts, for the attendee who holds a presentation;
- the *track* contexts, that reflects the fact that presentations are part of a track of the conference.

These three contexts are directly inspired from the example of CQL [1]. This example considered an auction system, for which we propose the mapping Table 1 in order to stick to our conference tracking system.

Table 2 gives a comparison between SensorScript and CQL queries based on the aforementioned mapping.

Table 1. Mapping to CQL example

Conference attendance monitoring model	Auction system model
Attendee	User
Presentation	Auction
Attendance	Bid
Country	U.S. state
Participant context	Bidding context
Speaker context	Seller context
Track context	Auction context

1. The first query allows to select presentations that occur after noon. It is conceptually very similar to the CQL query, as the condition between braces corresponds to the one declared in the *where* clause.
2. This second query aims at maintaining a running count of attendees to tracks 1 and 2 over the last hour. There is an important difference here as time windows can only be specified within conditions in SensorScript. This results in two conditions specified over the two sub-selections of the whole selection.
3. With this query we want to maintain a list of the current presentations. The main difference here is that SensorScript relies on attributes updated with the data stream over the nodes of the multitree, where CQL backs to table-like streams to manage the presentation state (*ongoing* or *over*).
4. Given that we want here to list the present attendees, we only need to add a sub-selection to the previous query with SensorScript, considering that a present attendee is an attendee that checked in a current presentation. On the other hand, CQL proposes a whole new, though significantly longer, query, based once again on streams that reflect presence or absence of attendees.
5. As presentations can be rescheduled during the conference, we consider now that speakers check-ins affect directly the state of presentations. This allows us to get a list of non-keynote presentations, as we can follow the presentations that started then stopped in a window range of less than 35 min. We see here that the pathfinding mechanism of the language allows to get rid of any explicit join condition.
6. This last query keeps the age of the youngest speaker for completed presentations. An interesting point here relies on the multitree structure. As we saw in Fig. 1, the graph follows two routes from attendee to attendance, depending on whether the attendee is the speaker or assists to the considered presentation. In fact, the multitree allows *partially ordered sets* (or *posets*) in the graph, as long as absolute order can be decided between every couple of types from a *poset*. Actually, we rely on this property here to get the list of speakers. When following the orientation of connections between types, the *nearest* matching nodes are selected. Therefore, for presentations *attendee*

Table 2. Comparison with CQL

	SensorScript	CQL
1.	`presentation{starttime > '12:00'`	`Select * From Ongoing Where` `    starttime > '12:00'`

2	`track{name.in('tr1', 'tr2')}/`
	`    attendance{checkintime > now()`
	`    - 3600}.sum(1)`
		`Select Count(*) From`
		`    attendance[Range 1 Hour] Where`
		`    trackname In ('tr1', 'tr2')`

3.	`presentation {starttime +` `    duration > now()}`	`Select * From Ongoing Where pres_id` `    Not In (Select * From Over)`

4.	`presentation{startime + duration`
	`    > now()}/attendee`
		`Select name, state From Present`
		`    [Partition By attendee_id Rows 1]`
		`    Where attendee_id Not In (Select`
		`    * From Absent)`

5.	`presentation{(status='ongoing' ;`
	`    status='over', '35min')}`
		`Select Istream(Over.pres_id) From`
		`    Over[Now], Ongoing[Range 35 Min]`
		`    Where Over.pres_id =`
		`    Ongoing.pres_id`

6.	`presentation{status='over'}/`
	`    attendee.min(age)`
		`Select Istream(Over.pres_it, A.age)`
		`    From Over[Now], (Select`
		`    attendee_id, age From attendee)`
		`    [Partition by pres_id Rows 1] as`
		`    A Where Over.pres_id = A.pres_id`

nodes, this is the speaker. That said, if one wants to look at the age of the youngest audience member of completed presentations, this can be done with the following query, as *attendance* nearest *attendee* nodes are accessed through the participant context rather than the speaker context:

`presentation{status='over'}/attendance/attendee.min(age)`

In comparison, CQL requires both a nested condition and an explicit join.

As we can see, SensorScript expressions minimize the concepts that are specific to the language. In fact, selections, accesses and conditions are specified by operators rather than english words. Moreover, it simplifies multi-stream selections based on the implicit link provided between nodes by the multitree, compared to union specifications of SQL. Finally, conditions and timed conditions are expressed the same way, as the language was designed to implement them, whereas CQL introduces a new syntax dedicated to time windows.

6.2   Rooms Lighting Scenario

We propose here to consider the whole model from Fig. 1 in order to orchestrate all the sensors, aiming at automating the conference rooms lighting management. These different sensors allow to monitor light, participants presence and power consumption. The room lighting management addresses a typical problematic of home automation, which brings our example closer to both [11,17] examples. We also consider that blinds and powermeters are equipped with actuators. This will allow us to illustrate SensorScript's actions specification in order to address functions of these actuators.

In this scenario we will consider that ambient light of the conference has to be adapted according to several concerns:

- First of all, to save energy we would like the lighting of room to automatically turn off when all attendees have left it:

```
/room{!has(attendee)}/lighting/powermeter.turnoff()
```

We see in the model that two paths exist between the *room* and *attendee* types. However, only one condition is required here. In fact, on one hand, if a speaker is found using the shortest path, the condition is false without having to check the assistance using the longer path. On the other hand, if the room has no speaker but still some people in the audience, listing these attendees will be the only path existing within the model, therefore it will be the shortest one. This saves us having to express and test the two different accesses within the condition.

- Second, for rooms with open blinds, when the daylight (measured by an out-side light sensor named *daylight* for each room) falls below a certain threshold, we want the blinds to close and, if the room is not empty, the inside light to turn on. This is provided by the following two queries:

```
daylight{light < out_threshold}/blinds.close()
daylight{light < out_threshold}/attendee/room/lighting/
    powermeter.turnon()
```

As a non-empty room is a room bound to at least one attendee, it is more efficient here to use implicit filtering on sub-selections (the /attendee/room/ part of the query) rather than an explicit condition on the rooms.

- As ambient light, *i.e.* the light measured within a room, can incommode the readability of projected slides during a presentation, the following two queries propose to close the blinds, if open, and turn off the lights, if required, when a presentation starts:

```
presentation{status = 'scheduled' ; status = 'ongoing'}/
    blinds{status = 'closed'}.close()
presentation{status = 'scheduled' ; status = 'ongoing'}/
    lighting/powermeter{status = 'on'}.turnoff()
```

- Finally, we want the blinds to open or the light to turn on, according to daylight, when a presentation is over:

```
presentation{status = 'ongoing' ; status = 'over'}/
    daylight{light > out_threshold}/blinds.open()
presentation{status = 'ongoing' ; status = 'over'}/
    daylight{light <= out_threshold}/lighting/
    powermeter.turnon()
```

As we saw, actuators functions are called as methods on nodes within the language. The method specification is provided through inheritance over the *Node* class in the system, which implements the multitree nodes. For instance, Listing 2 illustrates the way to specify the *open* method for blinds. The system is able to detect classes that extend the *Node* class, which allows it to use these classes to instantiate according typed nodes, *blinds* in this example.

Listing 2. Action specification example

```
public class Blinds extends Node {
[...]
  @SensorScriptMethod
  public boolean open() {
    // call to actuator switch to open the blinds
  }
}
```

6.3 Limitations

CQL [1], TinyDB [12] and Esper [6] take advantage of SQL to address both dynamic and persistent data. Considering SensorScript is designed over data streams only and ensures real-time processing of data, we could not afford to keep a history over the data. In fact, even timed conditions do not require a history to be checked. As we only have to make sure that the condition holds for the specified time, this is the unique information to keep during the lifetime of the condition, which is also discarded as soon as the condition is unsatisfied or the time is over. However, we do not aim at replacing traditional DBMS, that can be used in parallel, whether storing the whole data stream or data prefiltered by SensorScript.

Languages as AmbientTalk [19], REScala [15] or EventCJ [8] aim at integrating event specification into existing programming paradigms. In this sense, their scope extends far beyond the one studied here, as we focus on the multitree only as the underlying model of the language. Nevertheless this limitation is what gives SensorScript its concise language based on implicit model parsing.

7 Conclusions and Future Work

We presented here the evolution of SensorScript towards a language for complex event processing dedicated to sensor networks. While the model mainly relies on previous works, we highlighted how the new language builds on the multitree in order to provide complex event processing mechanisms. We are able to balance the syntactic concision of the language with a real-time complex event processor for sensor networks. By providing flexible selections over the nodes, with the possibility to filter them on complex conditions, possibly over a time window, we offer a strong alternative to traditional SQL used in the literature. Moreover, SensorScript does not focus only on data access. In fact it provides the possibility to widen the scope of the methods accessible on nodes to other features than sensors monitoring, including but not limited to addressing actuators functions. Finally we showed that SensorScript is able to address examples proposed in the literature, with simpler results than SQL, while highlighting its limitations, especially on history management.

Future works will focus on deploying SensorScript over a sensor network spread over two distant sites. This will allow us to test both scalability and performance. Another lead would focus on interfacing with a traditional DBMS in order to integrate history management.

References

1. Arasu, A., Babu, S., Widom, J.: CQL: a language for continuous queries over streams and relations. In: Lausen, G., Suciu, D. (eds.) DBPL 2003. LNCS, vol. 2921, pp. 1–19. Springer, Heidelberg (2004)
2. Boag, S., Chamberlin, D., Fernández, M.F., Florescu, D., Robie, J., Siméon, J., Stefanescu, M.: XQuery 1.0: an XML query language (2002)
3. Clark, J., DeRose, S., et al.: Xml path language (xpath) version 1.0 (1999)
4. Cugola, G., Margara, A.: Tesla: a formally defined event specification language. In: Proceedings of the Fourth ACM International Conference on Distributed Event-Based Systems, pp. 50–61. ACM (2010)
5. David, P.C., Ledoux, T.: Wildcat: a generic framework for context-aware applications. In: Proceedings of the 3rd International Workshop on Middleware for Pervasive and Ad-hoc Computing, pp. 1–7. ACM (2005)
6. EsperTech: Esper (2015). http://www.espertech.com/esper
7. Garnier, A., Pottier, R., Menaud, J.M.: Sensorscript: a domain-specific language for sensor networks. In: International Conference on Future Internet of Things and Cloud (FiCloud-2015) (2015)
8. Kamina, T., Aotani, T., Masuhara, H.: Eventcj: a context-oriented programming language with declarative event-based context transition. In: Proceedings of the Tenth International Conference on Aspect-Oriented Software Development, pp. 253–264. ACM (2011)
9. Klyne, G., Carroll, J.J.: Resource description framework (RDF): concepts and abstract syntax (2006)
10. Kwon, O., Song, Y.S., Kim, J.H., Li, K.J.: Sconstream: a spatial context stream processing system. In: 2010 International Conference on Computational Science and Its Applications (ICCSA), pp. 165–170. IEEE (2010)
11. Li, F., Sehic, S., Dustdar, S.: Copal: An adaptive approach to context provisioning. In: 2010 IEEE 6th International Conference on Wireless and Mobile Computing, Networking and Communications (WiMob), pp. 286–293. IEEE (2010)
12. Madden, S.R., Franklin, M.J., Hellerstein, J.M., Hong, W.: Tinydb: an acquisitional query processing system for sensor networks. ACM Trans. Database Syst. (TODS) 30(1), 122–173 (2005)
13. Perera, C., Zaslavsky, A., Christen, P., Georgakopoulos, D.: Context aware computing for the internet of things: a survey. IEEE Commun. Surv. Tutorials 16(1), 414–454 (2014)
14. Pottier, R., Menaud, J.M.: Btrscript: a safe management system for virtualized data center. In: The Eighth International Conference on Autonomic and Autonomous Systems, ICAS 2012, pp. 49–56 (2012)

15. Salvaneschi, G., Hintz, G., Mezini, M.: Rescala: Bridging between object-oriented and functional style in reactive applications. In: Proceedings of the 13th International Conference on Modularity, pp. 25–36. ACM (2014)
16. Shaeib, A., Cappellari, P., Roantree, M.: A framework for real-time context provision in ubiquitous sensing environments. In: 2010 IEEE Symposium on Computers and Communications (ISCC), pp. 1083–1085. IEEE (2010)
17. Textor, A., Meyer, F., Thoss, M., Schaefer, J., Kroeger, R., Frey, M.: An architecture for semantically enriched data stream mining. In: Bhulai, S., Zernik, J., Dini, P. (eds.) Proceedings of the First International Conference on Data Analytics, Barcelona, Spain (2012)
18. Teymourian, K., Paschke, A.: Enabling knowledge-based complex event processing. In: Proceedings of the 2010 EDBT/ICDT Workshops, p. 37. ACM (2010)
19. Van Cutsem, T., Mostinckx, S., Boix, E.G., Dedecker, J., De Meuter, W.: Ambienttalk: object-oriented event-driven programming in mobile ad hoc networks. In: XXVI International Conference of the Chilean Society of Computer Science, SCCC 2007, pp. 3–12. IEEE (2007)
20. W3C: SPARQL 1.1 Overview. (2013). http://www.w3.org/TR/sparql11-overview/

Author Index

Printed in the United States
by Baker & Taylor Publisher Services

Printed in the United States
by Baker & Taylor Publisher Services